THE BRIGHTON JAZZ LINE

EDITED BY
KEITH SAMUEL AND PETER SIMKINS

CONTRIBUTORS:
SID BAILEY, ROY BOWER,
HORACE MEUNIER HARRIS,
BRIAN HILLS, ROY MARTIN,
JOHN MUXLOW, TERRY WHITNEY

*To Campbell
A superb trombonist
and a stalwart
keeper of the flenne.*

10.12.02

EVERGREEN GRAPHICS
CRAIGWEIL ON SEA
ALDWICK

This paperback edition published in 2002 by
EverGreen Graphics
Kufri, 11 The Drive, Craigweil on Sea
Aldwick, West Sussex PO21 4DU

Distribution and sales:
Keith Samuel
26 Hazel Close, Chandler's Ford, Hampshire SO53 5RF
Tel/Fax 023 8026 5361 Email: keith.samuel@LineOne.net

ISBN 1-900192-05-5

Printed and bound in Great Britain by
RPM Print & Design
2-3 Spur Road, Quarry Lane,
Chichester, West Sussex PO19 8PR.

Book Design by Cecil Smith
Typeset in Esprit Book and Poppl Laudatio by
EverGreen Graphics,
Members Of The Guild Of Master Craftsmen

CONTENTS

This book is dedicated to

TED AMBROSE
DERRICK STEWART-BAXTER
MIKE COLLIER
JACK GILBERT
LES JOWETT
ARNOLD KING
BENNY SIMKINS
KEITH SLADE
BERNIE WATERMAN
CHRIS WORRALL

and all the other past stalwarts of

INTRODUCTION

KEITH SAMUEL AND PETER SIMKINS

BRIGHTON HAS NEVER BEEN SHORT OF CHARACTERS – people with an individual take on life, wisdom to impart, secrets to unveil, stories to tell, experiences to share. It is a place of princes and politicians, landladies, luvvies and labourers; of bookies, buskers and beachcombers, showgirls and students; of sailors and sportsmen, waiters and writers, playboys, porters and poets; of Rotarians and retirees, pleasure-seekers, pleasure-givers, pleasure-wreckers, roisterers, day-trippers and skinny-dippers.

The city's jazz musicians are part of this rich legacy of characters. And perhaps they owe some of their individuality to this unique environment.

It goes deeper than the breezy stimulus of the sea air. The racy, raffish character of Brighton generates its own cultural dynamics. Resort playground, political convention centre, it is the region's unchallenged capital of entertainment, the arts, sport, education, and, increasingly, a microcosm of alternative lifestyles.

In Hove it has a sedate neighbour that once peeked sniffily through the lace curtains but is now assimilated into the greater metropolis of the "City By the Sea", a status cheekily self-proclaimed before formal bestowal by the monarch in 2001.

The acknowledged Queen of Watering Places, where seaside holidays were invented, Brighton is cosmopolitan, stylish, non-metropolitan, yet never provincial or, perish the thought, dull.

This is the story of the musicians, the bands in which they played and the enthusiasts who helped develop an audience for traditional and mainstream jazz music in Brighton and mid-Sussex in the years from 1945 until the present-day.

It has been prompted by the realisation that this area has produced more than its fair share of fine bands, plus a handful of richly talented individual jazz performers – some of whom have gone on to achieve national and international prominence.

These star names are the shining talents to emerge from a much larger community of performers and enthusiasts whose passion for jazz has been largely a spare-time pursuit and whose missionary work has neither sought nor earned much reward or recognition.

If the Prince Regent awakened the spirit of Brighton, then its jazz musicians have made a small but potent contribution to sustaining it.

This is their story …

THE EDITORS have made every effort to present an accurate and balanced narrative and to consult all appropriate sources. From the outset, publicity was given to the project locally and nationally and appeals were made to help trace individuals who might be able to contribute. Most of these appeals were successful but one or two requests for assistance were declined or ignored. If this has resulted in misperceptions, gaps in the narrative or failure to give credit where due, this is in no way intentional.

Similarly, we have endeavoured to identify the sources of all photographs and illustrations and to give appropriate acknowledgements.

KEITH SAMUEL in 1958.

PETER SIMKINS in 1974.

ACKNOWLEDGEMENTS

Thanks A Million ...

THE EDITORS are indebted to many individuals for their assistance in bringing this project to fruition, not least the "Band of Angels" who have helped us to underwrite the costs of publication :

SID BAILEY	PETER GODFREY	JOHN MUXLOW
GEORGE BENNETT	JOHN GOODRICK	BILL PHELAN
ROY BOWER	HORACE HARRIS	TREVOR PHILCOX
JOHN BOYETT	JIM HEATH	ROGER POCOCK
JIM CHAMBERS	GEORGE JONES	BILL POLLEY
JOHN DAVIDSON	ALAN KENNINGTON	GEORGE WALKER
STEVE DAVIES	ROY LEITH	TERRY WHITNEY
MAURICE DENNIS	ROY MARTIN	ANDY WOON
PETER DORDAY	ALAN MCCALL	GORDON WREN
CHRIS DUFF	DON MCMURRAY	& THE NEW CITY
MIKE ETHERINGTON	DON MITCHELL	JAZZMEN
PAT FINCH	BARRY MORGAN	

Grateful Appreciation is offered to all those named above and the following individuals for their generous help and co-operation in assisting with research and providing background material, photographs and ephemera:-

MIKE ADAMS	BRIAN HILLS (our	JUDY SAMUEL
JUNE AMBROSE	discographer)	TERRY SHEARING
PAT BENHAM	GEOFF HOARE	GEOFF SIMKINS
MICHAEL BLAKER	BERNARD HODGSON	NEVIL SKRIMSHIRE
PAUL BONNER	JULIA KING	The late KEITH SLADE
DEREK BRIDGER	VERNON LEIGH	JILL STAPLES
PAT CHAPMAN	BARRY LEWIS	BRIAN TOWERS
BRIAN CLARKE	DEREK LITTLE	CHRIS WATFORD
GEOFF COATES	ROY LOVE	RON WESTCOTT
BEN COLLIER	CHRIS MACDONALD	DORY WHITFIELD
JOHN COLLINSON	BERNARD MOSELEY	The late DERRICK WOOD
BRIAN COTTON	DANNY MOSS	ANNE WORRALL
GRAHAM COX	DICKIE NEAVES	The late CHRIS WORRALL
JOHN FRUCHT	TED OWEN	
GERRY GEOGHEGAN	JIM PEGG	And the staff at
The late JACK GILBERT	JOHN POSTGATE	BRIGHTON & HOVE
BILL HARVEY	LEN PROSSOR	LOCAL STUDIES LIBRARY

*"We just wanted to play jazz
and I guess we had
an inner compulsion to do so."*

TED AMBROSE

THE FEETWARMERS
circa 1943-44.
Left to right:
KEITH JUPP (guitar), KEITH SLADE (clarinet),
ALEC KILMASTER (drums), TED AMBROSE (cornet).

PICTURE BY COURTESY OF KEITH SLADE

CHAPTER 1

VICTORY BLAST

KEITH SAMUEL

The narrative substance of this first chapter owes a considerable debt to the recollections of Keith Slade, who died aged 74 in August 2002 whilst this book was in its final stages of preparation. Keith was a talented, warm and witty man who left a rich legacy of creative work in the theatre and radio as well as in jazz. He saw and approved the texts of this chapter and Chapter 5 before his death.

THE DATE WAS TUESDAY MAY 8, 1945. And it seemed as if most of the population of Brighton and Hove had taken to the streets. The townsfolk were in party mood. The war in Europe was over, Hitler had been defeated and the celebrations on VE Day were a welcome respite from six long years of sacrifice and hardship.

"A Good Time Was Had By All" was the headline in the *Brighton and Hove Gazette*. It described the good humour of massive crowds that drank the pubs dry and "thronged the flag be-decked streets singing and dancing until the early hours".

As citizens and servicemen spilled on to the streets to celebrate, the unmistakeable surging beat of jazz music intermingled with the sounds of joyful merry-making.

From the flat rooftop of a guesthouse on the corner of York Road and Western Road, four teenagers blasted away with a rousing repertoire of jazz standards – *That Da Da Strain* and *Tin Roof Blues* among them.

They called themselves The Feetwarmers. On clarinet was Keith Slade, a 17 year-old apprentice printer. The cornet player was Ted Ambrose, an engineering trainee a few months older than Slade and about to be called up for Army service. The guitarist was Keith Jupp, later to switch to trombone, and on drums was Alec Kilmaster, whose parents ran the guesthouse.

Keith Slade still had clear recollections of this impromptu performance when he talked to the author 55 years later in August 2000. "It was considered a very daring and liberated thing to do in those days, even though the circumstances of VE Day were unique and everybody was in a party mood."

Freedom and jazz are natural bedfellows. And this very public performance by the Feetwarmers was a symbolic prelude to the post-war task that Ambrose and Slade were to embark upon with missionary zeal: to build an audience for live jazz in the Brighton area.

Their commitment to playing jazz was absolute. They rehearsed at the Ambrose family home in Upper North Street. Huge effort was devoted to unravelling the mysteries of the music – a sometimes-painful process of self-discovery. Conventional instrumental tuition was available – at a price. But there was nobody to teach a trumpet player how to lead a small jazz group in the style of King Oliver or Muggsy Spanier, or a clarinettist to weave counterpoint in the manner of Johnny Dodds or Rod Cless. And jazz chord sequences were a code to be cracked every bit as mystifying as Sanskrit.

The Feetwarmers were pumped up with missionary fervour and were not going to be diverted into the commercial dance music world, which offered comparatively lucrative rewards. "We just wanted to play jazz and I guess we had an inner compulsion to do so," Ted Ambrose told Mike Collier in a BBC Radio Brighton interview broadcast in 1980. "We certainly had no ambition to do it for profit or we would have been playing in dance bands."

KEITH JUPP (trombone), TED AMBROSE (trumpet) and KEITH SLADE (clarinet) circa 1950.

PICTURE BY COURTESY OF TERRY WHITNEY

In this faltering, fumbling but ultimately triumphant manner they became the pioneers of The Brighton Jazz Line, a long and unbroken sequence of musicians and bands who have dedicated themselves 100 per cent to playing jazz and have carried a torch for the music in its traditional and mainstream idioms for over half a century.

Yet from the time of their victory blast in 1945 it was to be nearly five years before the Feetwarmers were ready to take the historic step of launching the first live jazz club in Sussex.

The founding quartet of Ambrose, Slade, Jupp and Kilmaster had played together from 1943 onwards whenever opportunities occurred. Their employers included Canadian and American servicemen billeted in Brighton around the D-Day build-up, who paid them 10 shillings each – a princely sum in those frugal times. And they promoted their own jazz dances at The Lantern, a small hall belonging to a welfare organisation in Preston Road. "Nobody danced," remembered Keith Slade. "We billed these sessions as dances as a piece of subterfuge. They would not have hired out the hall for anything as scurrilous as a jazz session."

Ted Ambrose and Keith Slade had been inspired to play by a mixture of influences – by hearing swing bands on the radio, seeing British stalwarts such as Nat Gonella and Harry Parry performing in the variety theatres,

A Dance
at
"The Lantern" 141 Preston Road,

7 p.m——11 p.m.

Featuring—
✷ TED AMBROSE and his JAZZ BAND ✷

Admission 1/-   Light Refreshments.

An admission ticket for the
wartime dances at THE LANTERN in Preston Road, Brighton.

COURTESY OF KEITH SLADE

but most significantly by listening to the records of the great jazz innovators such as Louis Armstrong, Earl Hines and Duke Ellington.

The broker of their friendship and their mentor was the ebullient, pontifical Derrick Stewart-Baxter, high priest of the Brighton & Hove Rhythm Club, which he helped start in 1936 then revived in the middle years of World War II. It was a kind of masonic lodge for jazz record-collectors* in which live music played an occasional minor part, usually in the form of a jam session featuring local dance band musicians.

Ambrose and Slade met as 15 year-olds at these gatherings. They were held at the Brighton School of Music in St Peter's Place, and then later at the London School of Dancing in Cambridge Road, Hove. Kilmaster was another member. Jupp was a school friend of Slade's. They listened intently to the jazz record recitals by Derrick Stewart-Baxter (variously known as DSB or Derry), John Wheater, Horace Harris, John Van Praagh and other enthusiasts who delivered lectures of scholarly intensity.

*HORACE MEUNIER HARRIS's portrait of DERRICK STEWART-BAXTER in Chapter 11 recalls in more detail the heyday of the BRIGHTON & HOVE RHYTHM CLUB and reflects the impact of the visit to Brighton by Graeme Bell's AUSTRALIAN JAZZ BAND in 1947-48.

Messrs. Jupp, Slade and Ambrose
model late –1940s men's fashions.

PICTURE BY COURTESY OF JUNE AMBROSE

Records such as Armstrong's *West End Blues*, Ellington's *Rockin' in Rhythm* and Muggsy Spanier's *At the Jazz Band Ball* made a big impression on the young converts.

"Amby (Ted Ambrose) was keen to get some music going, but when we first got interested in hot jazz, there was nobody to guide us, nobody to lead us and we didn't know what we were doing," recalled Slade.

Wartime shortages kept jazz records in scarce supply and also made musical instruments hard to come by – and expensive. "Money was as scarce as bananas in those days," remembered Slade, who was entranced both by the sight and sound of Harry Parry's clarinet when he saw him perform at the Brighton Hippodrome. "It had a sort of Christmas tree quality with all those lovely shining keys." Armed with a Teach Yourself book he started out on a battered soprano sax that cost 10 shillings (50p) before he could afford a second-hand clarinet – a simple system model he bought for £3 (then equivalent to a man's weekly wage) from a shop in Sydney Street. Ambrose acquired a double bass from his cousin Len Prossor as a stepping-stone to buying his first second-hand cornet, which he saw advertised in a local paper.

Gradually they made sense of their instruments and began to build a repertoire. By 1945, the year of their VE Day open-air performance, they were confident enough to travel up to London to make a couple of discs for private consumption. In his 1980 Radio Brighton interview Ambrose described these recordings as "a gallant attempt by a bunch of 17 year-olds" to play authentic jazz. Around that time, records by George Webb's Dixielanders had shown a way forward for British musicians who aspired to play jazz in the classic tradition. "It was spellbinding," said Keith Slade, recalling the impact of the Webb records half a century later. "Rough, brash, but what spirit! It's the spirit of the music that is everything. This is when the traditional jazz revival in Britain was really born."

However, there was to be a frustrating gap before Brighton's contribution to this revival could continue. Call-up to the armed forces loomed at this point and it was 1948-49 before Ambrose, Slade, Jupp and Kilmaster could re-group to resume their mission.

In those days jazz record collectors tended to be scornful of attempts by hometown musicians to play the music but Derrick Stewart-Baxter, then and for the remainder of his life, proved a doughty patron of all serious endeavours by local

THE TED AMBROSE JAZZ BAND at the Richmond Hotel, Richmond Terrace, Brighton, 1950-51, showing
TED AMBROSE (trumpet), **KEITH JUPP** (trombone), **KEITH SLADE** (clarinet), **DAVE WIGZELL** (guitar),
ALEC KILMASTER (drums), **TERRY WHITNEY** (piano), **GEORGE JARVIS** (bass).

PICTURE BY COURTESY OF TERRY WHITNEY

musicians to play live jazz. "He came to The Lantern sessions to support us, and he sat in the front row on the first night when the Brighton Jazz Club opened and he was there every week," remembered Slade.

As a writer, Derry had access to the columns of *Jazz Journal* and other specialist publications and he was the first to give publicity to Graeme Bell and his Australian Jazz Band, a group of exuberant young musicians who made a big impact on the British jazz scene in the late 1940s and acquired many followers and friends in the Brighton area. Their first visit to Brighton early in 1948 helped prepare the ground as

A self portrait by **TED AMBROSE**
in the mid-1950s.

PICTURE BY COURTESY OF KEITH SAMUEL

Ambrose, Slade and Co. completed their postings in the services. In particular, the Bell band encouraged dancing to their music, forging a strong bond between jiving and traditional jazz that survives to this day. It gave jazz a social appeal to young people from which it was to benefit greatly. This music also carried the faintest whiff of rebellion against stuffier codes of behaviour and dress that made it doubly attractive. A generation later rock'n'roll would seize the same ground in a much more spectacular way.

Organised by Ambrose, Slade and the band members, the Brighton Jazz Club opened for business late in 1949 (some reports suggest February 1950) at the Sussex County Arts Club in Bond Street, Brighton and it was to last for some seven years. The club was soon a big success, its weekly Friday night sessions patronised by young people, many of them students. It was a daring, exciting venture that brightened the drab days of post-war austerity in Brighton and Hove. Membership was approaching 400 by the time of the club's first birthday.

The Ambrose band by then had been augmented by a bass player from Crawley (George Jarvis) and Dave Wigzell on guitar. This enabled Keith Jupp to switch from guitar to trombone to complete an orthodox traditional three-piece front line.

Most significantly, the band had been strengthened in late 1948 by the recruitment of pianist Terry Whitney, a 16 year-old sixth former who auditioned in his Brighton Grammar School uniform and was promptly offered the job. Once again Derrick Stewart-Baxter was the conduit for this link-up. Terry, from Hassocks, first made contact with Derry in 1946 when he saw an article in the *Melody Maker* appealing for support in re-launching the pre-war Rhythm Clubs. He wrote to Derry, the listed Brighton contact, and was invited along to Sunday afternoon record sessions at Derry's Withdean home. "The first time I went along there were people there like Horace Harris,

**A young
TERRY WHITNEY
(piano)
in the early 1950s.**

PICTURE BY COURTESY OF JUNE AMBROSE

Derek Bown and John Wheater. They played wonderful records all afternoon. They were an amazing group of people for a 14 year-old to encounter, and they were very kind to me, Derry especially. Some time later he told me that Ted Ambrose had come back from fighting the King's enemies and was starting up a band. He put me in touch, I auditioned and got the job."

Another big influence on Terry was John R.T. Davies, the multi-instrumentalist, discographer and recording engineer who later played trombone with the Crane River Jazz Band and was then living in Ditchling. "Derry introduced me to John when I was about 15 and I remember walking across the fields from Hassocks to Ditchling to see him. John lent me a jazz chord book, which was a complete revelation."

. Visiting firemen – and women – helped establish the reputation of the new Brighton Jazz Club and put the town firmly on the jazz map. Mick Mulligan, George Melly and Beryl Bryden travelled down from London to sit-in with the Ambrose band. The small Arts Club (still in existence), with its rickety first floor room, was ill-equipped to cope with this burgeoning success and a move to the Richmond Hotel in Richmond Terrace followed. Here, a more spacious upstairs function room offered better facilities. More importantly, dancers had room to jive in the style becoming increasingly popular and part of the social allure that attracted young people to the clubs featuring British traditional and Dixieland jazz groups. The most famous of these was the Humphrey Lyttelton Club at 100 Oxford Street in London.

Many local musicians and fans have warm memories of the Brighton Jazz Club in its first incarnations at the Arts Club and the Richmond (it returned to the Arts Club for a further winter season). Among the sitters-in were many musicians seizing their first opportunities to play to a dedicated jazz audience – clarinettist Les Wood, banjoist/guitarist Tim Streeton, pianist Dory Whitfield (Dory Nutter before she married Portsmouth trumpeter Doug Whitfield) and trombonist Derek Staton among them. And more experienced players such as trumpeter Les Jowett and pianists Eddie Buckwell and Bernie Waterman also contributed to the entertainment.

Les Jowett, born in Bradford in 1925, was a fully formed talent when he moved to Brighton in 1949. He had learned the cornet and trombone from an uncle who played in the Black Dyke Mills Band and gained early jazz experience by sitting in at the Bradford Rhythm Club. He served in the Royal Navy during World War II, winning a Navy scholarship to King's College, Cambridge. Further study at the London School of Economics marked him out for an academic career – which included an appointment as a lecturer in Social Studies at Brighton Technical College.

Writing in 1982, John Wilson remarked on Les's keen intellect and how, in a short life-span, he became both a respected academic and an accomplished musician. "He delighted in debate on any topic, particularly all forms of jazz."

The same writer described how Les came to live in Brighton, where he met his wife Ida at a jazz concert at the Brighton Aquarium and also formed a close friendship with trumpeter Ted Ambrose. They shared the same house for a period – taking care not to practise the trumpet simultaneously! "At the Brighton Jazz Club," continued Wilson "Les played with the Ambrose band and also performed duets with pianist Eddie Buckwell. One night Cy Laurie visited the club, played with Les in the interval and thus began the Cy Laurie Four ... He also took the opportunity to join the re-formed George Webb band. With them he played at a now legendary concert, before members of the Royal Family, at the Festival Hall, when Ralph Sutton and Lonnie Johnson first appeared over here."

Back in Brighton, Les Jowett was destined to set a benchmark as a local band-leader in the mid-1950s, before his early death aged 35 in 1960. These later accomplishments are analysed more fully by Terry Whitney in Chapter 3.

Les Wood was destined to become one of the country's most admired jazz per-formers in the New Orleans idiom. He took clarinet lessons from Keith Slade, arriving early on Friday nights at the Arts Club before the sessions began. Later on John Boyett remembers Wood sitting in with the Ambrose band in Army battledress at the Richmond "with freshly blancoed bombardier's stripes on his arm". He was then completing his National Service with the Royal Artillery on Salisbury Plain.

Waterman later became a member of Les Jowett's fine band and Buckwell, admired for his technique and understanding of the complexities of modern jazz, joined the Ronnie Vine Quartet, which occasionally featured in two band sessions at the Brighton Jazz Club.

Such open-mindedness about mixing different streams and styles of jazz has been an attractive feature of the Brighton jazz scene. In other less liberal climes, jazz fans often segregated themselves into fundamentalist sects. Saxophones were frowned on (and sometimes greeted with boos!) and banjos were decreed mandatory by the tra-ditional jazz followers, whilst the modernists dubbed their counterparts "mouldy fygges" and sneered at their homespun instrumental technique.

Through banjo player Freddie Wheeler, trombonist Geoff Hoare and others, the Ambrose band had forged associations with Crawley and travelled up to the expanding New Town to play on several occasions. One performance there prompted sniffy comments in the local weekly news-paper from a reviewer whose notice was billed

LES JOWETT (trumpet) soon after his arrival on the Brighton jazz scene. He brought sartorial taste as well as musical talent to his new surroundings.

PICTURE BY COURTESY OF JUNE AMBROSE

An evening at the **CHALET CLUB** in Western Road, Hove, circa 1953-54.
As well as **KEITH SLADE**, **TED AMBROSE** and **TERRY WHITNEY**,
TIM STREETON (guitar), **BILL APPLETON** (drums) and **SAILOR SPICER** (bass) are also pictured.

PICTURE BY COURTESY OF TERRY WHITNEY

under the heading "A Musician Meets The Jazzmen". Under the initials R.H.M he wrote: "Members of the band very kindly come all the way from Brighton (for little or nothing except the love of the thing) to play at Three Bridges, and someone has got to tell them to play less fortissimo or else stay in Brighton – from which distance they will be heard with less chance of lasting damage."

The *Brighton and Hove Gazette* was kinder but the reviewer seemed a little preoccupied by "the man with bright red trousers" (Ambrose), "the pianist with the cigarette" (Whitney) and "the fair-haired trombonist with a Salvation Army instrument" (Jupp) when the band appeared in the Music Room at the Royal Pavilion. The uncredited reviewer observed that when the band burst into *I Wish I Could Shimmy Like My Sister Kate* " the plush red draperies of the Music Room shivered slightly as they took the full blast of the first 'hot' music ever to be played in King George IV's Marine Palace". In full flight, the writer then added that "the resined floorboards that once took the weight of curtseying ladies and bowing gentlemen before each minuet now groaned under the tapping and banging of 50 left feet belonging to not-so-graceful sweater girls and their blazered beaux".

STU EMSLEY
(alto saxophone),
with
SAILOR SPICER
(bass),
shortly after
joining the
TED AMBROSE JAZZ BAND,
circa 1954.

PICTURE BY COURTESY OF JUNE AMBROSE

In 1953 the Brighton Jazz Club moved to its third home, the Chalet Club at 114a Western Road, Hove. This first floor establishment, approached up a narrow staircase was spacious but in John Boyett's memory "one of the sleaziest places imaginable, with tired and musty sofas and dilapidated decor". By then Alec Kilmaster had moved to Essex and been replaced on drums by Bill Appleton, who worked in advertising. Tim Streeton, whose mother was a Hove councillor, was on guitar, and the portly Alf "Sailor" Spicer had taken over on bass. Whitney remained on piano but Jupp (now living in Australia) dropped out of the band after a disagreement following a ragged performance on a riverboat shuffle at Southampton. This left only two of the original pioneers from the Feetwarmers – Ted Ambrose and Keith Slade.

No regular trombonist succeeded Jupp, although both Derek Staton and Mel Henry were heard with the band on occasions. Derek, originally from Portslade, was a Brighton telephone engineer who took up the trombone when serving with the Army in Tripoli. He was forthright – both as an individual and a stylist – and, that comparative rarity, a trombonist who played left-handed. Mel Henry eventually qualified as a doctor and practised in London. He came from Hove, where his parents ran a café near the Granada in Portland Road. More frequently featured were Les Jowett, who played memorable trumpet duets with Ambrose (often echoing the classic King Oliver/ Louis Armstrong collaborations), and Stewart "Stu" Emsley, a fine clarinettist and alto sax player who became a regular member of the Ambrose band but, perhaps more significantly, developed a good musical understanding with Jowett.

Stylistically, the band had moved into broader territory, absorbing elements of the

Chicago and Harlem traditions as well as the conventional classic jazz and New Orleans influences. I first heard and enjoyed the band at the Chalet Club in 1955 and joined the Brighton Jazz Club that September on receiving my first pay packets after leaving school.

Interestingly, it was the audiences rather than the musicians that attracted most comment in the Press in the Brighton Jazz Club's latter period.

In the summer of 1955, Len Prossor, writing as Musicus in the *Brighton and Hove Herald*, described how the influx of foreign students from France, Sweden, Germany and Portugal had given the club "an international reputation possibly not bettered by even the London clubs". Sessions had then expanded to Tuesdays as well as Fridays and in the same article Prossor described how his cousin, the 26 year-old Ted Ambrose ("Amby in any language") "enjoyed immensely the success the club has achieved in promoting the truly universal appeal of jazz". The *Melody Maker* (then an authoritative voice in the jazz and dance band world) featured Brighton

Keith Samuel's BRIGHTON JAZZ CLUB membership card, 1955.

in an article by Tony Brown in January 1955. He observed "a sizeable student population, by predisposition or merely following the mode, has taken the Traditional to its heart. At the Trad nights at the Chalet Club in Western Road, devotees of the Real Stuff can be seen stomping it with typically formal informality to the usual vigorous trumpet, trombone, clarinet frontline".

But the stomping and the vigour had nearly run its course. In March 1956 a fire destroyed the Chalet Club and the Brighton Jazz Club was suddenly without a home. Attempts to keep things going at the Montpelier Hotel lasted for a few months, but by then Terry Whitney had been in hospital for a long spell, Les Jowett and Stu Emsley had formed a new, exciting band and Les Wood was already putting down a strong marker for a more purist form of New Orleans jazz at the Coney Hill Jazz Club sessions at the Park Royal Hotel in Montpelier Road.

The torch was being handed on, but there were now more jazz musicians to carry it and, just as important, a local audience for live jazz now existed, built up over the preceding decade by the pioneering work of Ted Ambrose, Keith Slade, Terry Whitney and their colleagues. Significantly, all three musicians would have major roles to play in later developments.

HOVE
ROUND
TABLE

No. 244

PRESENTS

★ A Festival of Jazz

Humphrey Lyttelton

with

DILL JONES   NEVA RAPHAELLO

THE DOME
BRIGHTON

Saturday, 18th June
1955
at 7.30 p.m.

Programme for
"A FESTIVAL OF JAZZ",
the first jazz concert to
be staged at
The Dome, Brighton.
It was a sell-out.

COURTESY OF KEITH SAMUEL

HOVE TOWN HALL

THURSDAY, 8th NOVEMBER, 1951

Concert of Jazz

FEATURING

GRAEME BELL
AND HIS
AUSTRALIAN JAZZ BAND

HUMPHREY LYTTELTON
(GUEST ARTISTE)

PROGRAMME

SIXPENCE

The cover of the programme for the concert at the
Hove Town Hall on November 8, 1951, featuring
GRAEME BELL'S AUSTRALIAN JAZZ BAND and guest
HUMPHREY LYTTELTON. This was the first jazz
concert in the area to post "House Full" notices

COURTESY OF HORACE MEUNIER HARRIS

The Brighton Jazz Line

BREAKTHROUGH

KEITH SAMUEL

SATURDAY JUNE 18, 1955 PROVED A SIGNIFICANT DATE for those who had laboured to build an audience for live jazz in the Brighton area since the end of World War II.

For the very first time, jazz musicians were invited to perform on the stage of the 2000-seat Dome, the South Coast's most prestigious concert hall.

The occasion was A Festival of Jazz, staged by Hove Round Table in aid of local charities, and the performers were Humphrey Lyttelton and his Band, the pianist Dill Jones and the singer Neva Raphaello.

The concert was a sell-out. This was an astonishing achievement, a genuine breakthrough in raising the profile of jazz in Brighton and mid-Sussex. In symbolic terms it was the local equivalent of the celebrated Royal Festival Hall jazz concert attended by HRH Princess Elizabeth in 1951.

In the building that once served as the riding school and stables for the Prince Regent, jazz music offered up powerful evidence that its appeal and its following in the Brighton area had grown to substantial levels in a few short years.

There was some useful official recognition. "Jazz Gets Civic Support" was the headline in the *Brighton and Hove Gazette* on June 25, 1955. It was reported that civic patronage had been bestowed on the first-ever jazz concert at The Dome. The mayors of both Brighton and Hove attended and agreed that this fund-raising event had been a big success. There was a picture of Humph and his newly recruited trombonist John Picard, and, the report stated that "the Dome was packed and every programme sold".

If it was Ted Ambrose, Keith Slade and the Brighton Jazz Club stalwarts who built the first levels of support in the area for regular live jazz, it was Humphrey Lyttelton who became the first charismatic draw card capable of swelling that support to concert hall audiences exceeding 2000. By 1955 the appeal of "hot jazz" (as it was still rather quaintly called) was reaching undreamt-of proportions – and the boom would continue until the early 1960s before suffering major setbacks. More of that in Chapter 4.

Jazz concerts had taken place sporadically at the old Hove Town Hall from the

HOVE TOWN HALL

Wednesday, DEC. 3rd at 7.30 p.m.

WILCOX ORGANISATION LIMITED PRESENT

JAZZ AND BLUES

With the World Famous American Singer of
BLUES—FOLK SONGS—BALLADS

"BIG" BILL BROONZY

Final Concert in England prior to return to America.

Supported by Europe's Greatest Jazz Band direct from London Jazz Club

CHRISTIE BROS. STOMPERS

featuring Trombone Star KEITH CHRISTIE

plus " The Group Within The Band "

THE IAN CHRISTIE TRIO

Compere :—The well known B.B.C. Jazz Authority, Disc Jockey, Critic and
Pelican " Jazz " Author

REX HARRIS

TICKETS AVAILABLE AT LYON & HALL, 92 WESTERN ROAD, BRIGHTON
Telephone 22251

5/6, 4/6, 3/6, 2/-

BOOK NOW FOR THIS GREAT ATTRACTION

Arthurs, Woodchester

**REX HARRIS was a major arbiter of
post-war jazz tastes. He compered this concert
at Hove Town Hall in December 1952.**

COURTESY OF HORACE MEUNIER HARRIS

early 1950s. They are still warmly remembered. Graeme Bell's Australian Jazz Band made two appearances in 1951. This carefree and talented group of revivalists from Down Under made many friends locally on their first visit to Britain in 1947-8 (the impact of their music is described by Horace Meunier Harris in Chapter 11).

The short-sighted union embargo on UK tours by American jazz musicians and bands was not effectively lifted until the late 1950s, but one or two artists (mostly singers) managed to evade these restrictions. This made possible appearances at Hove Town Hall by such splendid blues performers as Lonnie Johnson and Big Bill Broonzy in 1952.

Humphrey Lyttelton, whose band grew impressively in quality and stature as the 1950s progressed, developed a sizeable following in Brighton and mid-Sussex. Humph was a guest at the Graeme Bell concert on Thursday November 8, 1951.

Thanks to my elder brother John (he played cricket in the same team as fellow jazz lovers Derrick Stewart-Baxter, Jim Pegg, John Wheater and Alan Robson), I was taken along at the tender age of 12 to experience live jazz for the first time. My abiding memories are of a robust, brassy sound emanating from the musicians and of audience members tapping their feet *en masse* in response to the surging beat.

Significantly, this concert was a sell-out, the first for a jazz event in the area. Writing in the *Brighton and Hove Gazette* as N.P.B., Nick Breach reported that "the house full notices were outside the hall ten minutes before the concert started. Previous concerts have been well attended but have never approached this level. Promoters would do well to note that concert hall jazz can be made a success in Brighton and Hove if handled in the right way".

Lyttelton returned at least twice with his own band to raise the musical temperature at the stately old Town Hall. This splendid red brick Victorian building, sadly destroyed by fire in 1966, could seat over 1100 people in its main hall and its resonant acoustics suited the forthright sounds of revivalist jazz. Other concerts held there in the early and mid-1950s featured the bands of Freddy Randall, Sandy Brown and Ken Colyer.

For a period trumpeter Freddy Randall was Humph's chief rival in the hierarchy of British traditional and Dixieland jazz. Illness interrupted his career and he moved to

"Mr. Five by Five"
JIMMY RUSHING –
pictured in action
with the
HUMPHREY
LYTTELTON BAND
at The Dome on
September 21, 1957.

PICTURE BY COURTESY OF
KEITH SAMUEL

Brighton and ran a guesthouse in Montpelier Road in the late 1950s whilst he recuperated. Happily, Freddy was able to resume his professional career and accompanied American trumpeter Wild Bill Davison on his first appearance in Brighton in 1965.

It was the seven-piece Lyttelton band that scored another triumph in the history of Hove Town Hall jazz concerts with a sell-out appearance to mark Brighton students' rag week on Monday October 4, 1954. Writing in the *Brighton and Hove Herald* as Musicus, Len Prossor said: "The man who, as a boy, deserted the Eton-Harrow cricket match to go wandering in top hat and striped trousers down Charing Cross Road in search of his first trumpet, had more than a thousand people stomping for an extra helping of his music at Hove Town Hall... the band finally ripped into *Get Out of Here and Go On Home* before the clapping, stamping audience finally took the hint."

Humph had become the British standard-bearer for traditional or revivalist jazz as the 1950s progressed and it was fitting that Hove Round Table should select him for the honour of starring at the first jazz concert at The Dome in June 1955. In view of his triumph at Hove Town

By 1957, Hove Round Table were confident enough to book American blues singer **JIMMY RUSHING** to appear with Humphrey Lyttelton's Band at their FESTIVAL OF JAZZ held at the Dome.It was a memorable performance.

COURTESY OF HORACE MEUNIER HARRIS.

JAZZSHOWS LTD
present
TRANSATLANTIC JAZZ

BIG BILL BROONZY
with
CHRIS BARBER'S JAZZ BAND
& OTTILIE PATTERSON

Thursday   *Town Hall*
November 3rd   *Hove*
1955
Souvenir Programme   *One Shilling*

By the time of BIG BILL BROONZY's
second visit to Hove, in November 1955,
CHRIS BARBER's popularity alone was
sufficient to guarantee a sell-out.
The concert was also the first of a
long-running series presented locally
by Jazzshows Ltd.

COURTESY OF KEITH SAMUEL

Hall the previous autumn, the decision made commercial as well as artistic sense. That the Round Table should throw its weight and prestige into promoting jazz concerts for charity was due almost wholly to the initiative of Horace Harris, whose passionate devotion to jazz stretched back to the days of the wartime Brighton & Hove Rhythm Club. The Round Table, guided by Horace, promoted four memorable annual jazz festival presentations at the Dome between 1955 and 1958, including a terrific performance by American blues singer Jimmy Rushing and the Humphrey Lyttelton band on September 21, 1957.

In 1955 Humph wore the mantle of traditionalist emperor with some unease. A questing and adventurous musician he was to plunge, within a couple of years, into a radical overhaul of his personnel, hiring three saxophonists and rhythm section players judged by the standards of the day to be "modernists". This dismayed some of his more fundamentalist supporters who regarded this evolutionary process as an act of high treason. "Bomb the H Band" was inscribed on one of the banners hoisted in protest when Humph and his battery of saxophonists encountered one group of dissidents, no doubt sporting beards and sandals. Fortunately, with odd exceptions, such shafts of wit have served to keep in proportion the schisms and fervent factionalism that have often divided jazz supporters.

As Humph pursued his artistic vision – at some commercial risk – a new champion of traditionalist values was waiting in the wings. Having noted the success of the 1955 Dome triumph, Jazzshows Ltd. staged the first of a long series of concert promotions in the area, starting with "Transatlantic Jazz", a double bill pairing Big Bill Broonzy with Chris Barber's newly formed Jazz Band and Ottilie Patterson at Hove Town Hall on Thursday November 3, 1955. It was the blues master's second visit to the area.   Reviewing the concert in the *Brighton and Hove Gazette*, J.F.P. (Jim Pegg) said, "Hove Town Hall rocked to the rhythms of the Deep South", and that Broonzy and the Barber band produced music that "thrilled a packed house". The potency of the Chris Barber band's appeal was immediately apparent and in 1956 Jazzshows were confident enough to begin a regular series of concerts at the Dome featuring this talismanic performer. Derrick Stewart-Baxter was appointed the local consultant for Jazzshows, an organisation run by Ted Morton and that perky pioneer of the revival, George Webb.

DSB and Barber shared an equal passion for the blues and this helped secure local appearances in the late 1950s and early 60s by Memphis Slim, Sister Rosetta Tharpe, Louis Jordan, Curtis Jones, Speckled Red, Sonny Terry, Brownie McGhee, Champion Jack Dupree – a wonderful roster of blues and gospel artists mainly from the Deep South. Many of the concerts were compered by DSB in a committed but often artless fashion. Jim Pegg, who reviewed some of them, recalled in later years how Derry would amble ponderously on to the stage of the Dome and proceed to undermine his immense critical stature by indulging in the distracting habit of scratching his head with one hand and his backside with the other.

These guest blues performers were a delight, but the chief draw card remained the emergent Barber band – with its sprightly, clean style and piano-less rhythm section. Its roster of talents – including Lonnie Donegan, Monty Sunshine and singer Ottilie

CHRIS BARBER'S
JAZZ BAND,
with
OTTILIE PATTERSON,
were a major draw
by the time they made
their debut at
The Dome, Brighton
in 1956.

PROGRAMME BY COURTESY OF
KEITH SAMUEL

JAZZSHOWS *present*

Chris Barber's Jazz Band

Mick Mulligan and His Band

CHRIS BARBER'S JAZZ BAND

Friday 8 p.m.   Dome
August 24th 1956   Brighton

SOUVENIR PROGRAMME — — ONE SHILLING

HAROLD DAVISON & NORMAN GRANZ present

KID ORY
AND HIS CREOLE JAZZ BAND

SOUVENIR PROGRAMME · PRICE TWO SHILLINGS

The programme for the
appearance of veteran New Orleans
trombonist KID ORY at
The Dome on October 23, 1959.
His CREOLE JAZZ BAND included the
trumpet star HENRY "RED" ALLEN.

COURTESY OF KEITH SAMUEL

Patterson – would make a worldwide impact with hit recordings before the decade ended.

Within the short space of five or six short years the Dome became the South Coast's premier showcase for a breathtaking range of performers drawn from every jazz idiom. By 1961 the range had embraced the Count Basie and Stan Kenton Orchestras, Kid Ory, Henry Red Allen, Dizzy Gillespie and John Coltrane. And in the wake of Chris Barber, two more British bands made an indelible mark. Acker Bilk and his Paramount Jazz Band and Kenny Ball's Jazzmen attracted large followings among traditional and Dixieland fans, and matched Barber with hit records of worldwide appeal.

That Brighton's chief concert hall could play host to so many big jazz names in this period and deliver audiences of an appropriate size was, at one level, a simple expression of market forces. There was a public appetite for jazz and these concerts satisfied that demand. Records and radio played their part in spreading the popularity of the music, but what must not be underestimated is the patient work by local musicians, bands, record recitalists and enthusiasts who worked week-in, week-out over a decade from 1945 to foster a core audience for the music.

For younger people, jazz was an exciting discovery. Here was music of passion and vibrancy that packed an emotional wallop – a liberating and rebellious contrast to the glutinous sentimental material that dominated the hit parade at that time. And with the increase in the number of British bands capable of playing jazz with spirit and competence, so young people began to flock to the jazz clubs to listen to the music, talk about it, dance to it, romance to it – to the extent that it became part of the social fabric of their lives. Some of them were also inspired to try to play it.

The elevation of jazz to the concert hall was all very well. It gave the music hard-won status and a slightly spurious air of respectability. Audiences sat down to listen politely to music spawned in saloons, cotton fields, whorehouses and on Mississippi riverboats. Some parents even expressed approval of jazz in its concert hall wrapping (a sure-fire way to encourage greater extremism). Many young people wanted to express their responses to jazz in a more uninhibited way – by dancing to it – and by the mid-1950s jiving to traditional jazz had become commonplace, spreading rapidly from the London jazz clubs to the provinces. Jiving had its variations and some accomplished practitioners (it still has) but it served mainly as an agreeable variant of the eternal mating ritual. This intensified the social allure of jazz music and the jazz club.

This growth of support in the mid-1950s developed most strongly among students, sixth-formers and young white-collar workers (a social term well understood in the days when young men who toiled in offices, shops or the professions were expected to wear a collar and tie to work). These new converts embraced the music with a some-times-intense passion, prompted perhaps by the limited social and economic opportuni-ties in the decade of austerity following World War II. Students from other European countries helped swell jazz club attendances further when they flocked to Brighton in the summer months to attend language schools.

To this day, many people whose love of jazz was first kindled in this era remain devoted to it. They attend jazz festivals and residential jazz weekends at holiday camps, and many of them still like to dance. They drink less alcohol and eat more discerningly than they did in their youth. But they still support jazz and bands are hired for their retirement parties, their silver and golden weddings and – as the 21st century moves on – for their funerals.

In the mid-50s natural justice demanded that the local musicians who helped to nur-ture this audience should share some of the limelight with their professional colleagues, albeit in a supporting role. Jazzshows were gracious enough to book the Les Jowett Seven at the height of their comparatively short life to support Sandy Brown's Jazz Band, pianist Dill Jones and the Mike Daniels Delta Jazz Band at a Dome concert on Friday December 6, 1956.

Australian jazz pioneer GRAEME BELL
a firm favourite among
revivalist jazz fans in Brighton and Hove.
PICTURE BY COURTESY OF KEITH SAMUEL

It is generally accepted that this splendid band – arguably the best to emerge in Brighton – failed to live up to its strengths on this occasion. Writing in the *Brighton and Hove Herald*, Len Prossor said that they gave signs of becoming a concert force to be reckoned with but that "their music had little of the verve and fat tonal quality normally present in their playing at the intimate Vanguard Club". Terry Whitney writes in detail about the significance of the Jowett band and its lasting musical impact in Chapter 3 but does not dwell on the fact that people danced to the band at the Vanguard Club, just as they had danced to Ted Ambrose's band at the Chalet Club earlier in the 1950s. And when the Coney Hill Jazz Club started in 1955, dancing was an integral part of the audience proposition.

The Graeme Bell band pioneered dancing to traditional jazz in the UK in the late 1940s and the London clubs run by the likes of Humphrey Lyttelton and Cy Laurie became famous for the gyratory antics of some of their regular customers. The contention that many musicians draw inspiration from dancers (and that dancing is good for jazz music as well as good for business) remains an interesting one.

By the summer of 1955 the *Brighton and Hove Gazette* was sufficiently influenced by this social phenomenon to devote a whole page to a Focus on Jazz Clubs with a large picture of jivers dancing to the music of the Ted Ambrose band at The Chalet Club. "Jazz appreciation, like coffee drinking, is on the upgrade in Brighton and Hove," said the anonymous reporter. "Jazz clubs are springing up to satisfy the youthful craving for rhythm. Jeans and beards are standard adornments in the clubs where youngsters perform physical marathons in keeping time with the music." Interestingly, the piece also observed that dancers "go through the same routines" when dancing to "cool" jazz but failed to comment on the contrast in energy levels. Those that preferred to dance to traditional jazz invariably did so in a much more animated fashion than their cooler counterparts. Also overlooked was the quaintly snobbish disapproval of jiving in the big dance halls. Absurdly, it was even banned in some of them, where notices baldly stating NO JIVING were displayed.

It was to be five long years before another Brighton jazz band (the Riverside Jump Band) was given the next opportunity to take the stage at a major Dome concert. By then (1961) the full force of the so-called Trad Boom had gathered pace and audiences and their expectations had changed greatly.

The Jowett booking at the Dome in 1956 acknowledged the achievements of one local jazz pioneer and his colleagues. But there was no comparable recognition for another stalwart – clarinettist Les Wood, from Portslade, who took his first lessons from Keith Slade and had begun to make an impression by 1954.

The impact made by Wood, Les Jowett and the Ted Ambrose band was well chronicled in the pages of the two principal local weekly papers at the time, the *Brighton and Hove Herald* and the *Brighton and Hove Gazette*. By the mid 1950s both newspapers had begun to run regular and well-informed pieces about the area's jazz activities. Early *Gazette* pieces were written by Nick Breach, Jim Pegg, Mike Church and Bill Hall, whereas the *Herald* employed local bass-player Len Prossor (then a proof reader at the newspaper) to write a weekly column, Rhythm & Jazz, under the pseudonym of Musicus. I was privileged to follow in Prossor's footsteps at the *Herald* from early 1958, and then switched to the *Gazette*, writing as Sam Edwards for this publication until 1976. Much source material for the early chapters of this book comes from these newspapers.

Clarinettist **LES WOOD** (left) leads his band at the **CONEY HILL JAZZ CLUB**
at the Park Royal Hotel, Montpelier Road, in the mid-1950s.

PICTURE BY COURTESY OF CHRIS WATFORD

Les Wood is an enigmatic figure, who severed his connection with the jazz world
entirely at the beginning of the 1970s and whose present whereabouts are unknown.
But he occupies an honoured place in the hierarchy of The Brighton Jazz Line. For a
period he was a major stylistic influence, revered by musicians in Sussex and beyond
who followed the fundamentalist style of New Orleans jazz exemplified by Bunk
Johnson, George Lewis and, in this country, by Ken Colyer. Les steeped himself in the
Lewis clarinet style but often found difficulty in gathering together sufficient musicians who shared his enthusiasm for this idiom. This prompted him to commute to
London to play with musicians such as Ken Colyer and the Storyville Jazzmen (later
to be led by Bob Wallis), with whom he recorded for Doug Dobell's 77 label.

Wood's main base of operation was The Coney Hill Jazz Club, which opened in the
basement at the Park Royal Hotel in Montpelier Road, Brighton, in the spring of 1955
and flourished for the next three years or so. It evolved from a social club at Patcham
run by a former policeman, Peter Arden-Burrowes.

The leader of the club's resident band at the outset was pianist Bernie Waterman, a
cherubic Brighton hairdresser whose background was in the broad mainstream of jazz
and dance music. He, together with the Coney Hill band's trombonist Derek Staton,
bassist Roy Evenett and drummer Dickie Neaves subsequently joined the Les Jowett

Another shot of **LES WOOD** at the **CONEY HILL JAZZ CLUB**, showing **JOHN COLLINSON** (banjo),
SAILOR SPICER (bass), **BILL BRUNSKILL** (trumpet), **COLIN DAVIS** (drums) and **BRIAN "HENRY" HEAGREN** (trombone).
PICTURE BY COURTESY OF CHRIS WATFORD

Seven when it was formed in May 1956. Les Wood took over the leadership duties at the Coney Hill and with banjo player Tim Streeton gradually built up a band with musicians more attuned to the purist New Orleans idiom.

Les recruited John Collinson, then resident in Hailsham and working in a Brighton bank at this time, playing both banjo and piano. Collinson also played with the Dolphin Jazz Band in Hastings and contributes this short memoir of the period:

"I cannot for the life me recall exactly how I came to be involved with Les Wood's band at the Coney Hill. I suspect that the grapevine was working and, having rolled up to listen, I was recruited. And thereby increased my income by £3 a week! Sessions took place twice weekly on Tuesdays and Fridays and always appeared well supported.

"Another great incentive to travel to Brighton was the opening of Dobell's Jazz Record Shop in Western Road (in June 1957). Managed by Bill Colyer it became a focal point before the sessions began at the Park Royal Hotel.

"Great credit must be given to Les who at that time must have been the best George Lewis interpreter around. Eventually the club folded and the band broke up. The last time I saw Les was a chance meeting in Crawley in 1975 and he was living then in Chailey. I have never heard his name mentioned (except in recollection) on the jazz circuit in recent times so one must presume that he is musically inactive."

Quietly spoken, undemonstrative but fiercely committed to his concept of how jazz should be played, Wood fulfilled a lifelong ambition in 1957 when he was invited to play alongside his idol, George Lewis, who was on his first visit to the UK. Lewis complimented Wood on his playing, and he was still cherishing this memory when I interviewed him in October 1958 for an article in the *Brighton and Hove Herald*. He was then 26 years old, talkative, modest, just a touch humourless and believed his task, in his own words, was "to keep the flame of New Orleans jazz alive in Brighton". However, Jazzshows came in for criticism for staging their Dome concerts on Friday nights. Les pointed out that the Chalet Club and then the Coney Hill had built Fridays up as the night for traditional jazz and that Jazzshows hi-jacked this audience every time they staged a concert.

As well as Collinson he had by then recruited Colin Davis on drums, Sailor Spicer on bass (previously with the Ted Ambrose band), and Bill Brunskill (trumpet) and Mac McKay (trombone) were commuting from London to play at the Coney Hill club.

Hove banjoist Tim Streeton had moved to London but retained an association with the band and Dave Cutting and Henry Heagren were among other London trombonists who supplied the tailgate sounds that Les judged essential to his style of playing.

Several efforts have been made in recent times to track down Les Wood, the most assiduous by clarinettist Chris Watford, who played with the Dolphin Jazz Band in Hastings and travelled to Brighton regularly to hear Wood in his prime. Some of the contributors to this

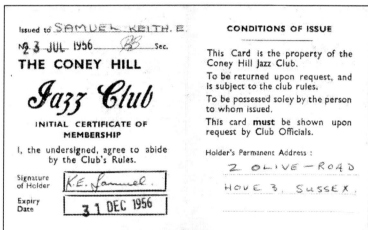

Membership card for the CONEY HILL JAZZ CLUB, 1956.
BY COURTESY OF KEITH SAMUEL

book helped Chris compile a detailed portrait of Les, which appeared in *Just Jazz* magazine in May 2001. Watford agrees with Collinson's critical appraisal of Wood and believes he was the finest George Lewis stylist that this country has produced.

Chris Watford's article is a good source for those who want more detail, particularly about Wood's recordings. It also prompted a "memory lane" contribution in the following November's edition of *Just Jazz* from Geoff Spencer, who met up with Wood in the mid-1950s. At that time Spencer was the proprietor of a newsagent's shop in New England Road, Brighton, where Wood, trombonist Hugh McConachie and others practised from time to time. In a telling anecdote, Spencer remembers accompanying Wood to the Stoll Theatre in Lyndon to hear George Lewis with Ken Colyer's band in 1957. "There must have been a second band that Les did not want to hear because, at his insistence, we spent some time in the theatre bar rather than listen to anyone but George Lewis. To say Les was a purist is putting it mildly!"

Les Wood first quit playing at the end of the 1950s. An architectural surveyor by profession, he was spotted by Terry Whitney on a building site near Hassocks in the mid-1960s. He told Terry that he had achieved the pinnacle of his ambition by playing with George Lewis in 1957 and had no wish to play again.

Surprisingly, he emerged from retirement in January 1969 – nearly ten years after he last played in public – to unveil a new five piece band at the King and Queen Hotel in Marlborough Place. With him were Gerry Geoghegan (banjo), John Boyett (bass), Geoff Simkins (drums) and London trombonist Pete Dyer. They later moved their regular Thursday nights sessions to the Gloucester Hotel in Gloucester Place but, by the middle of April, Les Wood's re-emergence as a bandleader was over. John Boyett recalled that the deciding factors were poor attendances plus the inability to find a suitable trumpeter and the added cost of transporting Pete Dyer from London.

Wood deputised for a few dates for Chris Jaques, clarinettist with the New City Jazzmen, who was recuperating from illness, then drifted into self-imposed exile.

This expansive mid-1950s period also saw "modern" jazz acquire a significant following in the Brighton area. Venues that flourished included the Lighthouse Club at the Montpelier Hotel run by Don Sollash and the Club Mambo operated by Stan Jacobs in Kings Road. In this field of jazz activity there was an overlap between the large community of musicians then employed professionally and semi-professionally in theatre orchestras and in satisfying the big market for dance music at venues such as the Regent Ballroom, the Aquarium and King Alfred ballrooms, and in the big seafront hotels. Concerts in Brighton by Stan Kenton (the first by an American band in the post-war era), the Modern Jazz Quartet, Dave Brubeck etc. in the mid and late-1950s stimulated enthusiasm for the more contemporary jazz styles. Many talented musicians played jazz locally in the modern/mainstream idioms in this period – among them Eddie Buckwell, Ronnie Vine, Don Pashley, Jimmy Taylor, Jo Hunter, Sammy Bryant, Lennie Watts, Norman Evans, Larry Wilton, Kenny Knight and Peter Gold. Some of them continue to play prominently but their activities are outside the scope of this narrative and their story must await another volume.

BAZ.

CHAPTER 3

THE LES JOWETT SEVEN: A PORTRAIT

TERRY WHITNEY

IN THE SUMMER OF 1955 the Ted Ambrose Jazz Band, with which I played piano, included two brilliant musicians – Les Jowett on second trumpet and Stu Emsley on clarinet and alto saxophone. Les, a Lecturer in Economics at the Brighton Technical College, was a charming and intelligent man and also a highly original trumpet player with considerable experience on the London jazz scene. I became very friendly with him and his wife, Ida.

I was hospitalised for some nine months in September that year and, when I re-emerged in the summer of 1956, it transpired that the Ambrose band had folded and Les and Stu had formed a new band called The Les Jowett Seven. Derek Staton was on trombone and Geoff Berry on guitar. The rest of the rhythm section consisted of the Bernie Waterman Trio – with Bernie on piano, Roy Evenett on bass and Dickie Neaves on drums – which had originally played dance music but had recently been part of a New Orleans-style band led by Les Wood at the Park Royal Hotel in Montpelier Road.

The Les Jowett band was playing every Saturday evening at a club called The Vanguard in the Dolphin Buttery under the Paris Cinema in New Road, Brighton. It was advertised as "Traditional Jazz – With A Difference". It quickly became apparent that a new force had entered the Brighton jazz scene. The music, based on the traditional repertoire and instrumentation, was fluent, melodic, cohesive and swinging. It was centered on the exceptional and exciting rapport

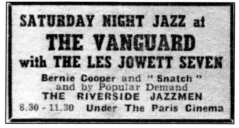

An advertisement from the
EVENING ARGUS, February 2, 1957,
publicising the LES JOWETT SEVEN's
regular Saturday night sessions at
the Paris Cinema in New Road, Brighton.
This was the heyday of the Jowett band.
COURTESY OF KEITH SAMUEL

between Les and Stu, which I had witnessed in embryo form the previous summer in the final days of the Ted Ambrose band.

The comparatively modern rhythm section gave the band a light and transparent texture quite unlike that of the banjo-based traditional bands to which Brighton was accustomed. The club was successful and attracted large crowds of listeners and dancers. Learned jazz scholars and local musicians – both traditional and modern – rubbed shoulders with the cream of Brighton youth, jiving to the pop music of the day. The whole atmosphere – enhanced by Don Sollash's witty compering and occasional Joe Williams-style singing – was electric and inspiring.

In December 1956 the band was the first in Brighton to be featured in a concert at the Dome and held its own against the competition of the nationally known bands of Mike Daniels and Sandy Brown. It subsequently made successful appearances at the Hot Club of London, the Humphrey Lyttelton Club, the Floating Festival of Jazz on the River Thames in 1957 and other London venues.

Derek Staton left the band early in 1957 and was replaced on trombone by Mike Collier soon after he moved to Brighton. Mike was well known in London, where he had led his own band. A dentist by profession, he would be an important figure in Brighton jazz for many years. His playing added authority to a front line which now went from strength to strength. When Geoff Berry emigrated to Canada in April 1957 the guitar chair was taken by the young, and gifted, Pat Benham. There were no other personnel changes during the band's short life.

**LES JOWETT receiving more attention from STU EMSLEY (right)
than from the audience at the PARIS CINEMA BUTTERY, circa 1956-57.**
PICTURE BY COURTESY OF KEITH SAMUEL

THE LES JOWETT
SEVEN aboard the
ROYAL DAFFODIL
during the FLOATING
FESTIVAL OF JAZZ on
the River Thames in
June 1957. It was one
of the year's hottest
days – in more senses
than one. With Jowett
on trumpet are MIKE
COLLIER (trombone)
and STU EMSLEY (clar-
inet). ROY EVENETT is
on bass.

PICTURE BY COURTESY OF
JUNE AMBROSE

DEREK STATON, the
LES JOWETT SEVEN's
first trombonist.

PICTURE BY COURTESY OF JUNE AMBROSE

OPENING SUNDAY APRIL 14th

"THE LES JOWETT SEVEN"
Traditional Jazz with a difference!!

HEAR the band's recording on
"Esquire Records."

HEAR the band backing the B.B.C.
television interlude film
"Spring Sends Them."

HEAR the band IN PERSON at :-

THE DOME BALLROOM, WORTHING.

EVERY SUNDAY MORNING 11 a.m. to 1.15 p.m.

Admission 2/-

The Hackney Press Ltd Printers, 407, Hackney Road, E.2

Handbill promoting the LES JOWETT SEVEN's
Sunday lunchtime sessions at the
DOME BALLROOM, WORTHING, in 1957.

COURTESY OF BEN COLLIER

I used to sit in occasionally and, at Les's request, I contributed several arrangements. I also wrote two blues-based original numbers for the band to play on the sound tracks of BBC television interlude films made by Les's friend Stephen Black. The BBC insisted that the performances should be taken from commercial recordings in order to save the Musicians Union residual fees that would otherwise have been payable to all the musicians every time the film was televised.

In conjunction with the first film, "Spring Sends Them", Les was able to persuade Carlo Krahmer to record the band for his Esquire label. The recording took place on 20 January 1957 at a studio in Bond Street, London. From

The cover for the EP issue of the LES JOWETT SEVEN'S first recording, released on the Esquire label. The tracks were recorded on January 20, 1957.

COURTESY OF KEITH SAMUEL

The front cover of the LES JOWETT TRIBUTE ALBUM issued by Flyright Records in 1982.

COURTESY OF KEITH SAMUEL

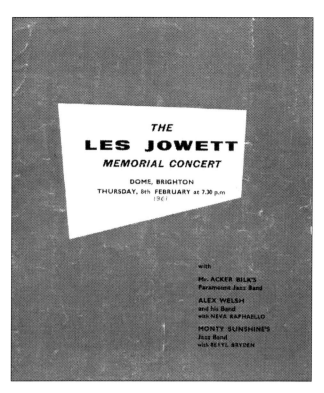

After LES JOWETT's tragic death at the age of 35 in November 1960, local bands and musicians rallied around to perform at a benefit session at the **CHINESE JAZZ CLUB** on December 16, 1960. A special tribute concert at The Dome, featuring the bands of Acker Bilk, Alex Welsh and Monty Sunshine, followed on February 8, 1961.

COURTESY OF KEITH SAMUEL.

this session, four tracks – *Spring Sends Them, Struttin' with some Barbecue, Call of the Freaks* and *Sidewalk Blues* – were released on an Esquire 45rpm EP. They were reissued in CD format in 2000 on 'The Great Revival – Traditional Jazz, 1949-58, Vol.4' [LAKE LACD 137]. They present a vivid and well-recorded reminder of the band in its prime. The driving lead and original and melodic solos by Les himself, as well as those by Stu Emsley, still sound very impressive.

For the second film, "Footsteps in the Sand", Les approached Doug Dobell, who agreed to record the band for his 77 label. The recording session took place in August 1957 in a room over Dobell's record shop at 104 Western Road, Hove. Four tracks – *House in Harlem for Sale, Louisiana, Footsteps in the Sand* and *Spain* – were released on a 77 EP. They were reissued with other material in 1982 on an LP, 'Les Jowett – A Tribute' [Flyright FLY 217], but so far as I know they have never appeared on CD. On these tracks the band sounded a little tense and Les himself had intonation problems, so the overall impression given is marginally less favourable than that presented by the earlier Esquire recordings. Much of the music, however, was excellent and Les's solo on *House in Harlem for Sale*, reminiscent of his idol Red Allen, is probably the finest recorded example of his playing left to us.

In an eloquent sleeve insert to the Flyright tribute LP, John Wilson recalled how the eminent critic Stanley Dance was impressed with the group, commenting that "their loose, open style" was reminiscent of the Luis Russell Band, and that they played traditional jazz in a mainstream context. Summing up Les's musical career, Wilson wrote: "Unfortunately, it is one of life's ironies that true perspective only comes with looking back, not forward. Les Jowett never really had his due share of recognition in life. Let us hope that this album may in some small measure, help redress the balance."

In October 1957 Les suffered two major blows. Stu Emsley left the area and, because the music was interfering with the cinema above, the band had to leave its excellent venue. Unable to find satisfactory replacements, Les lost heart and himself left the band – which was subsequently re-formed under the leadership of Ted Ambrose as The Vanguard Jazzmen. The demise of the Seven was a minor musical tragedy but, in the 18 months of its existence, it achieved great things and the Brighton jazz scene would never be quite the same again. Fortunately, we can still enjoy its qualities through its recordings.

Les continued to play brilliantly for a year or two longer in bands that never displayed the same quality or joie de vivre of the Seven and never achieved similar popularity with the specialist jazz audience or the general public. Les died of cancer in November 1960 at the tragically young age of 35. I lost a good friend, whom I still miss and frequently think about. I remain in touch with his son Miles, who still has, and treasures, Les's trumpet although, sadly, he does not play it.

LES JOWETT (left)
and STU EMSLEY
(right) flank the
LES JOWETT SEVEN'S
rhythm section in
1957:
ROY EVENETT
(bass),
PAT BENHAM
(guitar),
DICKIE NEAVES
(drums)
and
BERNIE WATERMAN
(piano).

PICTURE BY COURTESY
OF BEN COLLIER

CHAPTER 4

BOOM AND BUST

KEITH SAMUEL

ONE BENEFIT OF THE EMERGENCE of a new generation of jazz enthusiasts in the mid-1950s was the existence in their ranks of a fair number of aspiring musicians. These would-be performers were rarely missing from the audiences at the Chalet, the Coney Hill and Vanguard jazz clubs and at the Hove Town Hall and Dome concerts.

I was one of them. With rapt attention we listened to the professional and semi-professional jazz musicians, analysed their instrumental technique and watched for the gestures and signals they gave to each other to identify keys, tempos, solo routines and dynamics. It was an exciting search for clues that would unravel the mysteries of how to master a musical form whose essence defied setting down on manuscript paper. The parallel acquisition of basic instrumental technique was a much more straightforward – and duller – learning challenge.

In common with the first post-war generation of local jazz musicians we had no formal opportunities to learn how to play jazz. But we had the huge advantage of local role models to follow in Ted Ambrose, Les Jowett, Les Wood, Keith Slade, Stu Emsley, Terry Whitney, Mike Collier, Derek Staton, Bernie Waterman and others.

They had learned how to decipher the jazz code and – in most cases – were glad to share their hard-won knowledge with the next generation of players. They gave us encouragement and, sometimes, invaluable opportunities to play to an audience.

The Brighton Jazz Line was in good shape and its succession was being nurtured, thanks to the generosity of these first pioneers.

The emergent second generation contained some talented players and colourful characters. Many of them continue to play regularly in the 21st Century.

Youth clubs and community groups were often the seedbeds for these first stumbling developments as jazz performers. Steve Davies, Dave Margaroni, Steve Phillips, Spencer Holden and others were forming jazz and skiffle groups while still at Varndean Grammar School, another group sprang up at Hove Maccabi youth club containing John Frucht, Arnold King and Vernon Leigh, and at Burgess Hill the Delta Jazzmen were formed by a group of Rover Scouts including trumpeter George Jones

The first of two Brighton-based outfits to be called the MARTINIQUE JAZZ BAND was led by oboe-playing STEVE DAVIES (third from right) with Varndean Grammar School colleagues DAVE MARGARONI (trombone), BARRINGTON "SPADGER" JAMES (clarinet) SPENCER "GUS" HOLDEN (drums), STEVE PHILLIPS (guitar) and FELIX GORTON (banjo). The date is January 1957 and the location is St Peter's Church Hall, Brighton.

PICTURE BY COURTESY OF STEVE DAVIES

and trombonist Roy Love.

Skiffle music (briefly popular in the charts thanks primarily to Lonnie Donegan) sometimes featured alongside straightforward jazz in some bands. Its do-it-yourself elements had a rough-and-ready appeal to youngsters not yet able to afford orthodox musical instruments. It was a passing fad, but playing a kazoo or a tea-chest bass were the first steps down the path of performance taken by one or two jazz musicians who later gained prominence.

In Lewes, trumpeter Trevor Philcox had started the Barbican Jazz Band with Pat Whittle (reeds) and a contingent of young Seaford musicians that included Alan Parkes (guitar), Harry Herriott (bass), Tony Hood (drums) and the precociously talented Colin Purbrook. Colin was destined, after a music degree taken at Cambridge, to become a topflight professional jazz pianist and West End theatre musical director. Immensely versatile, Purbrook played clarinet and trombone in the Barbican band as well as piano and ensured that the band never lacked a wide range of instrumental voices. He died aged 62 in 1999. Richard "Dickie" Willcox, from Cuckfield, also played trombone with the Barbican band before moving to London to work as a BBC Radio producer.

"The Barbican band had only a short life from 1955 to 57," remembers Trevor Philcox. "But it was revolutionary in the sense that, in a sleepy old town like Lewes, nothing like a jazz band had ever existed."

After a few rehearsals at Pat Whittle's home a residency was started at the Brewers Arms in Lewes High Street, that quickly caught the enthusiasm of local youngsters. For a few months there were packed attendances but when support dwindled the band

The
BARBICAN JAZZ BAND
at the Brewers' Arms,
Lewes in August 1955.
Left to right are
MIKE LABERN
(guitar),
PAT WHITTLE
(alto sax),
JOHN FORD
(piano),
ALAN PARKES
(bass),
TREVOR PHILCOX
(trumpet),
COLIN PURBROOK
(trombone)
and FRED MITCHELL
(drums).

PICTURE BY COURTESY OF
TREVOR PHILCOX

moved base to The Barn at Seaford. "There were memorable sessions there with guest players such as Mike Collier, Derek Staton, Don Lawson and frequently Snatch Snashall," recalls Philcox. "But perhaps the band's main claim to fame was to allow Colin Purbrook to develop his considerable multi-instrumental talents. He could play any instrument in the band to a very high standard."

The bearded Gordon "Snatch" Snashall played an amplified viola and was a highly eccentric itinerant performer. He fiddled with intense energy and his primitive amplification equipment would often emit sparks and smoke and blow fuses. An eternal optimist, he appeared frequently in talent shows in an elusive search for wider fame.

Jazz fiddler GORDON "SNATCH" SNASHALL, pictured with his dog Bunny who accompanied him on gigs and sometimes "sang" along with the music. SNATCH played the viola and his rudimentary amplification equipment regularly blew the fuses when he sat in at the LEWES JAZZ CLUB in the late 1950s.

PICTURE BY COURTESY OF KEITH SAMUEL

The Barbican band's demise in 1957 was bought about by Purbrook's departure to study at Cambridge and the decision of the leader, Philcox, to throw in his hand with the Riverside Jump Band

The Riverside band grew out of the Aldrington Youth Club in West Hove – where from 1956 people like Mike Mounter, Pat Benham, Brian White, Barry Morgan, Brian Clarke and myself gathered together to play together for the first time.

Common to all these groups was a shared age range (broadly the late teens), and a sense that jazz brought excitement and a vivid mode of self-expression to our rather humdrum provincial lives. We also shared an impatience to progress as jazz musicians regardless of limited instrumental technique (in most cases).

Louis Armstrong and George Lewis were distant gods. Humphrey Lyttelton and Chris Barber had shown that British jazz bands could develop their own character. Les Jowett and Les Wood were examples of what could be achieved locally. We were impatient to take our places alongside them and, egged on by enthusiastic supporters of our own age, we were sometimes over-confident in believing we were good enough to play to paying audiences without ballasting support from the first generation players.

Nevertheless, talent began to shine through. Trumpeter Mike Mounter and guitarist Pat Benham quickly made their mark – Benham joining the Les Jowett Seven in its latter stages at the tender age of 17. As the leader of the Martinique Jazz Band (the first of two bands in the area to bear this name), Steve Davies's talent was evident early on but he was handicapped both by the novelty and the limitations of playing the oboe as his main instrument. It was not until he switched to soprano saxophone that his potential was realised. Both Mounter and Davies fell victim to National Service call-up for two years, and it was the early 1960s before they fulfilled their early promise.

For a period Mounter also played piano with the Delta Jazzmen, an enterprising band in the New Orleans tradition that flourished in Burgess Hill between 1955 and 1962. Led by George Jones on trumpet, the band's members were originally drawn from the 1st Burgess Hill scout group. With Jones at the outset were Roy Love (trombone), Geoff Draper (clarinet), Leon Figg (tenor sax), Derek Bridger (banjo), Dave Hertzig (piano), Mike Figg (drums) and Mike Doe on bass (one of many graduates from a tea-chest apprenticeship!). In time the band was to feature several more of the emergent talents of the Brighton and mid-Sussex jazz community

In March 1957, the Delta band started the

GEORGE JONES, trumpeter and leader of Burgess Hill's **DELTA JAZZMEN** and an early pioneer of street parade jazz in Sussex.

PICTURE COURTESY OF GEORGE JONES

THE DELTA JAZZMEN from Burgess Hill playing at LEWES JAZZ CLUB in 1959.
Pictured at the BREWERS ARMS, left to right, are: TED OWEN (clarinet), MIKE DOE (bass),
GEORGE JONES (trumpet), MIKE FIGG (drums), DEREK BRIDGER (banjo) and ROY LOVE (trombone).
PICTURE BY COURTESY OF KEITH SAMUEL

Burgess Hill Jazz Club at the Women's Institute Hall, by which time the personnel had been whittled down by the departure of Leon Figg and Hertzig, and Robin Edwards had succeeded Draper on clarinet. When Edwards left to attend university, Ted Owen travelled up from Brighton to play with the band for most of 1958 and it was during this period that George Jones was encouraged to form the Excelsior Marching Band. He was the first to gather 20 or so musicians from half a dozen traditional bands in Sussex to create the county's prototype New Orleans-style parade band. Roy Martin has subsequently carried the torch in the county for this kind of music with his Expedient Brass Band.

The Excelsior Marching Band paved the way with a ragged but memorable performance at the Brighton Rag Week procession in November 1957, followed by better-organised efforts at the Hayward Heath Dolphin Fair in April and Burgess Hill Goose Fair in September 1958. "We had to weed out the dead wood," commented George Jones after the Brighton parade. Whether or not this was due to indifferent musicianship or over-indulgence is not recorded. However, I recall (as a member of the front rank of trombones) a distinct loss of momentum as we trudged uphill via West Street and Queens Road to Brighton Station, followed by an exhilarating but musically chaotic descent downhill into Trafalgar Street. The band members wore ill-fitting peaked bus drivers' caps, borrowed by Jones from the Southdown Bus Company. With

Roy Love, Hugh McConachie and myself, Mike Collier also played in the front rank of the trombones (wearing dark glasses to avoid being recognised, claims Ted Owen).

By comparison, the Haywards Heath performance was a minor triumph. There were section rehearsals in advance, Les Wood lent impressive power to the reed section, the band marched in step (as a splendid photograph shows) and the parade route wisely avoided the hilly inclines that almost scuppered the Brighton effort.

With Gerry Geoghegan replacing Ted Owen on clarinet, the Delta band moved on to play at the Memphis Jazz Club at the Hayworth Hotel at Haywards Heath, in 1958; then a new club, The Jazzbar, at the Hassocks Hotel, in 1959. Derek Middleton made an impressive debut on the local jazz scene after succeeding Mike Figg as the band's drummer in 1959. He later saw service with most of the top Sussex bands, including the New City Jazzmen, Fourteen Foot Band and Riverside Jump Band.

As the Trad Boom gathered pace the band worked frequently across Southern England from Portsmouth to Hastings. One regular booking was at the unique Mermaid Club in Littlehampton. "The bandstand and dance floor were located in the converted engine room of a former motor torpedo boat moored by the harbour side," remembers George Jones.

Another impressive debut took place in 1960 when singer Anne Durrant first

THE EXCELSIOR NEW ORLEANS MARCHING BAND parading at the **HAYWARDS HEATH DOLPHIN FAIR** in April 1958. The band, led by **GEORGE JONES** on trumpet, wore caps borrowed from the Southdown Bus Company – and evidently marched smartly in step. **TED OWEN, LES WOOD, MIKE COLLIER, KEITH SAMUEL** and **HUGH McCONACHIE** can be glimpsed among the personnel.   PICTURE BY COURTESY OF BEN COLLIER.

THE NEW CITY JAZZMEN from Crawley have kept the jazz flag flying in Sussex for more than 45 years. This photograph was taken when they performed at LEWES JAZZ CLUB at the BREWERS ARMS on January 16, 1959. Founder members BERNARD HODGSON (trumpet) and RON WESTCOTT (trombone) were still with the band in 2002. Clarinettist JACK SHERRIFF left in 1960 and subsequently played with many groups in the Brighton area including the MARTINIQUE JAZZ BAND. He led his own ROYAL QUINTET for a number of years.

PHOTO BY COURTESY OF KEITH SAMUEL

appeared with the band on an occasional basis.

This pattern of work continued until 1962 when disbandment was brought about by pressures of work and most of the surviving original members moving from the area. By then the versatile Gerry Geoghegan had switched from clarinet to banjo when Derek Bridger was called up for RAF service, allowing Geoff Draper to rejoin the band on clarinet with his National Service behind him.

Most of these emergent musicians were inspired by a wide range of jazz masters and were happy to seize opportunities to play whether in the traditional, Dixieland or mainstream idioms. But a much more single-minded stylist emerged in the shape of Ted Owen, a diminutive young trainee silversmith from the Queens Park area of Brighton who was devoted to New Orleans jazz and became Les Wood's most avid disciple in developing a clarinet style inspired by their hero George Lewis.

In this mid-to-late 1950s period it seemed that Brighton and mid-Sussex was teeming with aspirant jazz musicians and bands formed, re-formed and broke up at a pace too swift to chronicle.

An avid jazz fan since his schooldays, John Boyett was a couple of years older than most of the second generation players and did not take up the tuba (and later the string bass) until after he had completed his National Service and was back in the secure environment of Barclays Bank. Red-haired, socially extrovert and indefatigably optimistic, Boyett has been an omnipresent character on the Brighton and mid-Sussex jazz scene for over 40 years. He has had unrivalled opportunities to assess the relative merits and contributions of many of the musicians who figure in this story.

John's first playing colleagues in the mid-1950s were a rehearsal band that gathered at the Hove Place Hotel, led by Hugh "Mac" McConachie on trombone, with Dick Deeley (trumpet), Frank Parker (banjo), and a younger talent, the fast-emerging Ted Owen.

Boyett went on to forge a longstanding friendship and musical partnership with Owen. "We were both inspired by Les Wood and his Gloryland Jazz Band when they were playing at the Coney Hill Jazz Club," recalls Ted. "John and I would meet in the evening at the 'Pav' (the Pavilion Hotel in Castle Square, Brighton) and talk endlessly about Bunk Johnson, George Lewis and Ken Colyer, and drink as much Guinness as possible!"

Ted Owen became an increasingly influential figure, playing with the Delta Jazzmen in Burgess Hill in the late 1950s then leading his own Excelsior Jazz Band for a couple of years, his New Orleans Rhythm Boys and various trios, quartets and other combinations. He played with the drummer Barry 'Kid' Martyn and with George Perry in Soho with a band that included Mike Cotton and John Beecham. He then turned professional for a couple of years at the height of the Trad Boom in 1961-62 to play with the Mike Peters Florida Jazz Band (which included Roy Williams on trombone). Banjo player Stu Morrison (later to play with Chris Barber) introduced Ted to the fine Portsmouth trumpeter Cuff Billett. Ted and Cuff maintained a close association and played together memorably in the Vieux Carré Jazz Band in the late 1950s. Owen believes that this band, more than any other he played with, captured best the spirit of the New Orleans revivalist approach.

After Les Wood's abrupt retirement at the end of the 1950s, Ted Owen carried the torch for the purist New Orleans style in Brighton and mid-Sussex. There was some poignancy in the fact that his decision to emigrate to South Africa in July 1969 came a few short months after Les Wood's short-lived re-emergence. The gap left in the ranks was that much wider.

After a career in insurance Ted now lives in retirement at Stanger on the Natal coast and has happy memories of his jazz life in Brighton and mid-Sussex. He played for a time in South Africa but told me in May 2002 that he no longer plays in public. "I get out my clarinet occasionally, look at it, play a little then put it away again."

On their return from National Service, Mike Mounter and Steve Davies (now playing soprano sax) were drawn into collaboration with Owen in the early 1960s, notably in a long running session at the Norfolk in Grand Parade. Gerry Geoghegan, who had succeeded Owen as the clarinettist with the Delta Jazzmen in Burgess Hill, became the regular banjo player in Owen's New Orleans Rhythm Boys and for the next 20 years or so he was prominent in the ranks of several more of the traditional and New Orleans bands in the area.

Etching by Michael Blaker of clarinettist TED OWEN in the late 1950s.

COURTESY OF MICHAEL BLAKER.

Mike Mounter's involvement in the area's jazz activities has lasted even longer. Steve Davies, after periods in exile, has returned to live in Brighton, to play locally – memorably with the Royal George Five at Burgess Hill in the late 1970s – and to perform with and manage the globe-trotting NatWest Jazz Band for more than 20 years.

"Ted Owen was a bit special," reflects Boyett. "He got us to focus on New Orleans jazz. Mike Mounter was and is a natural jazz musician. Like Cuff Billett he's *all jazz*. Gerry Geoghegan is another natural. As well as banjo and clarinet I've heard him make a useful stab at playing trumpet and he could probably get a useful sound out of a trombone if asked."

Another admirer of Ted Owen's playing was artist and fellow student Michael Blaker who has written an engaging book entitled " The Autobiography of a Painter-Etcher". (Beresford House Press). In it he recalls heady days at Brighton College of Art where jazz provided a substantial part of the sound track to student life.

Blaker observes that "Brighton in that period was somewhat like New Orleans might have been in its jazz heyday – or, at least, we did all we could to create such an atmosphere". He recalls the period from 1957 onwards when the skiffle and jazz revival was at its height. "Once a week every village and town in Sussex seemed to have its jazz club. The bands were local, dedicated and idealistically uncommercial, which was why they were so good.

"Ted Owen was a student of silversmithing at the college, and all day one could hear from the workshop the sound of the clarinet as he practised it."

Living in Ramsgate in 2002, Blaker retains his admiration for Owen's musical talents and produced for this book a new print of one of his 1950s etchings of Ted playing the clarinet.

Michel Blaker played the harmonium, piano and slide whistle in a succession of quirky student spasm bands, including the Eminent Victorians, the Spasmodics and the Portobello Jazzmen. His memoir includes colourful descriptions of the prominent part played by jazz in rag day processions and dances, and the launching by Brighton art students of the mammoth Jazz in June events at the Corn Exchange from 1958. Ted Owen is especially proud of his part in this initiative, which he believes helped to put Sussex jazz on the map.

JAZZ IN JUNE

brighton art students present a ball

brighton corn exchange

JAZZ
BAND
CONTEST

friday 20 june 1958

admission 5s

Brighton art students combined a flair for design with their enthusiasm for jazz. A ticket for the first Jazz in June event in 1958.

COURTESY OF KEITH SAMUEL

THE JAZZ ENTERTAINERS, a group of youngsters from the HOVE MACCABI CLUB, who were
coached by DEREK STATON (trombone) and JIM WALKER (piano). JASON PROPP is on clarinet,
ARNOLD KING on trumpet, CLIVE BUBLEY on drums and VERNON LEIGH on guitar.
The picture was taken in 1958. Bass player JOHN FRUCHT is missing.

PICTURE BY COURTESY OF VERNON LEIGH.

By 1958 the second generation of jazz musicians in Brighton and mid Sussex were
into their stride. The ad hoc mentoring by the local pioneers, together with plenty of
opportunities to perform in local clubs and community halls, had strengthened their
standards of performance.

Pianist Bernie Waterman and trombonist Derek Staton both helped the Maccabi
club youngsters at different times. Among the players were Jason Propp (clarinet and
alto), Arnold King (trumpet), Clive Bubley (drums), John Frucht (bass) and Vernon
Leigh (guitar). Jim Walker helped out on piano and another club member Carl
Simmons was also heard on drums.

Guitarist Vernon Leigh recalls how Staton's no-nonsense enthusiasm overcame the
band's early inexperience. "The first thing he said was 'OK, let's play a 12 bar in B
flat'. We looked at each other blankly. But thanks to him we began to understand what
it was we had been listening to at the Coney Hill and Vanguard clubs and we started
to improve." Staton, after leaving the Les Jowett Seven in 1957 drilled the Maccabi
club youngsters into a band called The Jazz Entertainers that played some sessions at
the Prince Albert in Trafalgar Street in 1958.

In due course Frucht turned professional for a brief period, and then he and Leigh
became long-stay members of the Riverside Jump Band. Simmons also saw service
with this band. Arnold King (or Arnie as he was universally known) went on to
become one of the local jazz scene's best-loved characters, operating as a sideman,
bandleader (renowned for his witty announcements), unquenchable enthusiast and
promoter of the Brighton Jazz Club during its 1970s incarnation.

THE VANGUARD JAZZMEN at the Hayworth Hotel, Haywards Heath, in 1959.
Left to right: DEREK STATON (trombone), DICKIE NEAVES (drums), TED AMBROSE (trumpet),
BERNARD MOSELEY (bass), BERNIE WATERMAN (piano), PAT CHAPMAN (alto saxophone/clarinet).

PICTURE BY COURTESY OF PAT CHAPMAN

Before he left the area in 1962 to work in East Anglia, Derek Staton was a lively and resolute presence in Brighton jazz circles. A capable trombonist in the traditional/Dixieland idiom, Derek held fast to his principles and did not always see eye-to-eye with his fellow musicians. He was replaced by Mike Collier in the Les Jowett Seven in 1957, but enjoyed a long spell of fulfilment when the remnants of the Jowett band came together under Ted Ambrose's leadership as the Vanguard Jazzmen from 1958. Mike Collier soon dropped out and Staton returned to the fold as the band's trombonist and efficient manager.

This band appeared widely at jazz clubs and at private events and made two broadcasts for the BBC West Region from the Burlington Hotel Jazz Club in Worthing in 1961. Often clad in smart maroon band jackets, the Vanguard band played an entertaining and versatile brand of Dixieland and mainstream jazz, but with less reliance on the kind of original arrangements that typified the Jowett Seven.

The Vanguard band worked steadily for the next four years or so, including a long residency at the Starlight Rooms at the Hotel Montpelier in Brighton, which extended across much of the week during the summer seasons in the early 1960s. Well before then the band had acquired two more stalwart members in Bernard Moseley (also known professionally as Bernard Marshall) who succeeded Roy Evenett, and Pat Chapman who eventually replaced Stu Emsley on clarinet and alto, after a brief stay by Bob Lomas. Ted Ambrose on trumpet, Bernie Waterman on piano and drummer Dickie Neaves remained constants.

Bernard Moseley, 80 years old in November 2002, recalls the heyday of the Vanguard band. "It was fortunate that when I joined the band it was just beginning to peak and I have memories of some great sessions. Our longest residency was at the Starlight Rooms where we finished up playing five or six nights a week, wearing different jackets, different shirts, but the same musicians playing Trad, mainstream and Latin American in our varying disguises, adding Stan "The Man" Jacobs on conga and timbales for authenticity.

"The men's toilet at the Starlight Rooms had an unfortunate tendency to overflow and flood the dance floor. When this occurred those of us at the back of the band who couldn't see what was happening were made aware of the threat by Ted Ambrose who – from his vantage point at the front of the stand – would shout out 'Come In Number Nine!'"

With this line-up the Vanguard Jazzmen became, in 1959, the first local band to win the mammoth Jazz in June jazz band contest held annually at the Corn Exchange. In symbolical terms this victory was a re-assertion by the senior contingent of Brighton jazz musicians of their hard-won status. Organised by Brighton art students for charity, the first Jazz in June event was held in 1958 and the format lasted for six years. Eventually the novelty wore off and the huge crowds they attracted were largely siphoned off in 1963-64 by the musical and social revolution set in motion by The Beatles phenomenon.

BERNARD MOSELEY conferring with producer **BRIAN PATTEN** (left) and presenter **GRAHAM SPIERS** (right) prior to a BBC West Region radio broadcast in 1961.

PICTURE BY COURTESY OF BERNARD MOSELEY

The zestful **Bernie Waterman**, who had been a charter member of the much-admired **Les Jowett Seven**, maintained a versatile presence in the jazz and dance music world for many more years, often playing in company with **Bernard Moseley**. Bernie took in his stride, literally, any style of jazz from New Orleans to bebop and accompanied performers as diverse in style as **Les Wood** and **Tubby Hayes**. He continued to help and encourage younger musicians, a commitment that extended back to the post-war days of the **Avalon Swing Club** at the Hotel Montpelier and sessions at the **Half Moon** in West Street where young-sters such as drummer **Peter Gold** were helped in their development. Bernie succumbed to cancer at the early age of 51 in 1973. So great was the affection in which he was held that two memorial sessions were held in his honour. The first, at the **Gay Highlander**, Peacehaven, featured three bands (**the Benny Simkins Sextet, Jack's Royal Quintet** and **Bill Polley's Phoenix Six**) and many individual musicians. The second, at the **Fox and Hounds**, Haywards Heath, starred **Bruce Turner** with the **Fourteen Foot Band**.

A characteristic shot of
BERNIE WATERMAN
at the piano keyboard
with the
VANGUARD JAZZMEN
at the Montpelier Hotel,
Brighton, in 1958.
Also pictured are
BERNARD MOSELEY
(bass),
DEREK STATON
(trombone),
DICKIE NEAVES
(drums),
TED AMBROSE
(trumpet)
and
BOB LOMAS
(clarinet).

PICTURE BY COURTESY OF
BERNARD MOSELEY.

The narrative of the story has raced ahead at this point. Significantly, just as the Vanguard band was getting into its stride in the early 1960s, the support of young audiences for traditional jazz – or Trad as it came to be glibly dubbed – changed from the steady incremental build-up that had characterised the post-war revivalist years to an almost frantic level of enthusiasm.

KENNY BALL (left) and ACKER BILK, whose recordings became worldwide hits
during the height of the Trad Boom in the early 1960s.

PICTURES BY COURTESY OF KEITH SAMUEL

Much has been written about the Trad Boom as it came to be known. The hard fact is that it was fairly short-lived. It can be conveniently bracketed between the huge Top 20 successes of three or four recordings – starting with Chris Barber's *Petite Fleur* in 1959, featuring Monty Sunshine playing the haunting Sidney Bechet composition. It was an international hit, selling a million in both in the UK and the United States.

In 1961 Acker Bilk went one better with his clarinet-and-strings cocktail *Stranger on the Shore*, which achieved multi-million sales and the No.1 spot in both the UK and the USA.

Interestingly, neither the Barber nor Bilk hit recordings featured the standard traditional/Dixieland instrumentation (trumpet, trombone, clarinet and banjo-focused rhythm) so integral to their public performances. But shortly afterwards Kenny Ball and his Jazzmen hit the tills in the record shops, first with *Samantha* and then the worldwide hit *Midnight in Moscow*, which reached No. 2 in the States in 1962.

By any standards these were major commercial successes. It was the first time that jazz (albeit marketed in a palatable form) had made such an impact on the record-buying public since the swing era successes of Benny Goodman, Artie Shaw and Glenn Miller. Barber's success was a something of a windfall but Bilk and Ball were skilfully marketed in the mainstream of the entertainment world and their financial rewards were no doubt substantial.

In the space of ten years or so the revivalist jazz movement, hitherto earnest, worthy, and a touch high-minded in a slightly fatuous way, suddenly found itself surrounded by marketing men, agents, and endless cheesey entrepreneurs hustling for a quick buck.

Where Barber, Bilk and Ball led the way, other – often inferior – imitators were drafted in to ambush the wallets of the new fans being drawn in by the high profile PR and wide exposure on national TV and radio. Bands dressed in funny hats, appeared on variety bills and TV with comedians and jugglers, and tills rang… for a while.

For local jazz musicians in Brighton and mid-Sussex there was a substantial spin off from this unexpected blossoming of interest. Sussex bands had become accustomed to running their own jazz clubs in musty backrooms of pubs and community halls – and often subsidising them out of their own pockets. Now they were propositioned to take residencies and bookings at swish clubs and ballrooms where the promoters took the risks… and the sometimes-large profits. There were even broadcasts and bookings in concert halls and posh hotel ballrooms for the better (and luckier) bands.

Apart from an increase in the number of jazz concerts held at the Dome, the start of the Trad Boom was most graphically symbolised by the launching of the Chinese Jazz Club at the Brighton Aquarium Winter Garden late in 1959.

The founder and promoter of the club was the colourful Bonaventura "Bonny" Manzi, who had run jazz sessions in Chertsey and Crawley but chose Brighton as an ideal place for his major investment in jazz. The Chinese Jazz Club opened on

"Chop Chop" The effervescent "UNCLE" BONNY MANZI, promoter of the Brighton Chinese Jazz Club. He is seen here at the Railway Hotel, Crawley circa 1959-60. TERRY LIGHTFOOT is the clarinettist and his brother PADDY is on banjo (right). The be-hatted young fans have clearly heeded Bonny's entreaties to wear "rave gear".

PICTURE BY COURTESY OF JOHN ROBERTS

November 27, 1959 and continued to operate, with various shifts of policy, until 1967.

From the outset, Trad jazz on Friday nights was the staple attraction and a procession of many of the best-known bands of the day was featured – Ken Colyer, Bob Wallis, Kenny Ball, Dick Charlesworth, Terry Lightfoot, Cy Laurie, Alex Welsh, Humphrey Lyttelton, Chris Barber, Mick Mulligan and George Melly, Monty Sunshine etc. Some local bands were given bookings, usually as supporting acts, and there were also interesting forays into modern jazz and rhythm 'n' blues on other nights.

"Uncle Bonny" marketed the Brighton Chinese Jazz Club in a surreal, seemingly chaotic but essentially clever way. Smouldering joss sticks and Chinese lanterns offered a quasi-oriental atmosphere, crocodile sandwiches were advertised (in the confident expectation that they would never be ordered) and Bonny's handbills and advertisements were irresistible in their lack of sophistication. "I always enjoyed the careless printing and Bonny's throwaway humour," remembers Michael Blaker who attended the club regularly.

A characteristic handbill from "UNCLE" BONNY MANZI advertising forthcoming attractions at the Brighton Chinese Jazz Club in 1960.

Nowadays Bonny's humour would cause ructions for its lack of political correctness.

"Chop Chop Velly Good" was his principal catch phrase when he sought to command attention in print or over the microphone. But smartest of all was his sly encouragement to young patrons to wear "rave gear" – which Bonny helpfully defined as including "bikinis, bowler hats, pyjamas, bear skins, suits of armour, football gear", with prizes offered for the best turn-out.

It was of course a recipe for an old-fashioned fancy dress party, re-positioned to encourage a participative, exhibitionistic, mildly erotic and camera-friendly role for young audiences as they danced and strutted to the music of the Trad Boom minstrels.

In his readable autobiography *Owning Up* published in 1965, George Melly cites Acker Bilk's bowler hat as the emblematic cult object of the Trad Boom and he credits the "eccentric jazz promoter" Uncle Bonny with coining the expression "rave gear" and for encouraging the wearing of it at his clubs by "ravers".

Melly, an astute observer of social trends, saw all this as fairly harmless anti-authoritarian behaviour, echoed by previous generations and those to come. He also argued that British Trad signed its own death warrant by reducing the music to a banjo-laden formula and by breaking through into the pop world with its demands for repetitive gimmicks, leading to inevitable over-exposure. Melly talked of Trad's "three year omnipotence" (meaning 1959-62). It was he said a "monotonous and dreary time" when the airwaves "were turgid with banjos".

Nevertheless, business boomed and many good musicians earned a better living as a result. But as the new audiences raved and cavorted to the British "Traddy-pop" bands their heedlessness of the inspirational sources of revivalist jazz (King Oliver, Louis Armstrong, Jelly Roll Morton, George Lewis etc.) was only too apparent.

In its appeal to young people, rock n' roll – dating from the emergence of Bill Haley, Elvis Presley and Jerry Lee Lewis – had been a potent rival to traditional jazz since the mid-1950s. This kind of music tended to have a bigger hold in the industrial towns. It also had much more clout in the film industry where its purveyors (particularly Presley) enjoyed the status of sex symbols, an area in which Acker Bilk and his bowler hat were totally outclassed. But rock music's next generation of stars would inflict much greater defeats on the jazzers.

Out of the blue in 1963 came The Beatles, sweeping all before them in an unprecedented wave of adulation that changed the entire music industry – and the way that younger people interacted with it – in a matter of months.

Their records swamped the charts. They sold 7 million discs in Britain alone in 1963, as "Beatlemania" swept the country. Then it was the turn of the United States and the rest of the world to fall under their spell. Nothing like it had been seen before and the entire show business world was turned on its head.

British Trad simply faded away in the face of this onslaught. Middle-aged men in fancy dress were no match for four raunchy young lads in their early 20s capable of claiming 60 percent of the airplay on US radio and selling 150 million single discs by the end of 1965.

Jazz clubs closed and promoters and agents fastened quickly on to beat groups cast in the Beatles mould. The most robust jazz bands survived, so did the Chinese Jazz Club until 1967. Canny as ever, Bonny saw the writing on the wall and switched to rhythm'n' blues as his main offering, but still kept a smattering of jazz going (Bonny flirted with jazz promotion again when he was running the Concorde Restaurant on the Aquarium premises in the late 1970s).

But, for the Brighton and mid-Sussex bands that had benefited from the windfalls of the Trad Boom in the early 1960s, it meant a swift return to the pubs, backrooms and the self-financing impoverishment of gigs without contracts and sometimes without any firm agreement on fees. The music and its spirit would survive if it could re-establish and sustain itself as a niche attraction. Later chapters show how this was achieved.

CHAPTER 5

THE RIVERSIDE JUMP BAND: A PORTRAIT

KEITH SAMUEL

Lewes is renowned for its boisterous Bonfire Night celebrations. But the fireworks were entirely musical on March 9, 2000 when the county town's Jazz Club played host to a reunion of The Riverside Jump Band, brought together to play again for the first time in 30 years.

Leader **Keith Samuel** *had tracked down and assembled all eight members of the 1960 line-up for a special millennium charity performance in aid of the Ear Foundation. All this detective work paid off when the House Full signs went up for the first time in the current Lewes Jazz Club's history. More than 150 people crammed into their Constitutional Club headquarters to cheer on the veteran musicians (average age by then 63) and raise more than £500 for the charity.*

For the band's clarinettist Keith Slade it was a poignant occasion. At 72, one of the founding fathers of live jazz in Brighton and mid-Sussex was back in action locally for the first time in a dozen years. His singing and playing in a burlesque performance of "The Golden Wonder Blues" proved a show-stopper and the Club persuaded the Riverside band to make their reunions an annual event.

With Slade on clarinet and Samuel on trombone, the Riverside Reunion Band raised a total of £2200 for charity with further annual get-togethers in 2001 and 2002. Other regular participants were Trevor Philcox (trumpet), Terry Whitney (piano), Vernon Leigh (guitar), Brian Clarke (drums), and Barry Morgan and John Frucht sharing the string bass duties. Pat Benham, Mike Mounter, Brian White, Robin Grayson and singer Karen Donovan were among other Riverside alumni who made guest appearances.

The death of Keith Slade aged 74 in August 2002 means the band can no longer re-assemble the exact personnel from its 1960s heyday but Keith's talent, warm friendship and impish humour will live on unwaveringly in the memory of the band's musicians and its supporters.

MILLENNIUM REUNION. In March 2000, the **RIVERSIDE JUMP BAND** re-assembled its 1960 line-up for a one-off charity performance at the Lewes Jazz Club. Pictured in rehearsal beforehand, left to right, are **KEITH SAMUEL, BARRY MORGAN, VERNON LEIGH, BRIAN CLARKE, TREVOR PHILCOX,** the late **KEITH SLADE, TERRY WHITNEY** and **JOHN FRUCHT.** The event was a sell-out and the Riverside reunions became an annual event, raising substantial sums for charity. Other alumni participants have included **MIKE MOUNTER, ROBIN GRAYSON, KAREN DONOVAN, BRIAN WHITE** and **PAT BENHAM.**   PICTURE BY COURTESY OF KEITH SAMUEL

Below, **Keith Samuel** *tells the story of the* **Riverside Jump band.**

T HE RIVERSIDE JUMP BAND – known initially as the Riverside Jazzmen – flourished in Brighton and mid-Sussex for 12 years between 1956 and 1968, playing a blend of Chicago-style Dixieland and swing. We performed weekly at the Lewes Jazz Club for 18 months in 1958-59 and appeared at concerts, festivals and prestige venues such as the Brighton Dome and Corn Exchange as well as at countless Sussex pubs, clubs, town halls and anywhere else where young people congregated.

The band made its public debut at the Green School Hall (now demolished) at Southwick Green in late 1956 and in the spring of 1957 enjoyed a hugely successful run at the Hangleton Manor Hotel, Hove. On successive Saturday evenings the place was packed to its medieval rafters. The proprietor took fright at such large numbers and placed an advertisement in the *Evening Argus* on three consecutive nights announcing the closure of the sessions due to "accommodation difficulties". We were all too young to appreciate the irony at the time. Success on this scale can elude musicians – and hoteliers – over an entire lifetime.

The ambition to form what became the Riverside band developed among a group of jazz-loving teenaged friends who attended Aldrington Youth Club in Glebe Villas, Hove. Our nearest local was The Adur pub near Hove Lagoon where, legally under-aged, we daringly drank half pints of cider or mild ale. It was beyond our most far-fetched dreams that, 20 years later, this workaday redbrick Kemp Town Brewery pub would feature in-person appearances by near-legendary American jazz stars such as Buddy Tate and Dick Cary. We flirted with the name of The Adur Estuary Stompers for a while and this whimsy survived long enough for Barry Morgan (then a trainee sign-writer) to letter an advertising billboard but we decided that The Riverside Jazzmen was less parochial and more ambitious.

Barry and I had known each other since playing football together for the 3rd Hove Cubs. At the same time that I bought my first trombone, he acquired a banjo. Louis Armstrong was probably our major hero, but the more accessible models for inspiration and emulation were Humphrey Lyttelton and Chris Barber. With only the crudest grasp of basic techniques and with breath-taking self-confidence we announced early in 1956 that we were forming a band. Various figures drifted into focus clutching instruments – none of them with much clue about how to unlock the exotic mysteries of playing jazz. Names I remember include Max Huzinga (later to become a local estate agent), Graham Gifford, Frank McManus, the Cook brothers – Willie and Arthur, Gordon Evans, Nigel Butler, Bruce Davison, Guy Robins, Pete Watson, Dave Shade, Spencer James and Dave Lloyd. We fumbled, clonked, burped,

THE RIVERSIDE JAZZMEN play to a packed house at the Hangleton Manor Hotel, Hove, early in 1957. Left to right KEITH SAMUEL (trombone), BARRY MORGAN (bass), MIKE MOUNTER (trumpet), BRIAN WHITE (clarinet) and PAT BENHAM (guitar). Drummer BRIAN CLARKE is obscured.   PICTURE BY COURTESY OF KEITH SAMUEL

THE
HANGLETON MANOR HOTEL, HOVE

Regret that the **RIVERSIDE JAZZMEN** will not be playing FOR A PERIOD owing to accommodation difficulties.

———

LUNCHEONS & DINNERS SERVED
Excellent Chef de Cuisine
Fully Licensed

———

TELEPHONE   -   -   HOVE   49428

Panic stations. This advertisement appeared in the EVENING ARGUS on three consecutive nights in March 1957. The truth behind the "accommodation difficulties" was that the jazz drew crowds beyond the hotel's capacity. The management's solution was to sack the band!

strummed, thrashed, honked, hooted and falteringly acquired the first semblance of a repertoire.

By then I was working as a reporter on the *Brighton and Hove Herald* and Len Prossor, who played the double bass semi-professionally, was a colleague (and responsible for the *Rhythm and Jazz* column in the paper). He sold his spare bass fiddle to Barry Morgan, fulfilling Barry's ambition to graduate from the banjo. We badly needed the company of more accomplished players – or at least fast-learners of our own generation. They came in the shape of Brian Clarke, a feisty drummer from Shoreham who helped me co-lead the band for nearly four years, Brightonians Mike Mounter (trumpet) and Brian White (clarinet, alto and tenor sax) and Hove guitarist Pat Benham. Already a grapevine was in place that pinpointed aspiring young jazz musicians in the area. Brian White worked hard at acquiring the cool demeanour of a professional musician. He was very sociable, loved telling jokes but was never a slave to punctuality – a handicap he clearly overcame when he made his career in full time music. Pat Benham, the baby of the band, exuded a calm, almost monkish dignity and never laughed at Brian White's jokes. For an art student he defied the conventional stereotype of Bohemian extroversion. The one tribal concession he made was wearing a duffel coat.

We soon had enough people to form two bands but a process of gentle culling, National Service call-up and natural selection boiled the personnel down to Mounter, White, Benham, Morgan, Clarke and myself – a conventional traditional/Dixieland six piece line-up, with Benham resolutely resisting inducements to play Morgan's cast-off banjo! Pat, already technically accomplished and later to become a respected music teacher, helped us understand chords but the key stimulus came from Mounter, who played piano as well as trumpet and was the eldest member of the group by a year or so (our ages ranged from 17 to 20). A toolmaker by trade he was nonchalant to the point of near-amnesia at times and, although completely non-directive, had a natural talent for jazz that rubbed off on the rest of us. He played the trumpet with a ravishing tone and exciting dynamics.

Accepting a somewhat foolhardy invitation to listen to this embryonic group, Musicus of the *Brighton and Hove Herald* observed (on 16.2.57) that the band had "much enthusiasm" and "a drummer who lays down a very good beat". Pat Benham's promise was noted and Mike Mounter won praise for his forceful trumpet and "good jazz feeling" but "thus far his attributes are not matched by the rest of the band. Tuning and intonation will no doubt improve when the other players have greater control of their instruments".

Encouraged rather than crushed, we practised hard as individuals and rehearsed together regularly in the basement gym at Davigdor Road School in Hove. We made good progress. This was the "first" Riverside band with a settled personnel (meaning that it didn't change every weekend!) and by the spring of 1957 – after a false start at the Palmeira Hotel in Hove – we were appearing as the Riverside Jazzmen and fulfilling a series of regular bookings at the Co-op Hall, Southwick, the Sundown Club in Brighton as well as the Hangleton Manor Hotel.

When the Manor sessions came to an abrupt end we moved on to the basement clubroom at the Hotel Montpelier in Brighton, playing a summer season under the banner of the Club Continentale and attracting good numbers of foreign students as well as our regular supporters. We played at private engagements, many of them student functions, and were honoured by an invitation to play at the opening of the new Dobells Jazz Record Store in Western Road, Brighton, in June 1957. Ken Colyer, brother of the shop's manager Bill, smashed a 78 record on the counter to declare the

Experience lends a hand. Clarinettist KEITH SLADE guests with the teenaged RIVERSIDE JAZZMEN at the Co-op Hall, Southwick in May 1957. His front-line companions are KEITH SAMUEL (trombone), MIKE MOUNTER (trumpet) and BRIAN WHITE (alto sax).

PICTURE BY COURTESY OF KEITH SAMUEL

Most drummers bring a smaller kit to rehearsals. Here, **BRIAN CLARKE** makes do with a minimalist array of equipment as he rehearses with the **RIVERSIDE JAZZMEN** at East Hove School in 1958.

PICTURE BY COURTESY OF KEITH SAMUEL

establishment open. We had fun guessing the name of the recording artist selected for this brutal treatment.

Together with youthful brash confidence, we carried with us a large group of friends and camp followers who filled the seats – and the tills – of establishments that hired the band. It was a marketing advantage that we did not fully appreciate at the time. Our supporters gave us noisy, partisan support. Their loyalty owed nothing to musical taste or appreciation; it was an expression of tribal affinity. Our musical ambition was simple. We just wanted to play in public and if we were rewarded for it, so much the better. The Hangleton Manor gave us £6 collectively for our sell-out performances there. At the time £1 for an evening's work seemed a handsome fee. None of us earned more than £3 or £4 a week in our day jobs.

We also had no means of transport – beyond the indulgence of one or two parents prosperous enough to own motor cars who occasionally consented to act as taxi-drivers. Mostly we travelled to gigs by train or on red Brighton, Hove & District double-deckers or the slightly classier green Southdown buses. Humphrey Lyttelton once stated that the difference between professional and amateur musicians was that the amateurs played on railway trains. Yes, we played in train compartments – and in waiting rooms for that matter, such was our youthful enthusiasm. And Barry Morgan stoically endured the jokey quips of bus conductors who were prepared to allow him aboard with his double bass ("How do you get that under your chin mate?").

I rode a tandem bicycle for a while, with my trombone case strapped to the rear section like a zombiefied companion. On one memorable occasion I "rushed" Don Weller to Hove station to catch a train to London, his overcoat billowing behind as he hung on with one hand to the rear handlebars, his saxophone case in the other hand. He caught the train. It was 1958 before I acquired a 1932 Austin 7. For the princely sum of £12 I became a member of the car-owning democracy that was to characterise the post war social norm. Into this tiny vehicle, with its rudimentary brakes and crash gearbox, we crammed Brian Clarke's drum kit, my trombone and Barry's double bass (with its scroll jutting out of the open passenger-side aperture) plus three well-built teenagers. It was a miracle that we never scythed down cyclists on our nearside with the protruding bass fiddle – not that we had sufficient acceleration to pass too many. The liberation from buses, trains and the tandem was worth the discomfort. By this time we had survived one or two upheavals in personnel and dedicated ourselves to starting a jazz club in Lewes.

It is humbling now to reflect on the generous encouragement we received from Derrick Stewart-Baxter, the local jazz author and critic, and trumpeter Les Jowett, who led the most distinctive of a succession of good bands to emerge from the Brighton area. In 1956-57 the Les Jowett Seven were at their all-too-brief high peak of attainment, holding a successful residency at the Paris Theatre Buttery in New Road, Brighton. Both Derrick and Les must have suspended all critical faculties to listen patiently to our L-plate efforts and to give friendly encouragement and valuable advice. Les generously invited the Riverside band to play the interval set on two occasions at the Vanguard club – and advertised our appearance in the *Evening Argus*. It was a mark of recognition and encouragement that we were not slow to appreciate, particularly when the Musicians' Union (in those days a power base for one or two old-fashioned Stalinists) threatened Les with dire penalties for playing alongside non-members. We were hugely flattered when Jowett hired Pat Benham as his guitarist when a vacancy occurred, particularly as Pat was not required to quit the Riverside band.

Even Musicus was in a more generous frame of mind when he reviewed the band in the autumn of 1957 in the *Brighton and Hove Herald*: "A second hearing last weekend proved very pleasurable and showed a quite remarkable improvement. They are now most promising and have some very good ideas." Barry and the two Brians were singled out for individual praise.

Disaster suddenly loomed when Mike Mounter was called up for National Service in late 1957. The possibility of conscription still lurked at this time for all of us after reaching the age of 18. Deferment for those in vocational training was usually possible

The first Jazz in June event at the Brighton Corn Exchange, 1958. The re-named RIVERSIDE JUMP BAND has two new recruits: trumpeter TREVOR PHILCOX and tenor saxist DON WELLER (second from the right). Also pictured are KEITH SAMUEL (trombone), BARRY MORGAN (bass) and BRIAN WHITE (tenor sax). Drummer BRIAN CLARKE and guitarist PAT BENHAM are hidden.

PICTURE BY COURTESY OF KEITH SAMUEL

and the call came more erratically as the political pressure to end conscription mounted. Out of the six of us only Mounter and Barry Morgan (both arbitrarily plucked from civilian life at the age of 21) were obliged to don khaki for two years. Mounter's call-up came very abruptly; either that or he forgot to mention it until the 11th hour. His imminent departure was reported in the *Brighton and Hove Herald* in October 1957 as a footnote to the sad news of the break-up of the Les Jowett Seven.

The most sensible move in the circumstances was to persuade Brighton jazz veteran Ted Ambrose, still without a regular band at the time, to fill the gap until we could find a permanent replacement. As well as playing at the contracted engagements, Ted rehearsed with us a few times and we benefited greatly from his experience and laconic advice. There seemed to be no local answer to filling the vacancy from among our own generation, prompting an unsuccessful experiment with Doug Hopkins, a trumpet player from Croydon. Doug's boppish approach was unsuited to the Riverside style, but he brought along with him a tall, well-built but somewhat absent-minded clarinettist and tenor player from Thornton Heath who had just left school and could already play a bit. His name was Don Weller.

Don, then 16, was keen enough make the train journey from Croydon to Brighton station most Sunday mornings for the next two years to rehearse at the nearby Cross Keys pub (now demolished). Even then it was clear that he had a very special talent and his subsequent outstanding career as a professional jazz musician with an international standing is no surprise. His public debut with the band at the Richmond Hotel, Brighton on March 14, 1958 caused a minor stir. By this time Brian White's appearances with us had become sporadic. Brian, now playing tenor sax and a passionate devotee of Lester Young's style, was keen to front his own group. Weller was a welcome and worthy successor and rapidly became the Riverside band's star attraction. There are one or two tapes in existence featuring Don playing Peanuts Hucko-style Dixieland clarinet, which now have a certain curiosity value. But even at this early stage his ballsy tenor sax playing was mightily impressive, a sound that would eventually carry to every part of the world where jazz is appreciated.

Hopkins soon made way for Lewes trumpeter Trevor Philcox who joined in the spring of 1958 just after the start of the band's 18-month residency at Lewes Jazz Club. This was a venture we promoted ourselves at the Brewers Arms in Lewes High Street. Trevor's availability was a windfall resulting from the break-up of the county town's Barbican Jazz Band following the ending of their residency at Seaford Jazz Club. A bank cashier with NatWest and soon to be married, he was four or five years older than the band's core members and brought to the proceedings a solid lead, inventive solo work and an all-round maturity. Playing alongside Colin Purbrook in the Barbican band, before Purbrook left for Cambridge and a professional career, had helped Trevor develop his musical pedigree. He was to remain a pillar of the Riverside set-up, utterly dependable both as a musician and an individual, until the band dissolved 10 years later.

Don and Trevor helped the band "catch fire" and they made their presence felt in June 1958 at the first of a succession of appearances we made at the annual Jazz in

Star soloist TONY COE (alto sax) guests with the RIVERSIDE JUMP BAND at Brighton Aquarium in March 1960.
Left to right: TREVOR PHILCOX, KEITH SAMUEL, BRIAN CLARKE (drums),
DON WELLER, ROBIN GRAYSON (piano) and TONY COE.

PICTURE BY COURTESY OF KEITH SAMUEL

June band competitions run by Brighton Art College students. We made a loud, exuberant contribution, playing bluesy jump material, which contrasted with the predominantly traditional jazz styles on offer. The crowd seemed to like the music, the beat was agreeable to the dancers and the judges gave us a pat on the head and a "special commendation". The Dolphin Jazz Band from Hastings were also impressive and it marked the start of a long-lasting friendship between the members of the two bands. There were six annual Jazz in June events, most of them held at the Brighton Corn Exchange. They were rowdy circus-style affairs straddling the peak years of the Trad Boom and attracted very large crowds. Our music failed to fit the conventional Trad matrix (no banjo for a start) but the judges seemed to like the contrast we provided and we always made sure our music was danceable. We won the contest outright in 1961, and were never placed lower than third, as well as gaining a clutch of individual awards for musicianship

Pat Benham moved to the West Country to continue his art studies, opening up an opportunity for Don's pianist friend Robin "Rubes" Grayson from Sanderstead in Surrey to join us in the summer of 1958. This cemented the regular line-up of the "second" Riverside band. Rubes, an engineer destined for a high-flying career with Rolls Royce, drove a classic Alvis car. He wore suede shoes, turned up with classy young ladies on his arm and exuded an air of poise and confidence that were to be envied. A droll wit, he surprisingly never questioned the band's choice of uniform – a gauche combination of white shirt, bright red tie and unmatching grey trousers. As they say in the movies, he was a good man to have on your side. Don Weller worked in a pet shop and once turned up on a gig covered in scratches after tackling an escaping ferret. He and Rubes were social opposites but rubbed along together very happily.

Predictably, the arrival of Weller, Philcox and Grayson began to re-shape the character and sound of the Riverside band – so much so that a change of name became a serious consideration. The repertoire was expanding to include more swing and mainstream numbers culled from records by Count Basie, Woody Herman and Duke Ellington. The overall sound ranged from Condon-styled Dixieland to the tight, bluesy small groups sounds of Johnny Hodges and Buck Clayton. After suitable debate Brian Clarke and I agreed that the new name would be The Riverside Jump Band. It was a sensible acknowledgement of our previous history and a more accurate description of the music we were endeavouring to play. Policy was not always made so easily. Brian, then working in the Southern Gas Board offices in Brighton, was full of nervous energy and had a habit of pacing the floor like a caged puma when confronted with problems and decisions. Sometimes he signalled his unease at rehearsals by pausing and then administering a thunderously loud thwack on his snare drum. Barry Morgan, the band's cheerleader and the most even-tempered of individuals, handled Brian's demons of doubt with ineffable humour and soothing aplomb and there were no serious bust-ups. Not at least until much later, in 1960, by which time Morgan had left the band to join the ranks of HM Forces.

The discipline of rehearsals and playing every week at Lewes Jazz Club in 1958-59 soon forged a clear identity for the "second" Riverside ensemble. Running the band and the club was a big responsibility. We would not have made much headway without the contributions of my Hove girlfriend, Judy Baker (we eventually got married in 1961). Judy was a combination of club secretary, doorkeeper, nurse, bouncer and scourge of the many liggers who tried to obtain entry without payment.

The Sussex coast contingent (Brian, Barry, Pat, Judy and myself) travelled by train to Lewes every Friday for the first few months, hauling equipment (drums, bass, amplification system etc) Sherpa-style as we scaled the steep hills of Lewes to reach the lofty perch of the Brewers Arms at the top end of the High Street. Later, intoxicated by a combination of the night's musical "highs" and various alcoholic beverages, the downhill descent to the railway station was a joyful contrast to earlier labours and exhaustions. It's easy to forget that, without such toil and commitment, many jazz clubs, then and now, would never last longer than a couple of weeks.

Star names who visited Lewes included Kenny Baker and Beryl Bryden. Many leading Sussex musicians and groups played there – including Les Jowett, trombonist Mike Collier, pianist Terry Whitney and the extrovert amplified viola player "Snatch" Snashall, whose primitive amplifier emitted menacing sparks and plumes of smoke before fusing the lights. There were guest spots for our fellow "territory" bands from elsewhere in the Sussex, with whom we made common cause – the Dolphin Jazz Band from Hastings, the New City Jazzmen from Crawley, Ted Owen's Excelsior Jazzmen from Brighton and the Delta Jazzmen from Burgess Hill. We played at each other's clubs and organised coach parties of supporters to swell the numbers and cover the expenses.

Islwyn Jones of the Brighton Youth and Community Service became a fan of the band and booked us to provide all the musical illustrations at a residential educational jazz weekend in November 1958 at which Les Jowett and Derrick Stewart-Baxter were the chief lecturers. A picture splash in the *Brighton and Hove Herald* from this event, conferred a curious sort of respectability on the (then) rare phenomenon of jazz education.

Lewes Jazz Club petered out in October 1959 and by then most members of the band were fully mobile. In addition to Rubes' classy Alvis, Trevor had a Vespa and Morris 8 and Barry, Brian and myself all ran huge six-cylinder Vauxhalls. On occasions our arrival at a gig had some of the flavour of scenes from gangster movies. This extra mobility transformed our musical horizons and we began to make our mark at single engagements along the Sussex coast and inland. We played at jazz clubs in Purley (billed as our "London" debut), Crawley, Hastings, Worthing, Bognor, and Eastbourne and briefly ran our own club in Horsham at The Star at Roffey. It is chiefly remembered for a spectacular punch-up involving local yobboes.

Horsham was not a happy hunting ground for the band. The wheels of Barry Morgan's jalopy were stolen on the same night that we quit this venue after threats of more trouble in December 1959.

As the Riverside sound acquired character and confidence, the Jump Band name proved a good marketing device. It aroused curiosity and bookers hired us to support guest stars and to be the warm-up act for some of the big draw cards of the emerging Trad Boom around 1960. In contrast to the customary pub back rooms and community halls we found ourselves appearing at much grander venues – enjoying the luxury of formal stages, lighting and amplification, even dressing rooms.

We were hired to play frequently at Bonny Manzi's bizarrely named but hugely successful Chinese Jazz Club, which opened, in late 1959 at the Brighton Aquarium Winter Garden. An educational jazz concert at the Pavilion Theatre, Brighton, yielded valuable publicity as well as prestige. The *Evening Argus* critic Roger Tilleray described us as "very competent" and Bill Hall in the *Brighton and Hove Gazette* praised the "happy, free-swinging quality" of the band and singled out Don Weller for special praise. According to the *Brighton and Hove Herald* we played with "real verve".

Amid this burst of well-received activity we agreed, in a fit of generosity, to play without a fee at a farewell party for a good friend who had followed the band loyally from our earliest days and was now emigrating to the United States. It was held in the Rothbury Cinema Hall, Portslade (now the HQ of Southern FM radio station). Many musicians have weathered adversity in the cause of jazz, but far fewer have faced head-on physical assault as we did on this occasion from a group of party-goers who wanted to hear rock 'n' roll rather than jazz. The term "front line", often used to describe the horn players in a jazz group, took on a new and menacing meaning for Trevor Philcox, Don Weller and myself as we warded off the blows before our assailants were restrained. By chance a tape recorder was running when hostilities broke out. This occurred during a slow-drag version of *Tin Roof Blues* (played for the benefit of dancers who enjoy what musicians call a "bum-clutcher"). One by one the instruments drop out of the ensemble as the recording captures the eruption of the bust-up. At the height of the rumpus Rubes can be heard picking out the theme of *The Archers* in droll accompaniment to the pandemonium.

We supported Acker Bilk's band at Shoreham Town Hall on April 11, 1960, Acker again at the Press Ball at Hove Town Hall on June 3, 1960 and we were the supporting band for a new and thankfully short-lived phenomenon, the All Night Rave. We enjoyed this dubious honour three times – at the Chinese Jazz Club with Dill Jones and Bob Wallis's Storyville band on March 19, then more grandly at an All Night Carnival of Jazz staged by Jazzshows at the Brighton Corn Exchange on April 1,1960 , supporting Kenny Ball, Ken Colyer, Terry Lightfoot and other name bands (fee £20!). We repeated our nocturnal duties at the Chinese club on July 23, this time sharing the bill with Dick Charlesworth's City Gents and the Bob Wallis band again. The glamour of it almost made up for the lack of sleep and the understandable need to stay awake in our daytime jobs.

Musically, a major thrill was backing alto saxist Tony Coe, then just beginning to

Representatives of the first and second generations of the **BRIGHTON JAZZ LINE** came together in the new line-up of the **RIVERSIDE JUMP BAND**. Pictured at Brighton Corn Exchange in 1961 are: **KEITH SAMUEL** (trombone), **TREVOR PHILCOX** (trumpet), **KEITH SLADE** (clarinet), **JOHN FRUCHT** (bass), **TONY HOOD** (drums) and **TERRY WHITNEY** (piano). Guitarist **VERNON LEIGH** is hidden.   PICTURE BY COURTESY OF KEITH SAMUEL

Despite the date it's not a hoax! All night sessions were a phenomenon of the Trad Boom and even the stately Corn Exchange was hired on one occasion in 1960 for one of these marathons. For part-timers such as the RIVERSIDE JUMP BAND's musicians it meant a bleary-eyed start to their daytime jobs on the following day.

COURTESY OF KEITH SAMUEL

CORN EXCHANGE · BRIGHTON

FRIDAY APRIL 1st

11 p.m. to 7 a.m.

JAZZSHOWS LTD. PRESENT

All Night Carnival of Jazz

Non-Stop Dancing Featuring

★ Ken Colyer's Jazzmen
★ Terry Lightfoot's New Orleans Jazzmen
★ Mickey Ashman and His Ragtime Band
★ Kenny Ball Jazzmen
★ Sonny Morris Jazzmen
★ The Riverside Jump Band

LICENSED BAR - CATERING BY LANGFORDS REFRESHMENTS

TICKETS 12/6 From Dome Box Office
Tel. 29337. Book early—Limited number of admissions

P(B)L.—602048

emerge as a major national figure, at the Aquarium Winter Garden Niterie on March 30, 1960. Perhaps, more sensationally, we became the first band from out-of-town to be hired to play at the Marquee Club in Oxford Street, where we were well received on October 5, 1960. This proved to be the high water mark for the "second" Riverside band.

Inevitably, Weller and Grayson decided that they had done enough commuting to Sussex for their jazz and moved on in the autumn of 1960 to form their own group. There was no ill will. It was a logical move. For Weller it was another step along the path that was to lead to a dazzling career as a professional jazz musician. By this time the end of conscription had been announced, but by some quirk Barry Morgan was among the very last of the post-war generation to be called-up for two years service. Thus we lost three key band members at much the same time. Wally Allen, a friend of Brian Clarke's from Shoreham, had joined by then as an "apprentice" on rhythm guitar (which meant he didn't always get paid!) and we had decided to hire Hastings singer Barbara Harmer after she sat in with us on visits to Eastbourne and Hastings. Barbara, an attractive Eurasian teenager, worked as a dress designer and sang in the Ella Fitzgerald style. For reasons now beyond recall it was decided that Barbara

Hastings singer **KAREN DONOVAN** brought some glamour
to the **RIVERSIDE JUMP BAND**'s performances in the early 1960s.
She is pictured singing at the Corn Exchange, Brighton, in 1961
backed by **TREVOR PHILCOX** (trumpet) and **KEITH SLADE** (clarinet).
In 2002 she was still performing in Kent – under
her real name, Barbara Placzek.

PICTURE BY COURTESY OF KEITH SAMUEL

needed a stage name. So she became Karen Donovan and sang (and broadcast) with us very successfully for the next couple of years, adding diversity and visual appeal to our performances.

However, the key problem was filling the void created by Weller's departure. There was minimal chance of attracting a saxophone player of similar virtuoso status. Keith Slade had deputised once or twice that summer in Weller's absence. A practical solution was to persuade Keith to come out of musical retirement and use his strengths as a fine clarinet player to emphasise the Eddie Condon-style Dixieland elements that remained part of the band's repertoire. A major bonus was that Terry Whitney was willing to throw his hand in with us, partly attracted by the chance to write new arrangements for the band and to accompany Barbara. We seemed to have a workable answer but Brian Clarke and Wally Allen still hankered to continue playing the bluesy jump material that had become an enjoyable part of our public proposition, and so we agreed to part company, meaning there were two more vacancies to fill. If Barry Morgan had been around he might have proposed some sort of compromise, but the break was made.

These were the circumstances in which I became the leader of the "third" Riverside band. It was an exciting opportunity to fuse some of the best talent from across two generations of the Brighton Jazz Line. Keith Slade and Terry Whitney had both played in Ted Ambrose's Jazz Band, which had done so much to build the audience for jazz in Brighton in the post-World War II years, and Whitney had also blossomed as a composer and arranger, providing the music for two BBC interlude films and local stage productions (some of them directed by Slade). Terry's input into the Riverside band's new repertoire was substantial. His arrangements covered a wide canvas – from Don Redman and Fats Waller compositions to those of Duke Ellington, Alex Hill and Hoagy Carmichael.

We rehearsed assiduously on Sunday mornings – usually at the Hove Place Hotel in Second Avenue or the Prince Albert in Trafalgar Street, Brighton. Terry would hand out the parts of new arrangements and whilst we fumbled our way through them, sit cross-legged at the piano stool, isolating himself from the surrounding dissonance while he studied that morning's *Observer* newspaper until we were ready for a run-down. Sometimes it was a long wait. Terry's shyness and seeming diffidence concealed a doughty enthusiasm and deep-rooted commitment to jazz music. A successful lawyer in his professional life, he also found the time for sufficient practice to build-up a formidable technique as a pianist, and he excelled in all departments of the game – as a soloist, accompanist, band pianist, arranger and composer.

Keith Slade, who had trained for the theatre but earned a more steady living in the printing industry, also brought many gifts to the table. In addition to his robust, bluesy clarinet-playing taking inspiration from masters such as Edmond Hall and Barney Bigard, Keith brought wit and energy to his vocals and – when the occasion suited – to a range of comic monologues and musical burlesques. Keith's cabaret turns, performed with a rubber-faced Buster Keaton-ish aplomb, became a secret weapon for the Riverside band, particularly useful for enlivening drowsy, unresponsive audiences in the quieter Sussex seaside towns.

In the new set-up Barry Morgan managed one or two dates when on leave but eventually John Frucht replaced him as our bass player. John, a sharp wit, came from a well known Brighton catering family, had trained as a chef at the Grand Hotel in Brighton and also spent a short spell on the road as a professional musician. The new drummer was Tony Hood, an amiable giant of a man from Seaford who drove long-

KEITH SAMUEL blows a fanfare outside the old **EVENING ARGUS** offices in Robert Street, Brighton to help publicise the 1960 **PRESS GANG JAZZ BALL**.

PICTURE BY COURTESY OF
KEITH SAMUEL

SHOREHAM *jazzbar*

present

THE
TEMPERANCE
SEVEN

★ ★ ★

KEN COLYER'S
JAZZMEN

★ ★ ★

THE
RIVERSIDE
JUMP BAND

★ ★ ★

MISS KAREN
DONOVAN

at the

DOME : *Brighton*

★ ★ ★

Monday, 20th November, 1961

In aid of Charity   PROGRAMME 1/6

Concert appearances at The Dome in Brighton remain a rare honour for local jazz groups. **THE RIVERSIDE JUMP BAND** earned this distinction in November 1961 when they shared the bill with the **TEMPERANCE SEVEN**, then riding high in the Top 20, and KEN COLYER'S JAZZMEN.

distance for a living, and had played with Trevor Philcox and Colin Purbrook in the Barbican Jazz Band. Vernon Leigh, another Brightonian, had played with John Frucht in the Jazz Entertainers, a group that had its origins in the Hove Maccabi youth club and also included trumpeter Arnold King. Vernon joined in mid-1961 to play rhythm guitar in the style of either Eddie Condon or Freddie Green depending on the choice of number. Always immaculately turned out and a born salesman, Vernon followed his father into the rag trade before making a successful career in insurance. He proved to be another long-serving Riverside stalwart – staying the full course with Philcox, Whitney, Slade and myself until the band dissolved seven years later.

The year 1961 proved the most fruitful in the band's entire existence. The warm-up jobs with the big names of British jazz proliferated, including sequences at both the Corn Exchange, Brighton and the Assembly Rooms, Worthing which paired us with all the major attractions of the day – from Acker Bilk and Kenny Ball to Ted Heath and Humphrey Lyttelton, and the British band we most admired – Alex Welsh's Dixielanders. The bands we supported most frequently were those of Bilk and Lyttelton, the latter again at two colourfully named events – a Left Wing Swing, promoted by the Brighton Co-operative party at the Corn Exchange on March 24, 1961 and a Jazz 'n' Splash at the old Black Rock Swimming Pool on August 25. The Co-op bash drew 1200 people but the poolside spectacular was ill conceived and sank without trace. The 1961 Press Ball at Hove Town Hall bracketed us with the

Temperance Seven, then very hot in the Top 20 with *You're Driving Me Crazy*. We also appeared in two Jazz Rendezvous broadcasts for the BBC West Region, recorded at the Richmond Room, Worthing, and were booked at two or three of the growing number of jazz festivals. These included one at Matchams Park, near Bournemouth, with Johnny Dankworth, Alex Welsh and the Temperance Seven, and the cheekily named Newport Jazz Festival at Newport, Isle of Wight, where Humphrey Lyttelton and the Avon Cites Jazz Band were also on the bill at a rather over-ambitious event held in a football ground.

The crowds were sometimes huge – 6000 at Matchams Park, 1800 at the Brighton Corn Exchange for Jazz in June. But a punch-up marred the latter event. "The delicate maidenhood of Brighton eagerly mounted chairs to witness the massacre," wrote Steve Race in a memorable account of the occasion in *Jazz News*. There had been a similar rumpus at the Press Ball at Hove Town Hall the previous month, evidence that the Trad Boom had its unwelcome elements. In my guise of Sam Edwards in the *Brighton and Hove Gazette* I reflected that the entry of jazz in to the Top Twenty and the pop music arena had backfired. "Frustration and disappointment is the only reward for those enthusiasts and musicians who have worked for years to bring jazz to a wider audience."

At the changeover point at the end of 1960 we could have reverted to the Riverside Jazzmen name but we had put a lot of effort into building up the Jump Band as a distinctive brand and we decided to stick with it. It also meant we did not have to order new stationery and business cards.

Retaining this name turned out to be a wise marketing move. It aroused curiosity and convinced some promoters of the merit in providing a contrasting sound to the big Trad draw cards at concerts, the big hops, all-nighters and festivals. They could be persuaded that the last thing they wanted was an imitation of the main attraction. Interestingly, we were never given anything less than a courteous reception by the most diehard of Trad audiences. And, astonishingly, critics and reviewers always resisted what must have been a tempting opportunity to suggest that we take a "running jump"!

Our most prestigious booking in Sussex was sharing the bill with Ken Colyer and the Temperance Seven at a sell-out Dome concert on November 20, 1961, presented by Shoreham Jazzbar, an organisation that adopted the Riverside band and gave us generous backing.

That summer we had abandoned our uniform dress of bright red ties and white shirts for garish striped blouses – "pirate shirts" as Keith Slade dubbed them. For a concert in front of a home crowd of 2000 people at The Dome, something more elegant was needed. Vernon Leigh's dad came to the rescue with a set of royal blue long-sleeved waistcoats (more accurately, cardigans) to be worn with pale blue ties and crisp white shirts. We never did get around to matching up the grey trousers. Nervous, but smarter than at any time in the past, we trooped on to the seemingly vast stage of the Dome and gave of our best. The audience took us to their hearts and the local reviewers were very kind. *The Evening Argus* critic gave us unstinting praise, comparing us favourably with the professional bands topping the bill. "Much more alive was the local-grown Riverside Jump Band whose numbers swung along smoothly and competently. A pity the band got minor billing and the shortest spot on the show." Bill Hall in the *Brighton and Hove Gazette* said that the band was "impressive". Soloists Trevor Philcox and Terry Whitney were "excellent" and the rhythm section "was far and away the most propulsive of the evening". It was our first – and last – major concert appearance and not without its share of honour. We won the Jazz in June band competition at the Brighton Corn Exchange the same year, prompting Hugo Martin in *The Brighton and Hove Herald* to describe us generously as "one of the most original and musical bands in this area".

THE FLORIDA   ADJOINING   BRIGHTON   AQUARIUM

SHOW CASE OF THE STARS   SAT. 20th—THE SCENE

CHINESE JAZZ CLUB   TOP OF THE HIT CHARTS

TONITE -- STUDENTS' RAVE

RIVERSIDE JUMP BAND   **THE WHO**

Our Guest this week 100 Nurses   Plus THE SYSTEM

LIC BARS   COFFEE BAR   JUKE BOX

Jazz and rock get equal billing in this EVENING ARGUS advertisement for THE CHINESE JAZZ CLUB in the mid-1960s. Public response and taste displayed no corresponding balance. The pulling power of groups such THE BEATLES and THE WHO eclipsed jazz in the affections of younger people as the 1960s progressed.

The relatively abrupt end of the Trad Boom in 1962-63 took its toll on part-timers as well as professional musicians. For "territory" bands that survived like the Riverside Jump Band it was back to the clubs, pubs and backrooms and the support of hard-core devotees. By 1964 the well seemed to be running dry and the band became virtually inactive for several months. Full-blooded revival became possible in 1965 thanks to an invitation from Mike Collier of the Sussex Jazz Society to help sustain a new plan for regular weekly sessions on Sundays at the Fox and Hounds, Haywards Heath. We agreed to a monthly spot in return for whatever the gate yielded and gave wholehearted support to this Society venture, and later ones at the Sackville Jazz Bar in Hove, described fully elsewhere in this book.

The nucleus of Philcox, Slade, Whitney, Leigh and myself had kept the band's character and repertoire intact. We added new material and became adept at accompanying solo performers as diverse as Bruce Turner, Lennie Felix, Danny Moss, John R.T. Davies, Will Hastie, Harry Walton, Alan Cooper, Jock Bain, Tony Coe, Jimmy Skidmore, Teddy Layton and Dave Carey. These were sometimes exhilarating occasions in which the challenge of backing star guests prompted all the musicians to raise their game. We were often paired with Dave Carey, a figure who occupies his own special niche in British jazz history. He was the knowledgeable and avuncular proprietor of the Swing Shop in Streatham as well as a drummer and vibes player of some accomplishment. Somehow, Dave never managed to anchor the wheels of his vibraphone and as the intensity of his playing increased he would advance across the shiny floor of the small back room at the Fox and Hounds, threatening innocent members of the audience with a menacing whirlwind of mallets and chimes.

The Fox was a companionable venue. Many musicians dropped in, sometimes forming ad hoc interval bands of high calibre. The Simkins brothers, Pete and Geoff, and Roy Bower were in the forefront of this alfresco activity and often sat in with the Riverside band. An advertised session backing piano legend Willie The Lion Smith at the Fox was eagerly anticipated by the band, but The Lion's tour was disappointingly cancelled due to illness and Danny Moss was hastily summoned to fill the gap.

There was a fresh spate of bookings at the Chinese Jazz Club in Brighton and more dates along the South Coast, at Hastings, Eastbourne, Lewes, Worthing, Portsmouth, Botley and the Concorde Club, Southampton. As well as Frucht and Morgan, other bass-players in this period included John Boyett and Alan Kennington. Carl Simmons, John Wood, John Rolf and Brian Clarke filled the drum chair after Tony Hood was

ANNE DURRANT singing with the RIVERSIDE JUMP BAND at The Ship Inn, Lewes Road, Brighton, in January 1963. Left to right: KEITH SLADE, VERNON LEIGH (guitar), ANNE DURRANT, JOHN FRUCHT, TREVOR PHILCOX, KEITH SAMUEL and drummer CARL SIMMONS. Pianist TERRY WHITNEY is not visible.

PICTURE BY COURTESY OF KEITH SAMUEL

lured into a hotel job at Eastbourne, but Derek Middleton eventually became the latter-day regular. Anne Durrant also sang very effectively with the band on occasions.

By the end of 1967 keeping the Riverside Band together was made increasingly difficult by the daytime career demands of the front-line members. The news that Trevor Philcox was being sent to Norwich by his NatWest Bank employers settled the issue. I was already working for ITV in Southampton, and Keith Slade had just been appointed to the production staff of the new BBC Radio Brighton station. After suspending activities for a while it was finally decided to disband but not before a final rousing farewell session was staged at the Sackville Inn in Hove on October 18, 1968, broadcast by BBC Radio Brighton in January 1969. Pete Simkins stood in for Terry Whitney at the piano on this occasion. Under the headline "A Swinging Farewell from a Great Little Band" Derrick Stewart-Baxter delivered a final epitaph in the *Brighton and Hove Gazette*. He observed that an air of nostalgia hung over the occasion, but "taking this into account the band played extremely well, as the broadcast will prove". Chris Duff in the *Mid Sussex Times* said that BBC listeners "would be blessed with 20 minutes of sparkling jazz from the now disbanded Riverside Jump Band".

The last musical reunion – until the Lewes millennium gathering in March 2000 – was held in September 1971 when Trevor Philcox returned to Sussex for a holiday. The line-up reassembled was completed by Keith Slade, Terry Whitney, Vernon Leigh, John Boyett, Derek Middleton and myself. This session was promoted by Arnie King and the Brighton Jazz Club at the Abinger Hotel, and again broadcast by BBC Radio Brighton. Present also were many of the leading characters of the Brighton jazz scene – Mike Collier, Derrick Stewart-Baxter, Benny, Pete and Geoff Simkins, Eddie Buckwell and many more.

The big Lewes reunion of the band in March 2000, a joyful and phenomenally successful occasion, was surrounded by a blaze of publicity, meriting a whole page news story in the *Evening Argus* and a two-page feature with colour pictures in *Sussex Life* magazine.

With further annual get-togethers in 2001 and 2002 at Lewes Jazz Club (and another special performance at Steyning Jazz Club in 2001), a link was re-forged in the Brighton Jazz Line.

Keith Slade performed at all these sessions with characteristic flair and humour, forming an unbroken connection with the mission he helped launch over half-a-century earlier to build an audience for live jazz in Brighton and mid-Sussex area.

CHAPTER 6

THE SUSSEX JAZZ SOCIETY YEARS

PETER SIMKINS

VIRTUALLY EVERY JAZZ PROMOTION since Buddy Bolden was a mere twinkle in his father's eye has been fraught with potential disaster. However good the bands and musicians being presented may be, factors such as an inaccessible location, a grumpy or impatient pub landlord, dodgy acoustics and uncooperative or indifferent local newspaper editors can give any club or concert series the life-span of a consumptive gnat. The story of Brighton and Sussex jazz in the 1960s and 1970s is full of such well-intentioned but short-lived ventures. Yet, amid the wreckage of these broken jazz dreams, there were some outstanding successes – and none more so than the activities of the Sussex Jazz Society at the Fox and Hounds, Haywards Heath, between 1964 and 1970. In this blessed case, a particular set of circumstances and personalities combined to provide the foundations for what might now be recognised as the first "golden age" of traditional and mainstream jazz in Sussex. For six years, a procession of legendary American jazz stars and top-flight British musicians appeared at the Fox each week under the Sussex Jazz Society's banner, offering local fans and record collectors the sort of sessions – on their own doorstep – that had previously only existed in their wildest fantasies.

The Sussex Jazz Society was *not*, as it name might imply, a subscription-levying body with elected officers and a membership list. In the beginning, the Society was one man – Mike Collier. On Sunday October 14, 1964, some eight years after moving to Sussex, Mike staged the first tentative session at the Fox with the Fourteen Foot Band. Initially the musical fare was served up by the Fourteen Foot Band and other local groups and sitters-in, but, within a few months, Mike – building on his experience with the Press Gang at the Fleet Street Jazz Club in the early 1950s – was increasingly eager to present regular guest artists, many of whom were friends he had

RUBY BRAFF
pictured at the FOX AND HOUNDS in July 1965.
PICTURE BY COURTESY OF BEN COLLIER

RUBY BRAFF

WITH

THE
ALEX WELSH BAND

PRESENTED BY

THE SUSSEX JAZZ SOCIETY

AT

THE "FOX AND HOUNDS"
HAYWARDS HEATH

ON

THURSDAY 8TH JULY 1965   AT 7-30 P.M.

ADMISSION £1

ADVANCE BOOKING ONLY

Leaflet advertising RUBY BRAFF's appearance
at the FOX AND HOUNDS, Haywards Heath
on July 8, 1965. Ruby was the first of many
American stars to play at the Fox.

COURTESY OF BEN COLLIER

made in the jazz world before moving to the South Coast. At the same time – thanks to the likes of impresario Harold Davison and Jazzways Ltd – tours by American jazz stars were becoming more frequent and the temptation to import them to Sussex proved irresistible. Never one to seek personal glory or publicity, the modest Mike avoided the limelight by staging truly ambitious jazz events under the anonymous umbrella of the "Sussex Jazz Society" and even enlisted the help of the well-known Derrick Stewart-Baxter to act as the Society's "spokesman" early on.

Mike's first really big step into the perilous world of jazz promotion was on 9 April 1965, when the great Earl "Fatha" Hines appeared with the Alex Welsh Band at the Florida Room of the Brighton Aquarium, supported by Mike's own Eighteen Foot Washboard Band. Over 350 people attended, paying a paltry six shillings a head for admission. Musically the evening was tremendous, with Earl Hines and the Alex Welsh Band in inspired form, but the session registered a financial loss of £22. The event was described by Keith Samuel (writing as Sam Edwards) as "a glorious failure" and one that might perhaps set a "new pattern" for jazz presentation in Brighton.

Meanwhile, Sunday jazz nights had become firmly established at the Fox, trumpeter Mick Mulligan being the first "name" guest with the Fourteen Foot Band on 30 May 1965. Less than six weeks later, the wonderful Ruby Braff appeared there with Alex Welsh. Seventy people paid £1 each to hear this memorable session. Derrick Stewart-Baxter's attempts to secure a photographic record of the occasion – especially low angle shots from the floor – prompted some tart comments from Braff, who was clearly both surprised and amused by the sight of DSB's not inconsiderable frame at his feet! For the next three presentations of American guests, the Sussex

Two of the most influential pianists in jazz history were guests of the
SUSSEX JAZZ SOCIETY in the mid-1960s: TEDDY WILSON (left) and EARL HINES.

PICTURES BY COURTESY OF KEITH SAMUEL

Jazz Society returned to the Florida Room in Brighton. Unfortunately, the first two of these sessions were marred in various ways. The appearance of tenor saxist Don Byas with the Bruce Turner Jump Band attracted a "smallish audience" of barely 150. Though he played well enough, Byas himself drove some customers to distraction with long, rambling and almost inaudible announcements between numbers while, backstage, he was a somewhat unpleasant, aggressive individual who delighted in showing everyone the knife he was carrying. John Roberts, writing for the *Crawley Advertiser*, criticised the "constant chatter" of many of the customers, and the Bruce Turner group was generally considered to be below par. The biggest cheer of the night came when DSB contrived to fall noisily off the stage into a pile of stacking metal chairs!

Worse was to follow in October 1965 when Mike and the Sussex Jazz Society presented American trombone star Dicky Wells at the Florida Room with the Alex Welsh Band. Dicky was obviously so drunk or high on other stimulants that he could only stagger through four numbers. At one point in the first number he dropped the slide from his trombone and could not get it back on. The Alex Welsh Band – and especially trombonist Roy Williams – saved the event by playing brilliantly but the Society offered to refund money to patrons or admit them to the next session at a reduced price. An embarrassed DSB praised the Alex Welsh Band but said that it nearly broke his heart "to hear Dicky Wells play like that. It is impossible for me to describe the performance because it hardly existed".

The legendary Chicago
tenor saxophonist
BUD FREEMAN (left) with
MIKE COLLIER (centre) and
DAVE CAREY (right) at the
**FLORIDA ROOM,
BRIGHTON AQUARIUM,**
on December 8, 1965.

PICTURE BY COURTESY OF BEN COLLIER

In many respects, the Wells fiasco represented the low point of the Society's major jazz promotions. An appearance at the Florida Room in December 1965 by Chicago jazz legend Bud Freeman – again with the Alex Welsh Band – was an artistic success but, although there was a fair-sized audience, the evening was another financial failure. The Sussex Jazz Society had now lost between £150 and £200 since April – a lot of money in the mid-1960s. "We did not intend to make a profit," said Mike Collier, who had personally borne most of the loss, "but as things stand we just cannot go on."

Happily, salvation was at hand. At this juncture, a small group of musicians, collectors and enthusiasts – including DSB, Ron Sweetman, Ken Bryant (proprietor of the "Studio Four" record shop in The Lanes), Terry Whitney, Keith Samuel and myself – pledged financial support to Mike, enabling him to continue presenting American guest stars. In addition, the Sunday night sessions at the Fox were by now very popular and were attracting growing audiences. Violinist Bob Clarke was living nearby, and tenor sax star Danny Moss had also returned to the area, both becoming regular and welcome visitors. Other guests at the Fox in the early months of 1966 were Bruce Turner, Sandy Brown, Bob Wallis, Mick Mulligan, Nevil Skrimshire, Freddy Randall and Lennie Felix. Most were backed by the resident Fourteen Foot Band or the Riverside Jump Band, though Crawley's New City Jazzmen also began to make regular appearances. So far as one can recall, local musicians and bands never demanded or negotiated a set fee, always remaining content to take a fair share of the door receipts on the night.

As the Sunday sessions flourished, it therefore seemed a good idea to present the next visiting American star in the friendly and intimate surroundings of the Fox's clubroom rather than at the more cavernous and impersonal Florida Room. Trumpeter Bill Coleman duly appeared with the Bruce Turner Jump Band at the Fox on Thursday 14 April, thus setting a pattern of sessions which lasted until mid-1968, with American stars being presented on occasional Thursdays and British bands and guests being featured every Sunday.

Much of the credit for the success of the Fox venture was due to the genial and extremely tolerant landlord Chris Worrall. Worthing-born Chris – soon dubbed "the patron publican of Sussex jazz" by Keith Samuel – was originally an engineer by profession and took over the licence of the Fox in 1965. Chris himself admitted that his interest in jazz only developed after he came to the Fox. As he told Keith Samuel for an article in the *Brighton and Hove Gazette* in 1967: "I was very pleasantly surprised by the sound the boys made and also by the type of people who came along to listen. I've made a great many friends among them since. There's never been any trouble at the pub on a jazz night nor any opposition to the club from regulars or local residents". John Marley, of the *Brighton and Hove Herald*, wrote of the Fox: "The session room is intimate, the country inn atmosphere prominent, and the music good".

DANNY MOSS plays to an appreciative audience at the Fox.

PICTURE BY COURTESY OF THE LATE CHRIS WORRALL

CHRIS WORRALL, jazz-loving landlord of the FOX AND HOUNDS, Haywards Heath. Chris, who kept the Fox for 18 years, died at the age of 74 in 2002.

PICTURE BY COURTESY OF ANNE WORRALL

Three Steyning residents played host to American trumpeter BILL COLEMAN in 1966.
From left to right are: DANNY MOSS, BILL COLEMAN, TERRY WHITNEY and
RON SWEETMAN. Ron now lives in Canada.

PICTURE BY COURTESY OF KEITH SAMUEL

Helped by the fact that the clubroom was separate from the rest of the pub and had its own bar, the Fox, by mid-1966, had developed its own "personality" as a jazz venue and was earning a deserved reputation, among musicians and fans alike, as one of the best clubs south of London. In his sleeve notes for the album *The Good Life*– recorded at the Fox in October 1968 and subsequently issued on Doug Dobell's 77 Records label – Keith Samuel said that what made the Fox unique was the imagination that went into the planning of routine Sunday night sessions. The formula was to "bracket together guest soloists with musicians of broadly sympathetic styles, who are never heard playing together in normal circumstances. The upshot of this deliberately contrived atmosphere of challenge has been a series of highly stimulating sessions in which as many as three, four and even five visiting instrumentalists have combined to produce jazz of a highly original character."

The Bill Coleman session saw yet another financial loss but, with a stronger safety net beneath it, the Sussex Jazz Society bravely persisted with its policy. After Bud Freeman had visited the Fox with Alex Welsh in June, one-armed trumpeter Wingy Manone appeared there with Alan Elsdon's band on 22 September. "This is the best spot yet", Wingy informed Derek Enscoe of the *Mid Sussex Times*. "The club is just right for size and has the best atmosphere of any club since I have been in England," he added. Clarinettist Ed Hall, in November, drew an attendance of 125 – a house record at the time – enabling the Society to enjoy the rare luxury of covering overheads and recouping earlier losses. This encouraged Mike and the Society to forge ahead with renewed confidence and when famed cornettist Wild Bill Davison came to the Fox to play a storming session with the Alex Welsh Band on 8 December, the place was so crammed with fans that all previous attendance records were shattered and people were actually turned away from the door. "There was barely room to lift a pint", wrote John Roberts in the *Crawley Advertiser*. For a brief but glorious period of some eighteen months, the sessions at the Fox were almost a victim of their own success and Chris Worrall even considered having an extension built.

These were the halcyon years for the Sussex Jazz Society. In 1967 the American visitors included Albert Nicholas, Henry 'Red' Allen (recently recovered from illness), Eddie Miller, Peanuts Hucko and Teddy Wilson (on Terry Whitney's own piano, specially imported from Steyning for the session). Apart from those already mentioned, other British and American musicians who were presented at the Fox were: Jimmy Skidmore, Dave Shepherd, Pat Halcox, Teddy Layton, Beryl Bryden, Dick Sudhalter, Alan Cooper, Will Hastie, John R.T. Davies, Ronnie Ross, Barry `Kid' Martyn, Kathy Stobart, Bert Courtley and George Chisholm. The venue was now attracting the attention of national jazz critics and Sinclair Traill, then Editor of *Jazz Journal*, wrote a glowing appreciation, describing a trip to the Fox as an "easy drive from London" offering the "certainty of a good jazz session with little danger of becoming thirsty". He added that the well-known DSB was often in attendance "buzzing around like a good-natured blues bottle". Regular newsletters, written for the Society by the articulate Chris Duff (now in Canada), began in September 1967 and the amiable George Vine (now living in Hanover) provided a good P.A. system for

Three of the outstanding American jazz soloists presented by the **SUSSEX JAZZ SOCIETY** at the Fox and Hounds, Haywards Heath, in the mid-1960s: clarinettist **ED HALL**, trumpeter **HENRY "RED" ALLEN** and tenor saxist **EDDIE MILLER**.

PICTURES BY COURTESY OF KEITH SAMUEL AND PETER SIMKINS

DANNY MOSS (tenor sax) and SANDY BROWN (clarinet) at the FOX AND HOUNDS, December 18, 1966.

PICTURE BY TED AMBROSE, BY COURTESY OF KEITH SAMUEL

JEANIE LAMBE, the Glaswegian jazz singer who frequently added a touch of style and glamour to proceedings at the Fox. She married Sussex tenor man DANNY MOSS in 1964. Resident in Perth, Australia, since 1989, Danny and Jeanie continue to tour internationally as a duo.

PICTURE BY COURTESY OF KEITH SAMUEL

the Fox sessions. Danny Moss and Jeanie Lambe were now frequent guests, as was altoist Wing Commander Jack Jacobs and drummer-turned-vibraphonist Dave Carey (proprietor of the "Swing Shop" in Streatham). Dave's early version of car boot sales in the car park at the Fox did much to swell the record collections of brother Geoff Simkins and myself while lightening our youthful pockets!

Heartened by the success of the Fox, and by the enthusiasm of another friendly landlord, Charles 'Brad' Bradshaw, the Society lent its support to the opening, in May 1967, of the Jazz Bar at the Sackville Hotel in Hove. Local groups, such as the Fourteen Foot Band, the Riverside Jump Band, the New City Jazzmen and the Martinique Jazz Band, were regularly featured and, in October, an ambitious jazz festival was organised, presenting – among others – American reedmen Budd Johnson and Earle Warren. The following year, Australian pianist Graeme Bell appeared at both the Fox and at the Sackville Jazz Bar, backed, on the latter occasion, by the Martinique Jazz Band.

British trombone giant **GEORGE CHISHOLM** –
from whom **MIKE COLLIER** took lessons – was
a frequent guest at the Fox.

PICTURE BY COURTESY OF THE LATE CHRIS WORRALL

It was, of course, too good to last. The devaluation of the pound hit the American tours and, after appearances by New Orleans altoist Captain John Handy and by Graeme Bell, veteran Boston alto saxist Al Sudhalter, who visited the club in May 1968, became the last American guest to play at the Fox for several months. Jazz at the Sackville in Hove folded in November 1968, after eighteen months of operation, when only twenty-eight fans paid to attend a session featuring Jack Jacobs. The Fox continued activities for a while, with mixed success. Pianist Alton Purnell appeared there with Barry Martyn's Band in March 1970 but falling attendances meant that the end could not long be delayed. By June 1970, Mike Collier had again been subsiding sessions from his own pocket for some time and it was decided to bring the Society's presentations at the Fox to a close. The SJS tried to maintain its previous policy at alternative venues – such as The Crypt at the University of Sussex or Jimmy's Restaurant in Steine Street, Brighton – during the ensuing few months, yet these attempts failed to match the level of success achieved at the Fox two or three years earlier. Though Chris Worrall somehow kept the Fox alive as a jazz venue, the Sussex Jazz Society itself had no regular "home base" by December 1971. It seemed that the great days (or nights) of the Sussex Jazz Society and the Fox had gone beyond recall. However, a second – if shorter-lived – "golden age" for both lay just ahead.

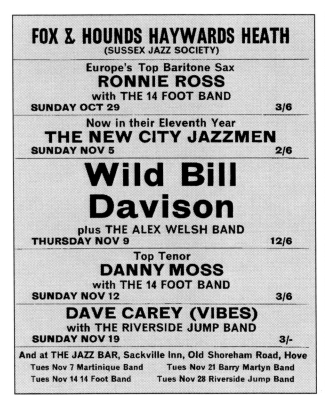

This leaflet promoting the SUSSEX JAZZ SOCIETY's sessions at the Fox in November 1967 reflects the ambitious and imaginative nature of MIKE COLLIER's programming skills by that date.

COURTESY OF KEITH SAMUEL

Handbill for the
SACKVILLE JAZZ BAR
in Hove, summer 1967.

COURTESY OF KEITH SAMUEL

Footnote. CHRIS WORRALL, landlord of the FOX AND HOUNDS in its jazz heyday, died aged 74 in April 2002. Before his death he offered the Editors photographs from his collection for inclusion in this book. Many friends from the jazz world attended his funeral at St Wilfrid's Church, Haywards Heath. During the service music was played by a quintet comprising ROY BOWER, ALAN KENNINGTON, JOHN MUXLOW, GEORGE WALKER and PETER GODFREY.

HAVE TENOR, WILL TRAVEL ...

Of the many musicians who first caught the jazz bug and developed their instrumental talents on the Brighton and Sussex scene, a few have gone on to win national or even international recognition. The late Colin Purbrook, Don Weller and Geoff Simkins are three of the names that spring immediately to mind in this connection. A fourth member of this select group is Danny Moss MBE.

Born in Redhill, Surrey in August 1927, Danny moved to Southwick as a small child and grew up locally, taking up the clarinet at the age of thirteen. Three years later he was working on tenor sax and clarinet with the Wal Rogers Quintet at Sherry's in Brighton. After serving in the RAF Band between 1945 and 1948, he played with Vic Lewis before spending a brief spell with Dennis Hale's Band back in Brighton. From 1949 and throughout the 1950s Danny worked essentially as a big band sideman, playing successively with Tommy Sampson, Oscar Rabin, Vic Lewis (again), the Squadronaires, Ted Heath and Geraldo. He was then with the Johnny Dankworth Orchestra from March 1957 to December 1961. By this stage, Danny's full-toned and authoritative tenor sax sound – influenced by Coleman Hawkins and Ben Webster – had marked him out as one of the major solo voices in British jazz.

In the early 1960s Danny's musical focus switched more to small group jazz. He was a member of the Humphrey Lyttelton Band from January 1962 to November 1963 and subsequently often appeared with the bands of Alex Welsh and Sandy Brown. In 1964 he married singer Jeanie Lambe and shortly afterwards returned to Sussex, settling in Steyning. The presence of Danny and the stylish Jeanie immediately gave an enormous boost to the local jazz scene and, in the latter half of that decade, contributed significantly to the success of the Sussex Jazz Society's sessions at the Fox and Hounds, where they were frequent and welcome guests. Indeed, Danny gave a great deal back to the local scene, sitting in and playing happily with a variety of bands – including those of a more traditional persuasion – and providing all concerned with spontaneous 'master classes' in swing, taste and timing. His readiness to encourage and support younger musicians and to share the spotlight with fellow Brightonians was illustrated by his recording with the Fourteen Foot Band for the 77 label and the two fine albums he later made for Flyright with altoist Geoff Simkins.

A treasured memory for Danny is the occasion in November 1970 when he was summoned from the ranks of Tony Bennett's backing band to play clarinet with Louis Armstrong at a special charity concert at the Astoria, Finsbury Park. It turned out be the great jazz virtuoso's last appearance in Britain before his death in 1971. "It was a marvellous thrill to play with Louis," said Danny afterwards, completely unfazed by the fact that the clarinet is not his primary instrument.

"I would have found it easier to play tenor but the idiom Louis played in demanded a clarinet and I wasn't going to quibble when faced with that kind of opportunity. Without doubt it was the greatest honour of my career as a musician."

Besides leading his own quartet and occasionally reverting to big band work with

John Dankworth and Maynard Ferguson, Danny showed up in a wide range of musical settings in the 1970s and 1980s, recording with Tony Bennett, Bing Crosby and Ella Fitzgerald, becoming a founder member of the Pizza Express All Stars and being featured at the Nice Festival as part of the *Jazz Journal* All Stars. In addition, he toured Australia with Digby Fairweather and worked in the USA with drummer Bobby Rosengarden's Band. In 1989 Danny moved to Perth, Western Australia, and, the following year, was awarded the MBE for his services to jazz. Fortunately for all of us, Danny continues to tour internationally and to record. In fact, I am writing this short pen-portrait of Danny while listening to two CDs he made at trumpeter Bob Barnard's Jazz Parties in Australia in 1999 and 2000. Clearly the passing years have neither dimmed Danny's big tone nor stemmed his articulate and assured phrasing. He remains one of the Brighton jazz scene's best-ever exports and ambassadors

DANNY MOSS
in 2002.

PICTURE BY COURTESY
OF DANNY MOSS

CHAPTER 7

THE FOURTEEN FOOT BAND: A PORTRAIT

TERRY WHITNEY

IN 1961 THE LATE, AND MUCH LAMENTED, MIKE COLLIER, having witnessed the phenomenal boom of skiffle music, convinced himself that the next pop sensation would be washboard music. He therefore formed a washboard band, which he believed would make the fortune of everyone concerned. Other musicians were more sceptical – justifiably as it turned out – but they were nevertheless happy to be involved with some unusual but enjoyable music making. At first Mike himself played the washboard but was persuaded by the rest of the band that his talents lay elsewhere. The reluctant drummer chosen to diversify and replace him was Brian Clarke. Other original members of the band included Ted Ambrose (trumpet), Keith Slade (clarinet), Dave Wigzell and Wally Allen (guitars) and John Boyett (bass). Later additions were Ted Owen (alto saxophone and clarinet), Pat Chapman (clarinet) and myself on piano.

The name of the band varied according to the number of participating musicians – each of whom was presumed to make a contribution of two feet. What would have happened if a one-legged player had joined remains a mystery. The original band had six members and was known as 'The Twelve Foot Band'. It subsequently increased to nine members and the name changed to 'The Eighteen Foot Band'.

Three private recordings were made by the group. The first two featured the talented singer Anne Durrant and the third included some arrangements I made of classic jazz numbers with clarinet trios. The band won the Brighton 'Jazz in June' contest and reached the semi-final of the National Amateur Jazz Band Contest in 1963. Apart from these activities, it made few public appearances but rehearsed and jammed in private while Mike waited in vain for the telephone call from a great impresario.

SUSSEX JAZZ SOCIETY supremo and (slightly reluctant) leader of the FOURTEEN FOOT BAND , trombonist MIKE COLLIER, photographed by his long-time friend and musical colleague, TED AMBROSE.

PICTURE BY COURTESY OF KEITH SAMUEL

In 1964 the washboard idea was gradually dropped and the group, which then had seven members, became 'The Fourteen Foot Band', although it was sometimes billed in the early days as 'Mike Collier's Washboard Band' or 'The Fourteen Foot Wash-board Band'. The name stuck no matter how many members were involved – although, at my ill-advised suggestion and against Mike's better judgement, the band's name was, towards the end of its life, shortened for a while to the trendy 'Fourteen Foot'. The original line-up of the new band was conventional and consisted of Mike (trombone), Ted Ambrose (trumpet), Pat Chapman (clarinet), Brian Clarke (drums), John Boyett (bass), Barry Skinner (guitar) and myself. Quite soon Alan Kennington replaced John Boyett, and Mike Church replaced Brian Clarke – who was in turn succeeded by Derek Middleton. Wally Allen replaced Barry Skinner on guitar and Ted Owen took over from Pat Chapman but both of them then moved away. The remaining line-up – of Mike, Ted, Alan, Derek and myself – stayed unchanged for most of the band's life.

Regular Sunday evening sessions were started at the Fox and Hounds – Chris Worrall's great pub just outside Haywards Heath – on 4 October 1964 and continued for nearly six years. The Fourteen Foot Band alternated with other groups such as the New City Jazzmen, the Riverside Jump Band and the Benny Simkins Sextet. Shortly afterwards the Fourteen Foot ensemble became the house band of the Sussex Jazz Society, which Mike and a few other enthusiasts formed for the purpose of presenting American stars touring with professional British groups.

After Ted Owen's departure the band lacked a regular reed player, so a saxophone or clarinet player had to be brought in for every performance. The tradition was therefore established of presenting a British star guest at each session. Early guests included Alan Cooper, Sandy Brown and Bruce Turner. These three musicians subsequently made the trip to Sussex on many occasions. Danny Moss too became a frequent visitor after he moved to Steyning and he introduced Ronnie Ross, the world-class baritone saxophonist, who married Mike's sister. Other guests on reed instruments over the years included Johnny Barnes, Teddy Layton, Jack Jacobs (a serving RAF officer), Will Hastie, Bill Greenow, Al Gay, Sammy Rimington, Dave Shepherd, Johnny Toogood (whom I can't remember at all) and Dick Morrissey. Jimmy Skidmore came several times and his son Alan, soon to become an international *avant garde* jazz star, was brought along once by Sandy Brown. Pete King – then, as now, a sensational bebop alto sax player – came along two or three times, as did Kathy Stobart, who, on one occasion, was accompanied by her husband, trumpeter Bert Courtley. Joe Harriott and Don Rendell similarly represented the modern jazz world.

Guests who were not reed players, but who were usually teamed up with one, included Freddy Randall, Humphrey Lyttelton, Alan Wickham, Bob Wallis, Mick Mulligan, Pat Halcox and Dick Sudhalter (trumpet); George Chisholm and Roy Williams (trombone); Lennie Felix, Harry· Walton and, always with Dick Sudhalter, Henry 'Thins' Francis (piano); Bill Bramwell, Diz Disley and Terry Smith (guitar); Dave Carey (vibraphone); Tony

TED AMBROSE ("Amby"), a key figure in the BRIGHTON JAZZ LINE, pictured in mid-career as a cornerstone member of the FOURTEEN FOOT BAND.

PICTURE BY COURTESY OF KEITH SAMUEL

Archer (bass); and, on drums, Tony Kinsey, who once sat in with Ronnie Ross. Perhaps the most engaging guest was Bob Clarke, the Scottish hot fiddle player, who worked in cabaret at the Crazy Horse Saloon in Paris but had a house in Lindfield. The singers Beryl Bryden and Jeanie Lambe were also popular visitors. Mike's guitarist friend Nevil Skrimshire used to sit in and once threatened to bring along Philly Joe Jones, the former Miles Davis drummer who was then "drying-out" in London. We were quite relieved that it didn't happen! The greatest thrill came when Bill Coleman, the legendary American trumpet star and the nicest man one could ever meet, sat in together with Danny Moss and Freddy Randall. Bill was staying at the time with his friend Ron Sweetman in Steyning and I cherish a photograph of him with Danny, Ron and myself taken outside a local pub that weekend.

The band's style was essentially mainstream. However, the diversity of star guests shows that it was capable of playing both traditional jazz *and* more modern styles. The modern soloists posed the greater problem, partly because their normal repertoire was largely unfamiliar but more because the band's knowledge of modern harmonic progressions was limited. Nevertheless, the musicians coped and the soloists – with one exception, who shall remain nameless – were friendly and undemanding.

THE FOURTEEN FOOT BAND and guests photographed outside the Fox and Hounds,
Haywards Heath on October 23rd, 1968, the day that their LP "THE GOOD LIFE" was recorded.
Left to right are: DANNY MOSS, TERRY WHITNEY, drummer DEREK MIDDLETON,
JACK JACOBS, MIKE COLLIER, ALAN KENNINGTON and TED AMBROSE.

PICTURE BY COURTESY OF THE LATE CHRIS WORRALL

On 23 October 1968 the band recorded an LP 'The Good Life' at the Fox and
Hounds for Doug Dobell's 77 label. It featured Danny Moss and Jack Jacobs and was
well received. It has recently been released on CD by Progressive Records [PCD 7018]
with previously unissued material and alternative takes.

Towards the end of the 1960s audiences at the Fox and Hounds started to drop and
by 1970 the Sunday night sessions were no longer viable. The last one took place in
June that year. The official guests were Bruce Turner and Dave Carey but Pat Halcox,
Diz Disley and Bob Clarke turned up for old times' sake. The audience was good and
the evening was very successful but it was too late for the sessions to be saved and the
unbroken sequence of nearly six years came to an end.

The band had already played at other venues. It was regularly featured at the
Sackville Jazz Bar in Hove, which functioned from the summer of 1967 until
November 1968. A "new" face there was the Australian piano player Graeme Bell,
whose band I had enjoyed when it toured Britain in 1947 and 1951. In 1969 there

were a few monthly sessions at The Gloucester pub in Brighton and one-off visits to the Kensington Jazz Club, the Osterley Jazz Club and The Grasshopper at Tilgate.

In September 1970 the band started to play regularly at The Gay Highlander pub in Peacehaven, where jazz had been presented for some time, and sessions there continued until 1973. In October 1970 the University of Sussex Jazz Club began to book the band on a monthly basis, hoping for the support of local fans who were welcome to attend. However, few of them made the trek to Falmer and support from students was also poor, so the sessions came to an end that December.

In November 1970 the Brighton Film Theatre presented a 'Star Night Gala' at the Regent Cinema. The main attraction was a showing of D W Griffith's great silent film *Birth of a Nation* accompanied by the brilliant theatre organist Florence de Jongh, who played the original score. The warm-up film was *A Night at the Regent Ballroom 1924*. This was accompanied by the Fourteen Foot Band augmented, for the occasion, by Geoff Simkins on alto saxophone. In December that year the band took part in an 'All Star Jazz Extravaganza' at the Dome, supporting the Alex Welsh band and the blues singer Champion Jack Dupree. Guest players included George Chisholm, Danny Moss, Ronnie Ross and Jack Jacobs. Jeanie Lambe sang and Humphrey Lyttelton was the compère. The Fourteen Foot band acquitted itself well but public attendance was poor, mainly due to an unfortunate clash with a local appearance of the Woody Herman orchestra.

At the beginning of 1971 the band found itself without a regular venue

JACK JACOBS and **DANNY MOSS** listen intently to a playback of **"THE GOOD LIFE"** tracks that they had just recorded on October 23, 1968.

THE PHOTOGRAPH WAS TAKEN BY TED AMBROSE.
PICTURE BY COURTESY OF KEITH SAMUEL

MIKE COLLIER proudly shows the album cover of **"THE GOOD LIFE"** to American trumpeter **BILL COLEMAN** shortly after the LP's release in 1969.

PICTURE BY COURTESY OF KEITH SAMUEL

although it continued to make occasional appearances at The Gay Highlander. In March it played with guests Ronnie Ross and Danny Moss at a 'Jazz Film Night' at the Brighton Film Theatre. In May there was a totally unpublicised and poorly attended concert at the Adeline Genée Theatre in East Grinstead that featured Danny Moss, Jeanie Lambe, George Chisholm and Ronnie Ross. Then, in August, the band took part in an 'International Festival of Music' in Guildford, supporting a touring American high school big band. Meanwhile, in May, regular appearances had begun at Jimmy's Restaurant in Brighton, a venue that had previously presented modern jazz.

Three Sussex bands earned a place on the bill for this major charity jazz concert at THE DOME on December 11, 1970.

After a good start, audiences tailed off and the sessions came to an end in September. During the autumn of 1971 the band started to play at the reconstituted Brighton Jazz Club at the Abinger Hotel on Brighton sea front. These sessions continued until the club folded in 1972.

Musicians who sat in, or deputised for regular band members, at this time included Eddie Buckwell on piano and John Wood and Malcolm Mortimore (in his first public appearance) on drums. Derek Middleton left the band temporarily and was replaced by Mike Travis – a fine London session player who lived locally for a short time – and later by Peter Burton. On 13 November 1971, BBC Radio Brighton staged and recorded a two-hour public concert at the Gardner Centre on the University of Sussex Campus. Keith Slade was the Producer for this event. The Fourteen Foot Band was featured with Bruce Turner, Ronnie Ross, Danny Moss and Jeanie Lambe. Mike Travis was the drummer and Hastings-based trumpeter Del Turner also participated. Brighton jazz writer Derrick Stewart-Baxter was the compère on this occasion. The recording was broadcast in its entirety shortly afterwards. It was thought at the time to be the longest jazz concert ever broadcast in this country.

In 1972 the band again made occasional appearances at The Gay Highlander and, in February, the band – with Danny Moss and Ronnie Ross – was recorded by the BBC at the Gardner Centre for a Radio One Jazz Club broadcast. Also recorded at the same session was the formidable Bobby Lamb-Ray Premru orchestra, featuring the

THE FOURTEEN FOOT BAND's tenure at the FOX AND HOUNDS came to an end,
after a six-year run, on June 28, 1970. Seen at the packed farewell session
(left to right) are DIZ DISLEY (guitar), BRUCE TURNER (alto sax), DEREK MIDDLETON (drums),
TED AMBROSE and PAT HALCOX (trumpets), ALAN KENNINGTON (bass) and
MIKE COLLIER (trombone). Hidden is pianist TERRY WHITNEY.

PICTURE BY COURTESY OF BEN COLLIER

cream of London modern jazz players. To our consternation, they settled themselves in the auditorium to listen to our rehearsal! Some two months later, in April, the Fourteen Foot Band appeared at the Crawley Jazz Festival with Humphrey Lyttelton and Ronnie Ross. In June, the band accompanied the veteran American trombonist and blues singer Clyde Bernhardt, who, in his youth, had played with the immortal King Oliver. The following month, the band, with George Chisholm and Danny Moss, was recorded at another BBC Radio Brighton public concert at the Gardner Centre. The concert, which was subsequently broadcast, also featured no less than three American high school bands.

1973 saw the sessions at The Gay Highlander come to an end and the band ceased to have a regular local base. By this time it was performing infrequently and all the members were committed to other bands. However, the Fox and Hounds had started to present jazz again occasionally and the Fourteen Foot Band returned to its old home for sessions in March 1973 and September 1974. In 1975 an attempt was made to present jazz at the Boship Farm Hotel at Lower Dicker but, in the event, only two sessions took place. The first, on 27 November, featured Danny Moss and at the second, on 4 December, George Chisholm was the guest. So far as I can trace, this was the band's last performance. After spells with the Benny Simkins Sextet and the Jubilee Jazz Band, Mike Collier launched The MC Band – of which I became a member – in 1983. But that's another story.

GEORGE CHISHOLM (left) "gurns" for the camera while TED AMBROSE manfully strives to keep a straight face, at the Fox and Hounds.

PICTURE BY COURTESY OF JUNE AMBROSE

CHAPTER 8

A FAMILY AFFAIR

ROY BOWER

URING THE LATE 1940s and the early years of the following decade, the so-called jazz revival was in full swing and in Britain, as in other parts of the world, many young people who were indifferent to the contents of the weekly popular music charts developed instead a passion for traditional jazz that they retain to this day. Inspired by such luminaries as Freddy Randall, Humphrey Lyttelton and Chris Barber, some even had aspirations to perform the music, buying instruments and forming bands with that end in mind.

One such young man attracted to jazz was Peter Simkins, who was born in 1939 and who, at the time of the jazz revival, was still a schoolboy. He then lived in the West London suburb of Greenford with his parents, Benny and Peg, and his brother Geoff, nine years his junior. The Simkins were a close-knit family who, by tradition, held regular parties with Benny's brothers and sisters. At these parties everyone was encouraged to indulge in artistic self-expression – in other words, they were required to "do a turn". Much later I was a guest at a number of these get-togethers, which continued into the 1970s, and I retain a vivid recollection of Benny's renditions of the music-hall songs *Burlington Bertie from Bow* and *Percy from Pimlico*, complete with top hat, cane and soft-shoe shuffle.

Benjamin Alfred Simkins was born on

"THE LOUNGE LIZARD". This picture of a suave-looking BENNY SIMKINS was taken in the late 1940s when he was a member of the BILL BENNETT BAND in West London.

PICTURE BY COURTESY OF PETER SIMKINS

26 March 1911 into a musical family at Harlesden in North-West London. His father was employed, unusually, as an artesian well-borer and was an amateur performer in the old music hall tradition. By all accounts the whole family – there were four sons and two daughters – had a "showbiz bent". In 1974, during an interview with BBC Radio Brighton presenter John Henty, Benny recalled his own performances of contemporary popular songs at a time when, as he put it, "I would have been only five or six years of age". He also developed an interest in military music and took lessons on the clarinet, joining the Acton Silver Band at 18. Throughout the 1930s Benny held down a day job with the Post Office but in the evenings he was more likely to be found playing dance music in one or other of the many ballrooms which then existed in London. He was by this time playing the tenor saxophone in a style heavily influenced by the American jazz musician Coleman Hawkins, who appeared in London in 1934. Benny is reputed to have attended every single concert, armed with binoculars in the hope of identifying Hawkins's fingering patterns.

During the Second World War, Benny served in a field squadron of the Royal Engineers and saw action with the Guards Armoured Division. When hostilities ceased he was a member of the prestigious Guards Armoured Division dance band, touring Germany and broadcasting from Bonn and Hamburg. After demobilisation he returned to London, resuming his work with the Post Office and in local dance bands.

Peter, encouraged by his parents, had taken piano lessons from an early age but

A youthful PETE SIMKINS (top left) at the BLUE CIRCLE CLUB, West Ruislip, circa 1959-60 when he was the pianist with the ART WOOD COMBO. Art (centre of the front row) is the elder brother of Ronnie Wood of The Rolling Stones.

PICTURE COURTESY OF PETE SIMKINS

The male members of the Simkins mafia jamming at the family home in North Road, Brighton, in the mid-1960s. With BENNY (tenor sax), PETE (piano) and GEOFF (drums) is a very young MICHAEL SIMKINS – now a successful West End actor – on vibes. John Boyett helps out on bass.

PICTURE BY COURTESY OF PETE SIMKINS

admitted to difficulty in reading music. He discontinued his lessons, settling instead for a crash course in jazz harmony from Dad. "From then on I ate, slept and drank jazz", Peter has written. His first public appearance as a jazz musician took place in a church hall in Hayes, Middlesex, in 1954, with a band called – improbably – The Abominable Blowmen. Later, wisely renamed the Omega Jazz Band, the group enjoyed a successful residency at Eel Pie Island. A stint with the versatile Art Wood Combo followed, coinciding with Peter's enrolment at King's College, London, where he obtained his degree in Modern History and first began to specialise in War Studies.

In 1958 Benny took early retirement from the civil service and purchased a tobacconists' shop in Harrow. It was not long before the lure of the seaside beckoned and the family moved to a similar property in North Road, Brighton. The year was 1961 and Peter recalls that, whilst viewing the premises, a tenor saxophone and a pile of old *Downbeat* magazines were discovered in an upstairs room - an omen, for sure! In some respects the jazz scene in Brighton at the time of their arrival was none too lively and the activities of the family during their early years in the town were largely of a non-musical nature. At one stage Benny sold his tenor sax. By 1964, however, Peter had found himself a jazz niche in a band at the Teachers' Training College and it was not long before he was joined in the group by his brother Geoff on drums. Peter had been impressed by Geoff's drumnastics with knitting needles and rulers while playing along to records, so, when a chance came to manoeuvre the band's existing, sub-standard, drummer out of the group, a cheap kit was purchased for Geoff, who then swiftly took over the drum chair.

Peter, by this time, was employed as Keeper of Exhibits at the Imperial War

Museum in London. Despite having to commute daily he managed to continue playing the piano in his spare time. Prior to becoming a founder member of the Benny Simkins Sextet in 1968 he found an outlet for his talents with the comparatively short-lived Martinique Jazz Band. Peter now lives in Ipswich with his wife Jane and his mother Peg. His only daughter, Catherine, has married and now lives in Oxford. Peter retired from the Imperial War Museum in 1999. In the same year he was appointed Honorary Professor in Modern History at the University of Birmingham and received an MBE in the Queen's Birthday Honours List. Highly articulate, Peter now spends his time lecturing and writing on his specialist subject, the First World War. He retains a passionate interest in jazz and, though he has an equal affection for Ipswich Town Football Club, still plays fine piano.

GEOFF SIMKINS joined the **TEMPERANCE SEVEN** in the early 1970s and, 30 years on, is still a regular member of that well-known band. This picture of him was taken in Hong Kong when the **TEMPERANCE SEVEN** had a short residency there, circa 1974.

PICTURE BY COURTESY OF PETE SIMKINS

Geoff Simkins began to plough his own jazz furrow, initially on drums, playing with his brother Peter and veteran trumpeter Ted Ambrose in the Martinique Jazz Band and helping to form, in 1965, the Old Timey Washboard Band, with Megs Etherington on cornet. Brother Peter had somewhat optimistically bought himself an alto saxophone – a plastic Grafton model – but, while he was away at work, Geoff instead picked it up and appeared to master it with startling speed. His fluency on that instrument belied his tender years at the time and, although he continued to play drums, it became increasingly clear that the alto was Geoff's musical voice.

In 1968, together with Jim Heath and John Muxlow, he formed the Harry Strutters Hot Rhythm Orchestra, an aggregation whose remarkable longevity is celebrated in Chapter 12 of this book. Subsequently he began a long musical association with the famous Temperance Seven and in the 1970s he played for a while at a club in Zurich with bassist Lindsay Cooper and trombonist Campbell Burnap. This was the time, to quote him verbatim, when his attitudes towards "professionalism, practice, Lee Konitz and life in general started to alter drastically". His impressive CV now lists appearances at clubs and concerts in Britain and overseas and includes numerous collaborations with visiting Americans. In 2001, for example, he was heard at the Lewes Jazz Club duetting excitingly with US tenor sax star Scott Hamilton in a session that ran nearly an hour over time. Geoff has recorded two CDs with guitarist Dave Cliff, both of which received excellent reviews. Earlier recordings featured him with fellow Sussex reedman Danny Moss and as a guest with his father's Sextet on recordings with American visitors Billy

Butterfield and Yank Lawson. Geoff still lives in Brighton and currently leads his own quartet. He is also heavily involved in jazz education projects.

Michael Simkins, the youngest brother (born in 1957) is not a jazz musician although he likes music. A successful professional actor, he trained at RADA and in 2001 not only played the male lead in the West End production of *Mamma Mia* but also appeared in the musical *Chicago*.

The notable achievements of the Benny Simkins Sextet are described in Chapter 9 of this book. Benny died, aged 71, in May 1982, having disbanded his Sextet only two months earlier when his doctor ordered him to rest. At the height of the band's success in 1974 he described his wife Peggy as his "inspiration and perfect partner" during the aforementioned Radio Brighton interview. She certainly provided unswerving support to her husband and sons and deserves much credit for

Taking the pith?
PETE SIMKINS (left) and **GEOFF SIMKINS**
reflect the glories of Empire in
a Brighton Carnival parade
in the late 1960s.

PICTURE BY COURTESY OF PETE SIMKINS

THE BENNY SIMKINS SEXTET
in full flow during one of its regular Sunday night sessions at the King and Queen,
Marlborough Place, Brighton, circa 1980.
Left to right are
MIKE COLLIER, ROY BOWER, VIC RICHARDS, BENNY SIMKINS, ALAN KENNINGTON, and PETE SIMKINS.

PICTURE BY COURTESY OF PETE SIMKINS

their artistic successes. Socially, the Simkins home in North Road provided a valuable focal point for jazz musicians and aficionados. During the family's residency the building retained its attractive pre-war appearance and décor and many a "visiting fireman" was persuaded to descend into the Aladdin's Cave of a cellar beneath the newsagents' shop to sample Benny's home-made wine. This was consumed, sometimes in copious quantities, to the accompaniment of musical gems from the family's extensive jazz record library. Eventually, with the establishment of the Brighton Jazz Record Appreciation Society in April 1971 these meetings took on a slightly less haphazard form.

The family was affectionately known as the Brighton Mafia (Benny, naturally, was The Godfather) and they shared, along with their 1930s Chicago namesakes, a deep admiration for American jazz musicians. The full story of Peter and Benny's efforts to present top US musicians is told elsewhere, and, although there was clearly a scintilla of self-interest on the part of the Sextet members, it should be recognised that these promotions, sometimes involving considerable financial risk, gave enthusiasts a local opportunity to hear and see many jazz giants at a remarkably modest cost.

Few would dispute that the Simkins family brought an organisational and entrepreneurial flair to the Brighton area jazz scene in the 1970s, rivalled only by the heady days of the Sussex Jazz Society in the 1960s. Keith Samuel, writing as Sam Edwards in the *Brighton and Hove Gazette*, touched on the achievements of jazz families, identifying a number of American examples. Sadly, Britain has produced relatively few families of jazz musicians, although the post-war scene has been graced by the Dankworths and the Christie and Pyne brothers. The Simkins clan are a worthy addition to this small but distinguished roster.

THE JAZZ EMPORIUM : *a vignette by Peter Simkins*

32 North Road was the Brighton home of the Simkins Mafia from 1961 to 1983. The property was a newsagents and confectionery business which Benny took over in October 1961, the premises having once been the site of the first Brighton Co-operative Store in the late 19th Century. All of the family lived there, at one time or another, during the 1960s and 1970s, as there was ample room in the large basement under the shop, and in the three floors above, to house everybody in reasonable comfort. The front basement, directly under the shop, was the home of the Brighton Jazz Record Society for much of the 1970s, while Benny's band normally rehearsed in the lounge above the shop.

The front basement was usually a glorious mess. A stuffed moose's head – leaking sawdust – jostled for space on the walls with posters of Laurel and Hardy and W.C. Fields, baseball pennants and old musical instruments, and the floor and assorted tables were occupied by the family's creaking, third-best furniture, threadbare cast-off rugs and a number of bubbling and menacing demijohns which contained Benny's latest batch of lethal home-made wine or beer. The growing record collection of Pete and Geoff was stacked on shelves along one wall, and in the far corner was a mysterious

THE "JAZZ EMPORIUM",
32 North Road, in the late 1960s.
In the late 19th century – long
before Benny Simkins took it over
as a newsagent – the shop was the
first Brighton Co-operative store.
Under the avuncular Benny, the
Emporium dispensed good music
and liquid refreshment to friends
from the jazz world, as well as
newspapers, sweets and cigarettes.

PICTURE BY COURTESY OF PETE SIMKINS

and murky alcove, masked by a multi-coloured plastic strip curtain, which nobody ever dared to penetrate or inspect.

For the regular Wednesday-night meetings of the Brighton Jazz Record Society, the Simkins family would provide French bread and cheese and members would bring their own tipple, such as a Watney's 'Party Four'. Regulars included Ted Mechen, Maurice Fleming, Gerry Clayton, Pat Sheen and Edwin Hinchcliffe. The Dobell's "Rat Pack" – John Kendall, Brian Peerless, Brian Chadwick and Bill Colyer – would often come down mob-handed just for the hell of it, especially if one of them, such as John Kendall, was giving a record recital. A strong bladder was required if a long track from a Buck Clayton Jam Session was being played , for the loo was two flights up!

As well as housing the jazz activities, the same basement was also the home for the "Wandering Minstrels" Gilbert and Sullivan Society organised by young Michael Simkins. Most nights of the week therefore witnessed a constant procession of people filing in and out of the premises and up and down the basement stairs. Innocent onlookers might have thought that Benny was running a speakeasy (or worse). American guest stars like Dick Cary, Kenny Davern, Bob Wilber and Billy Butterfield were all introduced to the subterranean joys of the basement and, when playing with Pete at the Ipswich Jazz Club in the late 1980s, Kenny shared some of his memories of the place with the audience. Singer Adelaide Hall, who stayed with a neighbour while appearing at the Theatre Royal one year, similarly visited Benny's "jazz emporium" and memorably sang "Creole Love Call" to an accompaniment by Benny and Pete in the room above the shop. Fittingly, a boozy jazz party was held in the basement after Benny's funeral in May 1982 and the joint was really jumping! Benny, the "Godfather", would have thoroughly approved of the manner of the send-off.

THE MARTINIQUE JAZZ BAND : *a portrait by Peter Simkins*

As in my father Benny's case, the move to Brighton in 1961 temporarily halted my jazz activities. However, the start of the Fourteen Foot Band's residency at the Fox and Hounds provided a jazz haunt which was very much to my taste and, with my younger brother Geoff, I soon became a regular member of the growing audience at the Sunday night sessions there. Never having been too shy and retiring where jazz is concerned, it was only a matter of time before I asked to sit in and my choice of material – such as the old Frank Signorelli standard *I'll Never be the Same* – obviously impressed Mike Collier, as invitations to play with the Fourteen Foot band and the Riverside Jump Band became more frequent when Terry Whitney was otherwise engaged.

At roughly the same time, our parents had begun to take in student lodgers and through one of them, John Hodgson, I was enlisted to help coach a small jazz combo at the Brighton Teachers' Training College in Kemp Town. The student band included singer Vic Burgess, clarinettist Peter Saunders and banjoist Pete Holloway. I decided that the band's line-up would probably be best suited to the Jimmy Blythe-Junie Cobb-Clarence Williams small group style of the late 1920s but the drummer, unfortunately, was not even up to that undemanding role. Having been impressed

THE MARTINIQUE JAZZ BAND at the Imperial Hotel, Brighton, probably in late 1966.
DAVE CAREY guests on vibes with HUGH CROXFORD (clarinet), PETE MITTON (trumpet),
GEOFF SIMKINS (drums), TONY CLARK (trombone) and PETE SIMKINS (piano).

PICTURE BY COURTESY OF PETE SIMKINS

Part of the
MARTINIQUE JAZZ BAND's
rhythm section –
MIKE "ABBO" ADAMS (bass),
JIM HEATH (guitar) and
PETE SIMKINS (piano) –
back BENNY SIMKINS (far left)
at a BBC Radio Brighton
presentation at the
Corn Exchange,
early in 1968.

PICTURE BY COURTESY OF PETE SIMKINS

with brother Geoff's increasing prowess on wooden rulers, knitting needles and suitcase while accompanying jazz records, I helped him buy the rudiments of a drum kit from shops in Kensington Gardens and Queen's Road and recommended him as a replacement. Within weeks, Geoff's distinguished jazz career was under way.

Benny, Geoff and I all appeared at a concert arranged by Keith Slade for the inmates of Lewes Prison on 10 October 1965 and, a few weeks later, in November, backed Mick Mulligan at a session at the British Legion Hall in Peacehaven. Mike Collier was on trombone that night, and other musicians on the date included Hugh Croxford on clarinet, John Greenwood on guitar, Pete Holloway on banjo and Vic Burgess on vocals. The gig, in aid of the Brighton S.O.S (Save Our Swing) Society, was, in some respects, a disaster, as only sixteen paying customers turned up and the band and sitters-in actually outnumbered the audience. It did, however, encourage Geoff, Hugh and I to stick together and form what became, in 1966, the Martinique Jazz Band.

The band's first trumpeter was Pete 'Mitz' Mitton, with whom I had played in the Omega Jazz band in West London in the mid-1950s and who had himself recently moved to Worthing. John Davidson was the first trombonist with the Martinique. By the time the band began a short residency at the Quarterstaff Folk Club at Jimmy's Restaurant in May 1966, Jim Heath had been added on banjo and Mike "Abbo" Adams was on bass. The rhythm section was to remain the same throughout the band's existence. Shortly before the first gig at the Quarterstaff Folk Club, Jim Heath had persuaded Geoff and I to take part in a home movie about the American Civil War and, during a wild Sunday-morning bayonet charge on the Sussex Downs, I fell on a magnesium flare – just as it ignited – and severely burned my right hand. For the entire evening on the band's first full gig I could therefore play only with my left hand!

By August 1966 the Martinique Jazz Band had started to play at the Imperial Hotel in Queen's Road on Thursday evenings, switching to Wednesdays after a few weeks. The Imperial, which had a spacious ballroom at the rear of the premises and a grand (if somewhat elderly) piano, was to become the Martinique's home for the next two-and-a-half years. Ernie and Vi Field were the benevolent, if often bemused, hosts at the pub. Tony Clark took over the trombone chair for a while before being replaced by Ian Todd, and Jack Sherriff succeeded Hugh Croxford on clarinet. When Pete Mitton left to concentrate on his activities with the Arun Valley Jazz Band, the vastly experienced Ted Ambrose joined on trumpet in May 1967 – thus completing what was to become the band's stable line-up until its demise almost two years later.

From now on, the band's reputation and popularity steadily grew. Audiences of over one hundred were common at the Imperial on Wednesday nights by early 1967 and the Martinique also began to appear regularly at the Chinese Jazz Club – where we backed blues singer Jesse Fuller in May that year – as well as at the Fox, the Grasshopper at Crawley and the Sackville Jazz Bar in Hove. The band's repertoire was fairly broad within the overall hot jazz tradition and embraced New Orleans marches, material from the white New York bands of the late 1920s and tunes from the likes of Don Redman, Hot Lips Page and Duke Ellington. When Australian jazz pianist and pioneer Graeme Bell starred at the Sackville in February 1968, the Martinique was chosen to accompany him – the group's musical style and approach having much in common with that of the Bell outfits of the late 1940s and 1950s.

In a futile and downright silly attempt to turn myself into a multi-instrumentalist in the manner of Lazy Ade Monsbourgh, I bought myself a second-hand Grafton plastic alto sax but barely got beyond simple scales and never produced anything other than a tone like a coyote that had just been emasculated! While I was away daily in London at work, Geoff, on the other hand, mastered the basics of the instrument with astonishing speed and, by August 1968, Chris Duff – in the Sussex Jazz Society newsletter – was able to report that he was "coming along nicely" on alto sax, though Chris noted, in addition, that Geoff's principal ambition, at that time, was "to drum for Ken Colyer". Geoff's burgeoning interest in the alto sax, however, heralded a parting of the ways for, by the autumn of that year, he was active at the King and Queen, with the newly-formed Harry Strutters, on Friday evenings and Sunday lunchtimes. The Martinique Jazz Band continued for a few more months until falling attendances at the Imperial and mounting disagreements over musical policy precipitated its break-up. The band's farewell gig was at the Fox and Hounds on 23 March 1969. Nevertheless, while it lasted – and particularly during its 'vintage years' in 1967 and 1968 – it is perhaps not too immodest for me to suggest or claim that the band had done much to maintain and further the cause of good-quality traditional jazz in the Brighton area.

CHAPTER 9

THE BENNY SIMKINS SEXTET: A PORTRAIT

PETER SIMKINS

THE BAND that was destined to fly the Dixieland and mainstream flag in Brighton most prominently throughout the 1970s really began with two musical exiles – Benny Simkins (my Dad) and Roy Bower – who had moved south in the 1960s from London and Manchester respectively. As that decade neared its end, neither belonged to a regular band and trumpeter Roy, in particular, wanted more than infrequent sitting-in or "depping" with local bands.

Keith Slade could claim to have acted as midwife at the birth of the new group, for it was he who booked Benny and Roy to play together – backed by myself and some other renegades from the Martinique Jazz band – at the Sackville Jazz Bar on Friday 18 October 1968, for a session which was recorded, and subsequently broadcast, by Radio Brighton. After the gig, Roy said to Benny, "Let's form a band." And the deed was done. They managed to attract the interest of trombonist Harry Ledger, a former Army bandsman, and the first rehearsal of the band – then still only a front line – was held at the Simkins home at 32 North Road, Brighton, on 13 November, less than a month later. I joined the group on piano at a time when the Martinique Jazz Band was beginning to break up, and bassist Pete "97" Hill and drummer Terry Shearing were soon recruited to complete the rhythm section.

Roy Bower already possessed an impressive library of arrangements – including some by fellow Mancunian Alan Hare – as well as extremely broad jazz tastes (everything from ragtime to hard bop) and a genuine love of the American popular song in its classic form. These assets, combined with his intense desire always to play the *correct* chord changes and seek unhackneyed material, did most – especially in the early days

The original BENNY SIMKINS SEXTET, featured at the Gloucester Hotel, Gloucester Place, Brighton in 1969.
Back row, left to right: TERRY SHEARING (drums), PETE HILL (bass) and PETE SIMKINS (piano).
In front are HARRY LEDGER (trombone), ROY BOWER (trumpet) and BENNY (tenor sax).

PICTURE BY COURTESY OF KEITH SAMUEL

– to shape the band's repertoire and set its high musical standards. The band's main influences were probably the World's Greatest Jazz Band, the Condon outfits and the exciting band that Bobby Hackett had led at the Henry Hudson Hotel. However, the newly formed outfit also drew its repertoire from the classic jazz of Armstrong, Morton and Oliver, the music of Buck Clayton, the Basie and Ellington small groups, and even modern jazz – particularly the compositions of Benny Golson. Vocals in the tradition of San Francisco favourites Turk Murphy and Clancy Hayes spiced this musical *mélange*.

Apart from opting for a deliberately wide and original repertoire, the band collectively decided to hold regular rehearsals – which it kept up for much of its long existence – and to delay its first public appearance until all members felt it was good and ready. By March 1969, when the band was rehearsing at The Gloucester, in Gloucester Place, Brighton, only one problem remained, that of choosing a name. A huge list of names (some of them unprintable) was considered and, after much discussion, the title of the "Benny Simkins Sextet" was agreed upon – when Benny himself was actually out of the room!

The Sextet's first public appearance duly took place on May 4, 1969, appropriately enough at the Fox and Hounds, Haywards Heath. The long preliminary period of rehearsal clearly paid off. John Roberts, in the *Crawley Advertiser*, judged the band to be "a versatile, highly-polished, professional-sounding addition to the jazz ranks" and Chris Duff felt that its performance was "ample proof that there is no shortage of good jazz musicians in Sussex", though both observed, not unfairly, that the Sextet was perhaps a trifle over-arranged and therefore lacked excitement and spontaneity at this stage of its life. Fortunately, the band's style – while always sticking closely to its initial aims – got looser and more confident as the months and years went by, and such early criticisms were no longer levelled at it.

Having launched itself into the Sussex jazz world, the Sextet quickly gained momentum. Appearances at the Gloucester, a Wednesday-night residency at the Imperial in Queen's Road and regular gigs at the Fox helped to hone the band's repertoire and increase its impact on the local scene. In January 1970 Radio Brighton recorded the Sextet at the Imperial for a programme in its "Worth Hearing" series. The band backed the first of many guest musicians when Bruce Turner played with it at The Arlington, Marine Parade, on 13 May and, the same month, the Sextet began its first two-year, Sunday-night residency at the nearby Pier Hotel, where rugby-loving landlord Chris Blythe provided a new and central venue for various local groups.

In the summer of 1970, Harry Ledger left the band (having re-enlisted in the Army and joined the Band of the Irish Guards). He was replaced by Cuckfield-based Geoff Hoare, previously with Ian Bell, the DJ Blues Band and a seven-piece band led by tenorist Pete Walker and pianist Pete Martin. Whereas Harry played in a smooth Urbie Green manner, Geoff's style was altogether lustier and his Lou McGarity-inspired trombone immediately gave the Sextet a more pronounced Dixieland feel. The influence of the World's Greatest Jazz Band was reinforced when that outfit visited Brighton to play at the Dome in December 1971. Members of the Sextet, including myself, were among those who welcomed Yank Lawson, Bob Haggart and the rest when they arrived and helped to look after them before the evening concert. Little did we dream at this stage that, over the next few years, we would become firm friends with several of the stars from the WGJB.

By the time the Sextet had celebrated its third birthday with a session at the Fox in May 1972, other personnel changes had taken place. Terry Shearing had left in August and reserve drummer Gordon Wren had been posted to Brussels, so Peter Burton took over the drum stool. Pete Hill had meanwhile gone north to Haworth in Yorkshire and was succeeded on bass by Chris Gibb. In the summer of 1972, the Sextet undertook a short tour of Yorkshire – the first of three – playing at the Bridlington and Leeds Jazz Clubs, the gigs being arranged by former Martinique Jazz band trombonist Ian Todd, then living in Pateley Bridge. Chris Blythe left the Pier Hotel in May 1972 and, following an abortive attempt to establish Friday sessions at the Ladies Mile Hotel, Patcham, the band began a new Sunday-night residency in the autumn at Brian Barratt's Gay Highlander pub at Peacehaven. No doubt encouraged by the fact that the admission price was, initially, a mere 20p, audiences at the Gay Highlander picked up well and guest stars were soon being booked. Bruce Turner, Danny Moss and John Chilton were all featured there, with the latter telling the audience how lucky they were to have such a good band in the locality. Guitarist Ted Muxlow (father of John) now regularly sat in with the Sextet, while the experienced and propulsive Bernie Godfrey, who had previously played with Alan Littlejohn, succeeded Pete Burton on drums. John Chilton's visit marked the last guest session at the Peacehaven hostelry for, after a fourteen-month stint, the band returned to the Pier Hotel in November 1973. As Benny told the local press, it seemed a "good idea to move back to the centre of town with the onset of winter".

The second residency at the Pier (shortly to be re-named The Buccaneer) had a

A Sunday night session in the upstairs bar of the Pier Hotel, Brighton, early in 1972.
Left to right: GEOFF HOARE (trombone), ROY BOWER (trumpet), TED MUXLOW (guitar),
PETER BURTON (drums), BENNY SIMKINS (tenor) and PETE SIMKINS (piano).

PICTURE BY COURTESY OF PETE SIMKINS

very promising start. Through the good offices of Sinclair Traill, American stride pianist Dick Wellstood appeared there with the band on 20 January 1974, becoming the first in a long line of American guests to be featured with the Sextet. Dick informed the audience that he had played better pianos in Basutoland but overcame the deficiencies of the offending instrument to provide a memorable evening of jazz. In March and April, Bruce Turner, Freddy Randall and trombonist Chris Pyne visited the Pier. However, after the band's third northern tour in May, the residency came to an end as a result of a disagreement with the management over admission charges. As one of the most popular and proficient groups in the area, Benny and the boys now

believed that they merited a flat scale payment rather than the more uncertain share
of door receipts, so June 9, 1974 saw them
inaugurate a new Sunday-night residency at
the Northern Hotel in London Road,
Brighton, where Bernie Barton was the wel-
coming landlord. The Sextet was now
becoming very active and, in the second
half of 1974, besides establishing itself at
the Northern – where Bruce Turner and
John Barnes were early guests – the band
backed George Melly at The Hungry Years
in Marine Parade and brassman Bobby
Mickleburgh at Markwell's Bar in the
Queen's Hotel, King's Road, in October.

As things turned out, all this was simply
a foretaste of even more exciting times
ahead. The band's first "golden year" began
at Christmas 1974 when, at Gordon Wren's
request, I played piano at his office party in
Victoria Street, London. Later in the
evening I called in at the 100 Club to see
and hear the all-star American group, the
Kings of Jazz, which featured such luminaries as Pee Wee Erwin, Johnny Mince and
Dick Hyman. Bud Freeman sat in with that
wonderful band and during a break at the
bar – when I was no doubt emboldened by
the demon drink – I casually asked Bud if
he would care to do a gig in Brighton. "Sure,
just ask my agent," he responded. Bud's
agent, Robert Masters, who also represented
the Kings of Jazz, was at the 100 Club that

Benny's band undertook short tours of jazz clubs in the north
of England in the early 1970s. They are seen here in
Bridlington, Yorkshire in May, 1974. Seated on the wall
outside a local guest house are PETE SIMKINS, PETE HILL,
BENNY, BERNIE GODFREY and ROY BOWER. Brighton record
collector and band supporter Ted Mechen looks on.

PICTURE BY COURTESY OF PETE SIMKINS

night and, since he too lived in Sussex, the deal was sealed in the train on the way
home. I then announced to a startled Benny next day that he was committed to backing Bud Freeman at the Northern in less than a month! With Alan Kennington
having recently joined the band on bass – and augmented for the evening by brother
Geoff on baritone sax – the Sextet appeared with Bud on 12 January 1975. He must
have given the band a good report because Robert Masters thereafter offered us
numerous opportunities to support visiting American jazz greats – all of which we
gladly seized!

During a trip to America in January 1975 – when I was supposed to be concentrat-
ing on Imperial War Museum business – I somehow "found" time to sit in twice at

BRIAN HILLS (clarinet) sits in with the SEXTET in the downstairs bar at the Pier Hotel,
Marine Parade in 1974. By this time CHRIS GIBB had joined the band on bass and
BERNIE GODFREY had succeeded PETER BURTON on drums.

PICTURE BY COURTESY OF PETE SIMKINS

Jimmy Ryan's famous club on West 54th Street in New York, playing there with Max
Kaminsky, Joe Muryani and Major Holley, mainly on the strength of saying that I
knew Bud Freeman! As if this were not enough, the year actually got better. A visit
by Wingy Manone to the Northern in June was of curiosity value rather than a musical success. Wingy was incapable of playing more than one chorus at a time and was
leeringly unpleasant, particularly to the ladies in the audience, having a large false
phallus (at least I think it was false!) strapped inside his trousers and manipulating it
salaciously at regular intervals. The Sextet was also subsequently criticised by Derrick
Stewart-Baxter for supporting a "well-known racist". In fact, the Wingy visit was only
a hiccup. In May, with Vic Richards depping for Bernie Godfrey on drums, the Sextet
had gone to the Dunkirk Jazz Festival and won second prize in a competition for traditional and mainstream groups – the prize money proving sufficient to finance a

weekend in Paris and some jamming at a club in Pigalle, where *boulevardier* Vic, for some inexplicable reason, announced the band in broken English and with a false French accent that made him sound like a refugee from "*Allo, Allo!*" Three weeks after Dunkirk, the band recorded its first album, *Linger Awhile*, for Bruce Bastin's Flyright label. Bob Williams stood in on bass for Alan Kennington on three of the ten tracks issued.

From this point, American soloists appeared with the Sextet thick and fast, sometimes at the rate of two a month, with the Fox and the Northern (but mostly the Fox) providing the venues. Just as Mike Collier had done a decade before, Benny promoted the sessions under the banner of the Sussex Jazz Society. In terms of jazz legends starring in one's own local pubs – and, this time, with a local group – the next twenty-four months or so probably constituted a second "golden era". Billy Butterfield, Dick Wellstood, Wild Bill Davison, Bob Wilber, Bill Coleman and Ralph Sutton all appeared at the Fox with the Sextet before the end of 1975, and Ralph's storming session was recorded for the Flyright label by Brighton collector Ted Mechen. Geoff Simkins, on alto and baritone, and Randy Colville, on clarinet and soprano, were added to the band for the majority of these gigs. Meanwhile, trumpeter Bernie Privin guested at the Northern. Bernie Privin's New York Jewish "put down" humour was as good as his trumpet playing and all the boys in turn were subjected to

BOB WILBER appeared on clarinet and soprano sax with the **BENNY SIMKINS** band
at the **FOX AND HOUNDS**, Haywards Heath on November 2, 1975. Clearly visible here are
GEOFF SIMKINS, BENNY, ROY BOWER, BOB WILBER, ALAN KENNINGTON (bass) and **GEOFF HOARE**.

PICTURE BY COURTESY OF PETE SIMKINS

Another star American guest at the FOX AND HOUNDS in November 1975 was stride pianist RALPH SUTTON. PETE SIMKINS greets his idol, while propping up the bar are Sussex musicians PETER GODFREY, GORDON WREN and JACK SHERRIFF.

PICTURE BY COURTESY OF PETE SIMKINS

his barbed wit. "If you moved into our block, the taxes would go down," he told drummer Bernie Godfrey. Nevertheless, he later sent a note to tell Benny how much he had enjoyed himself with the band. "It makes it so easy when everyone knows what the hell is going on," he wrote.

In May 1976 the band made a second trip to Dunkirk, where Alan Kennington won the award for the best instrumentalist in the traditional/mainstream category of the competition for amateur and semi-professional bands. Little did the judges know that, seconds before the Sextet's opening number, Alan had frantically asked me, in a hoarse whisper: "What bloody key are we playing in?" That year too, Dick Wellstood, Bud Freeman, Peanuts Hucko, Kenny Davern and Benny Waters all starred with the Sextet at the Fox and baritone saxist Joe Temperley was featured at the Northern in a session interrupted by a bomb scare! The Norman Hay Hall at the St Francis Hospital, Haywards Heath, was the setting for an appearance by Ruby Braff on 27 June. Having heard the acerbic Mr Braff "rubbish" a fine rhythm section with pianist Mick Pyne earlier in the day, we approached the evening with more than a little trepidation. Musically the session was fine and we were still smugly congratulating ourselves on our survival when a taxi firm rang to inform us that Ruby had taken a cab back to London after the session and charged it to Benny! Bob Wilber, Kenny Davern and Pug Horton were much kinder to us when they were featured together at the same venue in October.

The residency at the Northern had ended in May 1976 but, by September, the band had begun to appear at the 125 Club at The Adur, Hove Lagoon, where sessions were being organised by Vic Richards. When Mike Collier replaced Geoff Hoare as the Sextet's trombonist, the band was resident at The Adur on Sundays and backed multi-instrumentalist Dick Cary there in March 1977, followed by reedmen Buddy Tate and Jim Galloway in April. That summer, the band began its last, and longest, residency at the King and Queen in Brighton. American jazz singer Joe Lee Wilson, who had moved to Kemp Town with his English-born wife, became a frequent guest at the King and Queen and often brought American jazz friends to hear, and sit in with, the band. One recalls, for example, modern jazz drummer Victor Lewis – later a regular

On November 6, 1977 American trumpet great
BILLY BUTTERFIELD recorded the album "Watch What
Happens" for the Flyright label, backed by Benny and
his band. Butterfield and Roy Bower are seen here
"swapping fours" while an appreciative MIKE COLLIER
listens intently.

PICTURE BY COURTESY OF PETE SIMKINS

Benny's band had the honour of supporting several
American and British stars at a concert at The Dome,
Brighton on February 21, 1981. Left to right are:
HUMPHREY LYTTELTON (trumpet),
VIC RICHARDS (drums),
BILLY BUTTERFIELD (trumpet),
BENNY WATERS and BENNY SIMKINS (tenors), and
DAVE SHEPHERD (clarinet). The trombone slide
belongs to MIKE COLLIER.

PICTURE BY COURTESY OF PETE SIMKINS

with Stan Getz – happily propelling the Sextet through Dixieland warhorses such as *Royal Garden Blues*. On 6 November the band backed Billy Butterfield at the Fox and, next day, went with Billy to a studio in Worthing to record the album *Watch What Happens* for Flyright. As Eddie Condon might have said of a bibulous but enjoyable and successful recording date: "Mr Smirnoff attended the session and left looking somewhat emaciated".

The final personnel change occurred in 1978 when Bernie Godfrey departed after some five years and was replaced by the ebullient Vic Richards, already a good friend of the Sextet. Vic's extrovert personality was one of the ingredients that maintained the band's popularity at the King and Queen. Trumpeter Pee Wee Erwin and clarinettist Johnny Mince, undeterred by a long, fog-bound delay in Amsterdam, arrived just in time to blow up a real storm at the King and Queen on October 15, 1978 and Eddie Miller graced us with his stylish presence on 15 November, Keith Samuel being among the sitters-in that night. Jim Galloway paid a return visit to the town in April 1979 – this time appearing with the band at the Concorde Bar – and a notable coda was added to the American connection on October 19, 1979, the day on which the band – with Stan Warboys depping for Alan Kennington on bass – recorded the album *Easy to Remember* with Yank Lawson.

BENNY SIMKINS digs the baritone sax playing of son GEOFF at the KING AND QUEEN.
The picture was taken towards the end of Benny's playing days.

The poster for the Dome concert in 1981 – a great showcase for Sussex jazz, with the BENNY SIMKINS' BAND and pianist HARRY WALTON'S TRIO backing a roster of big names.

COURTESY OF BEN COLLIER

Had we known it then, a final session with Yank at the Fox in November 1979 effectively signalled the passing of the Sextet's best days. The band continued at the King and Queen for another couple of years until, early in 1982, Benny's health began to deteriorate and his doctor advised him to give playing a rest. The Sextet carried on for a time, with Norman Evans ably deputising on tenor, but without its much-loved father figure, guru, fixer and worrier-in-chief, the band was never quite the same. Benny died, following a stroke, in May 1982 – the same year in which Ted Ambrose and Harry Walton also passed away. Thus ended another memorable period in the story of Brighton and Sussex jazz.

The cavernous mock Tudor environs of the KING AND QUEEN have witnessed a good deal of Brighton's jazz history – including this poignant occasion. The ANDERIDA JAZZ BAND are pictured performing at a special session on April 23, 1983, when the Brighton jazz community turned out in force to honour the memory of BENNY SIMKINS and TED AMBROSE, who both died in 1982. The visible players are JOHN GOODRICK (clarinet), GORDON WREN (drums), BILL HARVEY (trumpet), CHRIS GIBB (bass) and BAZ SEARLE (trombone). Pianist PETER GODFREY is hidden.   PICTURE BV COURTESY OF GORDON WREN

Sussex Jazz Society
presents   6

DICK WELLSTOOD

with

BENNY SIMKINS SEXTET

SUNDAY, JUNE 22nd, 1975

FOX & HOUNDS, HAYWARDS HEATH

BAR EXTENSION

7.30 p.m.   ADMISSION £1.00

Visits by leading American jazz musicians to the FOX AND HOUNDS at Haywards Heath have left a legacy of treasured memories for Sussex jazz fans. This is the ticket for stride pianist DICK WELLSTOOD's visit in 1975.

COURTESY OF PETE SIMKINS

CHAPTER 10

FACES, PLACES, CHARACTERS AND COMMUNICATORS

PETER SIMKINS

THIS BOOK IS NOT JUST A STORY OF MUSICIANS AND BANDS. Many places and faces have a treasured place in the collective local jazz memory. The pubs and hotels that have hosted sessions over the years are too numerous to list – even if one could remember them all – but some venues became, or still are, pivotal to the Brighton and Sussex jazz scene. The Chalet Club in Western Road, the Montpelier Hotel and the Paris Buttery are just three that will be recalled fondly by those of us now drawing bus passes. Falling into the category of "they don't build pubs like they used to" are the mock-Tudor splendours of the King and Queen in Marlborough Place, the cavernous Pier Hotel (a.k.a. The Buccaneer) and the Adur near Hove Lagoon, while who could fail to be impressed by the Art Deco chic of Shoreham Airport – the long-time home of the Harry Strutters and, more recently, Brian Cotton and his Cotton Club Jazzmen (supper included)? At Shoreham, one has always expected to glance out of the window to see Jack Buchanan and Gertrude Lawrence climbing out of a Tiger Moth and into a Lagonda. Then there was "Four Bars Inn" in St James's Street – a brave, if short-lived attempt by Vic Richards to combine a restaurant with a jazz cellar and bar. The cosy, if crowded, back room at the Fox and Hounds, Haywards Heath – covered elsewhere in the book – occupies a very special niche in Sussex jazz history, although when I called in to the pub in the 1990s, I was aghast to see that the old interior (including that sacred back room) had been gutted to make way for a restaurant.

Even more important to the story are the people who have embraced jazz with an undying passion and who have sought to promote it or share its never-ending joys. One must pay tribute to the many loyal fans and collectors who, usually with more sense than money, have added immeasurably to the scene over five or six decades and

LEN PROSSOR, the Sussex bass player and musical journalist, a cousin of TED AMBROSE and wartime colleague of SPIKE MILLIGAN. He emigrated to the United States in the early 1960s and in 2002 – having reached his mid-80s – was still active as an entertainer. This photograph was taken in 2000.

PICTURE BY COURTESY OF KEITH SAMUEL

without whose support local jazz would have found it hard to continue. A vital role, of course, has been played throughout by the communicators. Coverage of jazz in the *Brighton Herald* from the early 1950s onwards was looked after by Len Prossor, Keith Samuel (who both wrote under the pen-name of Musicus), Hugo Martin, John Marley and Jeff Rigby. Jeff should have won a VC at least for his Herculean efforts to foster modern jazz in the area. His ventures did not always meet with the success they deserved, but some, such as the regular sessions he presented at The Ship in the Lewes Road, featured music of the highest quality. Jim Pegg, Keith Samuel again (writing as 'Sam Edwards'), and Mary Stewart-Baxter chronicled local jazz activity for the *Brighton and Hove Gazette*, as did I for a couple of years in the mid-to-late 1970s. Keith's unrivalled stint lasted for eighteen years before he persuaded me to take up the reins in 1976, having first treated me to a prawn and egg curry at an Indian restaurant in Queen's Road. Some people are easily bought! The ebullient Chris Duff wrote a column in the *Mid-Sussex Times* while journalist/bassist John Roberts covered the scene in the *Crawley Advertiser*. The tall, bookish and articulate John Postgate, himself a trumpet player, has also written extensively on jazz and still contributes record reviews to *Jazz Journal International*.

Jazz record collectors are a unique, obsessive and masochistic group all on their own. Invariably blessed with saintly and tolerant wives/husbands/partners (delete as necessary), they have long formed the hard core of jazz audiences wherever the music has been played. The courteous and gentlemanly Maurice Fleming, Edwin Hinchliffe,

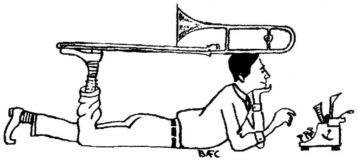

Trombonist and journalist KEITH SAMUEL, leader of the RIVERSIDE JUMP BAND, caricatured by the band's first drummer BRIAN CLARKE. This drawing accompanied early examples of the weekly columns that Keith wrote for the BRIGHTON AND HOVE GAZETTE – under the heading of Sam Edwards' Jazz Round-up – for 18 years.

ROY BOWER led the JAZZ FOUR in a long residency at THE CAT, West Hoathly, in the latter half of the 1970s. PETE SIMKINS (piano) and JOHN FRUCHT (bass) were regulars in the group. The landlord of THE CAT was former journalist ALAN ROBSON, who presented a concert featuring BUD FREEMAN at the Village Hall, West Hoathly, on May 2, 1977. Bud is seen here playing some licks to ROY BOWER (centre) and BENNY SIMKINS (left).

PICTURE CRAWLEY OBSERVER, COURTESY OF PETER SIMKINS.

Gerry Clayton, Pat Sheen, Horace Harris and the late Jack Hall are just a few who spring immediately to mind. The admirable Ted Mechen, a friendly and helpful guy with broad tastes but a decided preference for mainstream jazz, is another worthy of mention. The ever-obliging Ted was known to take time off work to drive the minibus containing the Benny Simkins Sextet on their occasional northern tours. His

THE ADUR in Kingsway, near Hove Lagoon, was a thriving jazz venue for a decade from 1973 onwards. The enterprising BILL POLLEY led the first band to feature at this roomy redbrick pub. They started out as the RIVERSIDE FIVE but had increased their number and re-named themselves the PHOENIX SIX by the time this picture was taken. Left to right:
MIKE MOUNTER (trumpet),
GERRY GEOGHEGAN (banjo),
JOHN DAVIDSON (trombone),
BILL POLLEY (drums),
PAT CHAPMAN (soprano sax),
ALAN KENNINGTON (bass).

PICTURE BY COURTESY OF GERRY GEOGHEGAN

This picture was taken at the old Hove Town Hall at the 1960 PRESS GANG JAZZ BALL and gives some indication of the size of audiences for traditional jazz at that time. It also illustrates an interesting range of dress styles – from the flamboyantly casual to the near-formality of collars-and-ties and party dresses. The band is the RIVERSIDE JUMP BAND.

PICTURE BY COURTESY OF KEITH SAMUEL

presence, as someone who could happily stay sober while those around him succumbed to the demon drink, was absolutely invaluable. Only once, when trombonist Ian Todd – then living at Pateley Bridge, Yorkshire – introduced Benny and the boys to the seductive charms of Theakston's 'Old Peculier', was Ted seen to be even slightly the worse for wear! Ted also had the good sense to buy a decent tape recorder and mixer and, with his customary quiet efficiency, set about recording sessions at venues like the Gay Highlander, the Pier and the Fox in the 1970s. Thanks to Ted, recordings of many of the American stars who guested with Benny at the Fox , the Northern Hotel and the King and Queen have survived. Indeed, Ted's tape of Ralph Sutton's session at the Fox in 1975 was subsequently issued by Bruce Bastin on the *Flyright* label. Bruce too merits special praise for his encouragement of local musicians and not only set up the *Flyright* recordings on which the Benny Simkins band backed Billy Butterfield and Yank Lawson but also brought out the two excellent albums on which Danny Moss and Geoff Simkins were paired.

Derrick Wood was one of the most determined of the long-standing Brighton collectors. Derrick, who succumbed to cancer in September 2002, became one of my earliest jazz friends in the town after the Simkins clan arrived on the coast in 1961. At that time Derrick and I were both single and spent an unhealthy number of evenings listening to his latest album purchases in his bachelor pad in Hampton Place - a flat with its own distinctive aroma of vinyl, curry and yesterday's socks. Derrick's commitment to jazz remained undiminished. The first-floor flat in Kemp Town he shared with his wife Sheila was literally stacked with CDs, LPs and state-of-the-art hi-fi equipment, quite apart from the good-quality wines or 25 year-old single malts which were the customary reward for anyone who managed to navigate a path through Derrick's collection to reach a comfortable chair. Derrick will forever hold the record for drinking Benny Simkins's lethal home brew - having quaffed four pints - although he was confined to bed for the rest of the weekend and had to admit to several violent confrontations with buildings on his way home.

The late Roy Dockrell, who died suddenly and prematurely a few years back, was legendary among local collectors for his unfailing one-upmanship. The likeable Roy was actually far too nice a chap ever to

The faces of drummers in larger jazz bands are often hidden in photographs. Here, BERNIE GODFREY of the
BENNY SIMKINS SEXTET
gets full frontal exposure in this picture from the late 1970s.

PICTURE BY COURTESY OF PETE SIMKINS

BRIGHTON JAZZ CLUB

PRESENTING
THE BEST IN SOUTHERN JAZZ
EVERY FRIDAY 8.00p.m. to 11.00p.m.
EVERY SUNDAY LUNCHTIME
12.00p.m. to 2.00p.m.

STAR ATTRACTIONS
1st FRIDAY OF EACH MONTH
BAR EXTENSION

Membership of £1.00 per annum
entitles free entry to normal sessions
and half price to STAR SESSIONS

I WISH TO APPLY FOR MEMBERSHIP OF
BRIGHTON JAZZ CLUB AND ENCLOSE
MY REMITTANCE OF £1.00

BRIGHTON JAZZ CLUB is a name that has graced a succession of promotional enterprises over half a century. This handbill advertises a 1974 version of the club organised jointly by bandleaders BILL POLLEY, BENNY SIMKINS and GUY FENTON among others. It was based in the elegant surroundings of Markwell's Bar, at the QUEENS HOTEL in Kings Road, where the ANDERIDA JAZZ BAND are pictured. Too elegant, perhaps. The management evicted the club at the end of the year.

COURTESY OF BEN COLLIER

In the mid-1970s the Northern in London Road, Brighton, was a hub of ambitious jazz activity. Drummer-band-leader GUY FENTON was a prime mover in this development and his colourfully named LUVOVADUR JAZZ BAND accompanied many guest soloists, including KEN COLYER (a frequent visitor), SAMMY RIMINGTON, PAT HALCOX and ALAN ELSDON. The band later changed its name – to the relief of those with shaky spelling – to GUY FENTON'S JAZZMEN. Pictured here are JOHN BOYETT (bass), GERRY GEOGHEGAN (clarinet), MIKE MOUNTER (trumpet), GUY FENTON (drums), DON WILLIAMS (trombone) and JIM HEATH (banjo), circa 1975.

PICTURE BY COURTESY OF GERRY GEOGHEGAN

do anyone down intentionally but he had an unrivalled talent for sniffing out the once-in-a-lifetime bargain in the second-hand racks of record shops. One could be absolutely sure that, if one went on a coach tour of the Highlands and chanced upon a dingy record shop in Mallaig, one would open the door only to be greeted by a grinning Roy, who just happened to be in the same area and would be clutching a rare Matty Matlock album which he had bought for 25p two minutes before you arrived!

Tony Bell – known to some of his mates, with heavy irony, as "The Reverend" – now lives in London, but is another collector and fan who seemed to be everywhere on the Brighton scene in the 1970s and 1980s. Tony's insatiable thirst for real ale, wine and good jazz (in more or less equal proportions) quickly became famous, as did his penchant for curried eggs and his capacity for breaking wind! His *bonhomie* would occasionally be dispelled by a cloudy pint or a jukebox spewing out pop music but he went far beyond the call of duty in willingly transporting impecunious or non-motorist jazz musicians to obscure gigs and far-flung venues. He would claim his reward by asking one to play a low-down, "knicker-tearing" blues. "Come on, Simkins, let's have a bit of filth!" he would bellow at me from the audience. Like those of Dave Carey before him, his one-man car boot record sales were irresistible to the Brighton musicians and collectors who gathered at the Napier or one of the other jazzers' watering-holes on Saturday lunchtimes. An LP was always hard to smuggle indoors past the rigorous gaze of a suspicious wife, particularly when one had imbibed a few pints of Harvey's Best! Thank God for the CD, say I!

Tony was a frequent traveller on the "Jazzboats", a slightly more grandiose and adventurous version of the old riverboat shuffles of earlier years, which the late Harry Walton organised for a while in the 1970s. Several Brighton bands participated in these voyages, which usually involved an overnight Channel crossing to Boulogne or Dunkirk, with bands playing in the ferry's lounge throughout. The legendary Bud Freeman was even persuaded to star on more than one trip. It required considerable dedication to the music to launch oneself into yet another tear-up jam session version of *Royal Garden Blues* on board a passenger ferry at five o'clock in the morning, yet, on longer trips, a cabin or two would sometimes be provided. One would duly be requisitioned by Tony Bell so that he could install a polypin of Shepherd Neame bitter

HANGLETON MANOR in Hove has played host to a number of jazz events over the decades – including an impromptu performance by American trombonist and singer CLYDE BERNHARDT in June 1972. Bernhardt, who had the distinction of playing alongside both KING OLIVER and CHARLIE PARKER during his career, joined MIKE COLLIER (left) and KEITH SAMUEL to form a trombone trio. ARNIE KING is the trumpet player.

PICTURE BY COURTESY OF KEITH SAMUEL

The front line faces of The
JUBILEE JAZZ BAND pictured in
1979 at **THE ADUR** in Hove.
Left to right:
SLUFF HAZELL (baritone),
ROY LEITH (alto),
PAUL BONNER (trumpet),
MIKE COLLIER (trombone).

PICTURE BY COURTESY OF BEN COLLIER

or Young's Ordinary for the benefit of musicians and friends.

On one such trip to a jazz festival in Middelburg, Holland, the Benny Simkins band was asked to back Bud Freeman at an evening concert. Trumpeter Roy Bower succumbed to the lurgi on the eve of the trip and Benny was forced to enlist the help of the organisers in finding a replacement at very short notice. When the band arrived

THE RAVENSWOOD HOTEL at Sharpthorne provided a distinctive setting for jazz sessions over a period of time. Pictured in this 1995 performance by an augmented version of **THE ANDERIDA JAZZ BAND** are (left to right): **PETER GODFREY** and **DORY WHITFIELD** (keyboards), **CHRIS GIBB** (bass), **DOUG WHITFIELD** and **BILL HARVEY** (trumpets), **GORDON WREN** (drums) and **DON WILLIAMS** (trombone). **DOUG WHITFIELD**, who started out with the **PORTSMOUTH JAZZ BAND**, died aged 72 in 2002. He and his wife Dory, who then lived in Portslade, first met at the **BRIGHTON JAZZ CLUB** in the early 1950s and subsequently set up home in Fareham. They figured strongly on the Hampshire jazz scene for more than 40 years, running their own group, the **RIVERSIDE JAZZMEN**, as well as commuting to Sussex to appear with the Anderida band.   PICTURE BY COURTESY OF GORDON WREN

at the ferry terminal at Sheerness on the appointed day, they discovered that the 'dep' was Alan Wickham – a splendid trumpeter but also a guy known to like a taste or twelve! All was well until a minute or two before the band was due on stage in Holland. At that juncture, an agitated promoter told Benny: "Your trumpeter cannot play!" "What do you mean?" asked an alarmed Benny. "He cannot play. He cannot stand!" came the reply. Somehow, Alan was induced to weave an erratic course onto the stage where, to everyone's relief, he played like a dream, even leading the front line down from the stage to march round the auditorium during a version of *Bourbon Street Parade*, to a storm of applause from the audience. The minute the set ended, Alan collapsed like a pricked balloon, although he was seen next day, on the voyage home, shaking his fist at a choppy sea! It was on this same trip that Tony Bell took with him two polypins of real ale, concealed in two large holdalls. Both polypins were emptied long before the weekend was over but, on our return, the face of the customs officer at Sheerness was a picture when, having ordered Tony to open the capacious holdalls, he found that the entire contents consisted of a toothbrush.

One character, above all, loomed over the Brighton and Hove jazz scene for several decades like some portly, kindly and passionate – if sometimes irascible – archangel. Whether he was holding court in the Druid's Head on a Saturday evening or ringing you at some unearthly hour to let you know every detail about the latest record he had heard, Derrick Stewart-Baxter was impossible to ignore. My brother Geoff and I were part of his circle at the Druid's Head for a few years and I also met him frequently at the County Ground, Hove, where we were both members of Sussex CCC. I understand that, before and after the war, Derry played cricket enthusiastically for Sussex Club and Ground and also Sussex Downs CC. By all accounts he was a reasonable slow bowler but

THE PALACE PIER, before it was renamed the BRIGHTON PIER, provides a backdrop to a performance by DON McMURRAY'S SOUTH COAST STOMPERS in November 1988. Left to right ALLAN SOKELL (sousaphone), DEREK LITTLE (soprano sax), McMURRAY (drums), JOHN EDSER (trombone) and BILL PARSONS (banjo). In this period, Horatio's Bar on the Pier advertised jazz twice weekly, featuring the STOMPERS, the ANDERIDA JAZZ BAND and MIKE COLLIER'S BAND among others.

PICTURE BY COURTESY OF DON McMURRAY

– not surprisingly for those who remember him – he was never the most agile of fielders and tended to find a perfectly valid reason for avoiding balls hit fiercely in his general direction.

My co-Editor Keith Samuel cherishes a characteristic anecdote about Derry dating back to a session at the Lewes Jazz Club HQ at the Brewers Arms in March 1959. The guest band were Ted Owen's Excelsior Jazzmen and Derry joined them on washboard for a couple of numbers. Keith remembers "a look of intense concentration on his face and whilst his head remained absolutely steady, like that of a class batsman facing hostile bowling, his jowls wobbled in time to the rhythm – an extraordinary spectacle". Keith wrote about this performance in friendly terms in his jazz column in the *Brighton and Hove Gazette*, describing it as a public debut. Never slow to open up a dialogue, Derry rang Keith to assert that he had performed on the washboard before, not only with his pal Graeme Bell but, even more impressively, with Sidney Bechet when the great man was persuaded to blow informally at a party during his London visit in the late1940s. Derry had the humility to admit that he only managed a few strokes with the thimbles before Bechet cast a thunderous look in his direction and inquired, "Who let the death watch beetle in here?" For once, Derry ducked the opportunity for an argument and retired gracefully to the sidelines!

For this book, Horace Harris, who knew him as well as anyone and who, for several years, was his next-door neighbour, has contributed an affectionate and sensitive portrait of DSB and his wife Mary in Chapter 11.

THE ROYAL GEORGE in Burgess Hill featured jazz prominently in the late 1970s.
THE ROYAL GEORGE FIVE, pictured here in 1977, was probably the last band of which TED AMBROSE was a regular member during his long-playing career.
He is pictured with STEVE DAVIES on soprano sax, DAVE GIBB (bass), RAY SCHOOLEY (banjo) and BILL POLLEY (drums).

PICTURE BY COURTESY OF STEVE DAVIES

CHAPTER 11

A MEMOIR OF DERRICK STEWART-BAXTER

HORACE MEUNIER HARRIS

I FIRST DISCOVERED *THE MELODY MAKER* LATE IN 1941. In those days it was a weekly tabloid-style newspaper for the dance band profession. However, due to wartime paper rationing, it was impossible to buy it at a news stand or from the newsagent. I sent off for a six-month subscription at threepence a copy, plus one penny for postage. It duly arrived every Wednesday morning and I found it a gold-mine of information about jazz as well as the dance band world. In August 1942 I saw a small announcement stating that it was intended to re-form the Brighton and Hove Rhythm Club. The very first Rhythm Club was launched in London in 1933 and became No.1. The movement grew rapidly and the Brighton and Hove Rhythm Club was started at a meeting in the restaurant above the Savoy Cinema in East Street in 1936, becoming No.107. The secretary then was Derrick Stewart-Baxter and it ran well until it closed with the coming of war in 1939. The 1942 notice which I spotted stated that anyone interested should contact the Honorary Secretary, Derrick Stewart-Baxter, at 47 Dene Vale, Withdean.

I duly wrote a letter and received a prompt reply – a letter followed by a postcard inviting me to attend an initial meeting on August 30, 1942 at the Brighton School of Music at 1, St Peter's Place. This I did and, to my surprise, I was elected as Honorary Treasurer. We met fortnightly, on a Sunday afternoon, for a record recital, the first being given by Derrick. My role as Treasurer was not arduous, as the subscription was only ninepence a meeting, with no joining fee. The rental of the first-floor room in which we met was one shilling an hour, but we had to take our own wind-up gramophone. It was a bare room with plenty of upright wooden chairs. We chatted about jazz and traded records. The fact that we tolerated such basic conditions indicates the level of our youthful love of the music.

DERRICK STEWART-BAXTER sucks characteristically on his pipe in company with New Orleans pianist ALTON PURNELL (centre) and MIKE COLLIER at the FOX AND HOUNDS, Haywards Heath in March 1970.

PICTURE BY COURTESY OF BEN COLLIER

Derrick, with his boundless enthusiasm, was the catalyst and kingpin. He gave the first few recitals and in due course persuaded me to do likewise. My first, in late September, was on Jack Teagarden – still one of my great jazz heroes – and my second, in late October, was on Count Basie. Then aged 16, I lacked the confidence and experience to give these recitals *ad lib* and painstakingly wrote out my scripts. Derrick invited me to visit his home to play records. The previous year he had married Mary Patchen, who was a few years younger, and their first home, paid for by Derrick's parents, was a semi-detached villa called "Deneside". The house was built about 1938 in what had been open country, with a view across fields towards Patcham windmill on the skyline. It was here I got to know him better.

Derrick was an only child, the son of Edgar Baxter – descended from the Baxters of Blackhall, a Baronetcy – and Maud Stewart, a proud Scot who enforced the hyphenation of their names. Edgar had never worked, while Maud had dabbled at being a concert pianist and a composer of light classical works. Before World War II they lived at "Downmere", Poynings, an estate which they had sold around the outbreak of war to Emile Littler, the theatrical impresario. As a boy Derrick had a tutor, but his academic progress was indifferent and there had been no obvious career for him. He became an assistant stage manager in the repertory company at the Theatre Royal, Brighton, where, amongst others, he knew Bill Owen, then acting under his real name, Bill Rowbotham. Derrick's parents bought him a Hillman saloon car, in which he travelled to meetings of the No.1 Rhythm Club in London. He used to say that the car knew its way back to Poynings blindfold.

This is where he conceived the idea of forming a Brighton Rhythm Club and, through his connections, persuaded Benny Carter – then in England for a year as Henry Hall's staff arranger – to become its first President in 1936. Benny Carter and Bob Howard both attended the first meeting. Other members of that first club were Wally Heulin, John Willis, Robert Waddy, Ken Lyon (subsequently a well-known Brighton dance band leader) and Reg Cooper (who, ten years later, took over from Max Jones as editor of the magazine *Jazz Music*).

With the coming of war, Derrick was called up in 1940 but was deemed medically unfit because of nervous problems. He was directed by the Ministry of Labour to

BERYL BRYDEN took this picture opposite
DERRICK STEWART-BAXTER's house in Dene Vale, Brighton in 1948.
Left to right: HORACE HARRIS, MARY STEWART-BAXTER,
OWEN MADDOCK (Mick Mulligan's tuba player) and DERRICK.

PHOTO BY COURTESY OF HORACE HARRIS

work as a civilian clerk for the Army, in a department requisitioning civilian property for military use. The office was in a converted house in Preston Road, just north of Harrington Road, and his boss was the amiable Major Levy, whose son Laurie was a jazz fan and one of our founder members in 1942. Other early members of the re-formed club included some who became stalwarts of the Brighton jazz scene: Ted Ambrose (always referred to as 'Amby', even in those days), Eddie Buckwell (an excellent pianist), Les Crawley (who played very acceptable jazz on the piano-accordion), Eric Carter (like Derrick, a great cricket watcher), Roy Dockrell, Les Gray, 'Duke' Sattin, John Wheater and John Van Praagh. Derrick and John Van P., as we called him, were both great recitalists.

47 Dene Vale had three bedrooms but the third was very small and Derrick used it as a den. It contained a table model wind-up gramophone and he introduced me to many recordings I had never heard – for example, those of Bennie Moten, Don Redman, Andy Kirk, Jimmie Lunceford and Jean Goldkette, the blues of Bessie Smith, the piano playing of Earl Hines and the wonderful Paris recordings featuring Bill Coleman, Dicky Wells and Django Reinhardt. Derrick also had wide cultural interests, not least in the theatre and films. After a meal we would sit and listen to the BBC Saturday night plays. He also introduced me to Dilys Powell's film reviews, *John O'London's Weekly*, the *Times Literary Supplement*, the poetry of Walt Whitman, the writings of John dos Passos, Thomas Wolfe, H.E. Bates, Rebecca West and many more. He loved the humorous stories of Robert Benchley, James Thurber and, above all, Damon Runyon.

Derry, as he was usually known, was not easy to live with and Mary bore his mood swings with great fortitude. He was capable of working himself into rages, often over some trifle, but they usually blew over as quickly as they started. Although highly literate, his handwriting was atrocious and his ability to do simple sums almost non-existent. He was quite useless at practical things, like knocking in a nail, and had no interest in gardening. He wore a blue pin-stripe suit for his Army job but otherwise dressed anyhow. Mary always cleaned his black office shoes, since the first time he attempted it after their marriage he got the polish all over his grey flannel trousers! Mary nobly put up with his shortcomings and, as a loyal wife, showed patience and good humour. Her support enabled Derrick, throughout his married life, to devote all his energies to listening to, and writing about, jazz – interrupted only by his passion for watching Sussex county cricket. While of medium height, he was inclined to stoutness, which increased as the years passed. He also acquired a very ruddy complexion, causing the boys in the Graeme Bell band, on their first visit to Europe from Australia, to christen him 'The Pink Balloon'.

At the re-formed Brighton and Hove Rhythm Club, there was a jam session once a month, prior to the afternoon recital. Derrick knew everybody who mattered and regularly prevailed upon musicians who played at the Regent Ballroom, Sherry's and The Dome to come and "have a blow", encouraged by the crate of beer which Derrick brought along in a taxi. He also arranged for various visiting recitalists known to him from his membership of the No.1 Rhythm Club. One was Leonard Taylor, who ran the Clapham Rhythm Club and who regaled us with his tales of pre-war visits to the jazz world in New York – which, we subsequently discovered, were entirely figments of his imagination! The monthly Sunday jam sessions were not popular with the proprietors of the Brighton School of Music, whom I think lived on the top floor, and after about a

BRIGHTON & HOVE

RHYTHM CLUB

Secretary: *Der:k Stewart-Baxter*

MEMBERSHIP CARD

Member's Name ....

Address ....

....

A membership card for the **BRIGHTON & HOVE RHYTHM CLUB**.
Circa 1942. Note the mis-spelling of "Derrick".

COURTESY OF HORACE HARRIS

year we moved to Hove and The London School of Dancing in Cambridge Road, off Western Road. This was also on the first floor but it was very comfortably furnished and contained a large radiogram. We carried on for another year but, gradually, conscription, or waning interest, led to dwindling membership. We produced a leaflet headed "Swing Fan? Like it Hot?" extolling the club's virtues, but eventually we had to close down. Nevertheless, the hard core of members remained friends and continued to meet informally at Derrick's house.

I saw less of Derrick during my own Army service, but when I was on leave we would get together. I was then buying my records from Elliott's in London Road, near Preston Circus, but Derrick introduced me and others to Wickham and Kimber in George Street, Hove. Unlike Lyon and Hall, and Murdoch's, both in Western Road, who specialised in classical music, Mr Wickham (a pre-war dance band pianist) leaned towards popular music and would go to no end of trouble to obtain items that were out of stock. He also ordered all the new monthly jazz releases as a matter of course. The shop became quite an unofficial meeting place for jazz lovers on Saturday afternoons.

Wartime, and the immediate post-war period, saw the proliferation of "little" jazz

DERRICK STEWART-BAXTER's friendship with Australian jazz pianist and bandleader GRAEME BELL stretched back to 1947. In this picture, DSB hovers behind as Graeme (left) and PETE SIMKINS play an impromptu duet at the SACKVILLE JAZZ BAR in Hove in February 1968.

PICTURE BY COURTESY OF PETE SIMKINS

magazines, all serving a useful function. One, however, which was launched in Harlesden, north-west London, in 1946 by Charles Harvey and which was called *Jazzology*, proved amateur and inept, to say the least. By this time Ralph Venables was a regular visitor to Brighton and he and Derrick hatched an elaborate practical joke which they played upon the unsuspecting Harvey. Using the pseudonym Shep Landes, Ralph submitted an article purporting to describe a previously unknown 1930 recording session for Okeh by Fred Gardner's Texas University Troubadours, featuring Bix Beiderbecke. Harvey printed it, so Derrick sent him another article, using his middle names, George Lucien, to disguise his identity and describing yet another Bix session. Harvey fell for it and became a general laughing-stock, helping jazz journalism in Britain thereafter to come of age.

During the war we became familiar with Australian jazz. Ralph Venables was in touch with Bill Miller of *Australian Jazz Quarterly* and I was writing articles for Ian Turner's *Jazz Notes*, both in Melbourne. Through them we were made aware that Graeme Bell was bringing his band to Europe, via Czechoslovakia. They arrived in London in December 1947 and we made use of our introductions to get to know them. Derrick and I were frequent visitors to the Leicester Square Jazz Club, where they played on Monday nights. They paid their first visit to Brighton in April 1948 and we introduced them to the delights of Applejohn's Cider Bar in Market Street, owned by George Thompson, a director of the Taunton Cider Company. This was a hangout for the jazz fraternity. Perhaps with the benefit of the amber fluid, Mel Langdon, their affable manager, and Graeme agreed for the band to undertake a private recording session which took place, after a rehearsal, at John King's basement recording studio below his shop at 1 East Street on 28 April. Derrick and John Wheater were responsible for financing the session. I was still in the Army but on leave and was suitably impoverished. The Bells very charitably played for no fee and two 12-inch and two 10-inch acetates were cut. It was understood that they would not be issued commercially and Derrick adhered rigidly to this stricture.

We saw a lot of the Bell boys both in Brighton and at the Leicester Square Jazz Club. A duplicated programme sheet was distributed at each session, which included an item called "The Weekly Puffo", written anonymously by Roger Bell. Shortly after that first Brighton visit it contained the following piece:

"Derrick Stewart-Baxter, the oldest inhabitant of Applejohn's, said that the Bell Brood introduced cider to Brighton folk last week. He introduced jazz to the Bell Band. It is not yet decided who won, and anyway, what AM I saying?"

They returned to Britain in 1950 for another very successful tour. On 9 December in London they recorded four sides for Tempo, one of which was "Shake that Thing", with Roger Bell doing the vocal and altering the words to: *"Old Derry Baxter, the Cakewalk King, got a hump on his back from shaking that thing!"*

Derrick supported all live local jazz in the Brighton and Hove area. This included sessions in the restaurant below the Dolphin Theatre in New Road, long since gone; downstairs at the Aquarium; and the Sussex County Arts Club in Bond Street, which moved to the Richmond Hotel, near St Peter's Church, where Amby led a band for a year or two. This was called the Brighton Jazz Club, which also presented recitals, but although Derrick and I obliged, I cannot remember the details of those evenings, other than that Keith Jupp was on trombone and Terry Whitney on piano.

Derrick also organised and ran a first-class recital club, on a fortnightly basis, which started life in the Territorial Army Drill Hall in Church Street, but soon moved to the function room above the portcullis at the King and Queen in Marlborough Place, where a buffet supper was included in the rental. It was named the Brighton Music Circle and admission was 1s. 6d. per session. Derrick wrote excellent leaflets describing each forthcoming session. I gave at least two recitals. Others who also did so at Derrick's request (nay, command) were Amby, Les Crawley, Les Jowett, Keith Slade, Eddie Buckwell, Ronald Sweetman, Ken Lindsay (the former manager of the Crane River Jazz Band), Dave Carey (who had been Graeme Bell's and Humphrey Lyttelton's drummer, and who owned the splendid "Swing Shop" at Streatham) and, of course, Derrick himself. There was also a programme called "The Two Voices of Jazz", comprising jazz readings and records by The Tentative Players, under the direction of Keith Slade and his wife, Pamela.

Derrick took an afternoon job as jazz adviser, with his own upstairs room, for Wickham, Kimber & Oakley, which had changed sides in George Street, Hove. They also employed Hazel Mundell, the wife of musician Harry Mundell, on the ground floor. Derrick's role was to recommend jazz recordings to the customers, but he was just as good at dissuading them from buying something that did not meet his high standards. Mind you, he probably persuaded them to buy something else instead.

By the 1950s Derrick had become passionately interested in all forms of the Blues, which was due to the strong influence of John Van Praagh. He got to know Paul Oliver, whose books on the subject are without equal. Paul edited a series of small books called Blues Paperbacks, which were published by Studio Vista Ltd of London. He persuaded Derrick to write *Ma Rainey and the Classic Blues Singers*, which appeared in 1970. Derrick dedicated it to Victoria Spivey, "Also to my great friend John Van Praagh who first gave me the taste for the Classic Blues".

By that time I had moved from Goldstone Crescent and was living in a chalet bungalow at 47 Maldon Road, Brighton. I had been there for several years when Derrick and Mary, in the mid-1960s, suddenly announced that they had bought the bungalow next door, at No.49. They moved in and re-named it "Fresh Fields". Derrick was not the ideal neighbour, fond as I was of him, since he would turn up on the doorstep or telephone at literally all hours, bursting to impart his latest jazz discovery or aching to pass on the latest piece of jazz news which had arrived by post. Graeme Bell and his new wife, Dorothy, stayed here when they came to Britain on their own in 1968. Derrick organised a superb jazz evening, featuring Graeme, at the Sackville Hotel, at the corner of the Old Shoreham Road and Sackville Road, Hove.

HORACE HARRIS in October, 2000.
PICTURE BY COURTESY OF HORACE HARRIS

As a result of correspondence, Derrick got to know Dr Al Vollmer and Sheldon Harris in New York and, with Mary, was able to visit New York several times in the late 1960s and 1970s. He would not fly and they usually travelled on the *Queen Mary*. Through Dr Vollmer and Sheldon Harris, he met Clyde Bernhardt, Victoria Spivey and others. Clyde Bernhardt subsequently recalled:

"When he [Derrick] came over to the States in June of 1968, I got together a few guys and rented a rehearsal hall so he could hear me play and sing...It was on Broadway and 52nd and Derrick brought along his tape machine".

Clyde stayed with Derrick and Mary in 1972 and on his return to New York formed the Harlem Blues and Jazz Band, which had a long run of success. Its birth can be very much attributed to Derrick. In a postcard from New York, dated October 1, 1970, Derrick told me that his book was "going like a bomb" over there, though he was bitter about the lack of interest in his own country and home town. Another card from him in 1972, sent from the Hotel Piccadilly on West 45th Street, reads:

"Am recording Viola Wells (Miss Rhapsody) on 22 April. I am using Cozy Cole's brother on piano – he's good. Also getting some tapes from Sheila Jordan for issue on Saydisc. Saw a superb concert by four pianists: Claude Hopkins, Teddy Wilson, Dill Jones and 89 year-old Eubie Blake. Dill is now one of the greatest piano men alive. He has improved SO MUCH. Eubie is a miracle. A great performer. Oh, how you would love it here! At this moment we are in a little drugstore with Clyde Bernhardt and Rudy Powell. I must be dreamin'! P.S. Sad news: Tony Parenti is dying of cancer. Willie the Lion is in hospital."

Derrick was the only person I have ever known capable of cramming so much on half one side of a picture postcard. What enthusiasm!

Derrick and I enjoyed discographical research and had various pieces published, including several collaborations. We also wrote articles on jazz for various publications. All of this was unpaid – not even expenses. In the August 1968 issue of Sinclair Traill's *Jazz Journal*, Derrick commenced a series of monthly articles entitled "Blues on Record". These continued, with changes of title to "Blues", then "Blues and Views", until at least January 1974, when I ceased taking the magazine. He also contributed a series called "Ramblin'Around" for Laurie Wright's research magazine *Storyville*, which appeared in bi-monthly issues from December 1974 to April 1977, as well as regularly reviewing records for *Jazz Journal* – not necessarily of blues material. In these later years, jazz writing came to dominate Derrick's life, and everything at "Fresh Fields" was subordinated to getting the column off to the editor on time. There were many panics.

The Australian version of "This is Your Life", on their Channel 7, featured Graeme Bell as the mystery celebrity in August 1978. At that time, Alex Welsh was touring Australia with a show called "Salute to Satchmo", with Roy Williams and Bruce Turner, plus Humphrey Lyttelton as star guest. Naturally they were all in the know and took part in the telling of Graeme's life story, but the best-kept surprise of all was the appearance of Derrick and Mary, who had been flown out from England for a week at the expense of Channel 7. Graeme often talks about Derrick and the great times we had. In his wonderfully informative and entertaining autobiography, published in 1988, Graeme wrote:

> *"Probably the most memorable date in England was when we played in the Aquarium Ballroom, Brighton. We met a most delightful character – jazz writer Derrick Stewart-Baxter, and his long-suffering wife Mary. For all his Englishness, of which I'm sure he is proud, Derrick, with his rorty love of life, jazz and cricket and an enormous propensity for hearty laughing, was immediately on the same wavelength as us Australians".*

I couldn't have put it better myself!

Sometime in the 1970s, life became more complicated for Derrick and Mary when he developed internal problems and had to have a colostomy operation. The surgeon assured him that it was reversible after six months but Derrick evolved a morbid fear of the knife and adamantly refused to return to hospital for the reversal operation. Mary was plagued with the problems of colostomy bags for the rest of his life. When I moved to Gloucestershire in 1976 I gradually lost touch with Derrick and Mary. My last letter to them in 1991 went unanswered. By then they were becoming infirm. Graeme Bell said that their Christmas cards petered out, so, in December 1991, he put in a stern note: *"Are you still there?"* Back came a card with very shaky writing:

> *"Dear old friends. Do not write us off yet! We have just celebrated our Gold wedding day, 50 years of arguing! Neither Derry nor I can walk but we still love one another and that is all we care about. Wait till I have my walking stick handy – I'll crown him with it. Mary and Derry".*

John Van Praagh came from the Isle of Wight to visit them two or three times a year and said they were both very poorly, having meals delivered daily and receiving regular visits by nurses. John reported that one was named Lorraine, so Derrick always called her "Sweet" – which had become her permanent name, even amongst her nursing colleagues. The bungalow looked very neglected but they refused to go into a home. Derrick died, ultimately of cancer, on November 16, 1992, aged 81. John went to the funeral but I could not as, that day, Edwina and I were travelling to Germany. At the time, John wrote:

> *"Warmth of personality, honesty of principles and a wonderful infectious enthusiasm for life – these are the qualities for which Derrick Stewart-Baxter will always be remembered by those who loved him. The jazz scene has sadly lost a charismatic figure who contributed much to its development in this country".*

Mary went into a nursing home but she was unhappy, as they did not like her smoking or drinking her daily glass or two of sherry. She only lasted another six months.

By all standards, Derrick was a considerable character, warm-hearted and in a sense larger than life. I am very glad to have known him so well and for so long.

Australian Channel 7 Television flew Derrick and Mary Stewart-Baxter to Sydney in August 1978 to take part in a "This is Your Life" tribute to Aussie jazz pioneer GRAEME BELL. Derrick and Mary, at the far right, are flanked by several British musicians then touring Australia with a Salute to Satchmo package – including Alex Welsh (with trumpet), Roy Williams and Bruce Turner. Ade Monsbrough is at the extreme right. Seated in the centre with Graeme Bell (wearing a tie), his wife and son, are brother Roger Bell (with trumpet) and, kneeling, drummer Johnny Sangster. Humphrey Lyttelton (wearing a white tie) is visible in the centre background. Other stalwarts of earlier Graeme Bell bands such as Jack Varney, Pixie Roberts and Lou Silbereisen are also present. Graeme, still going strong in 2002, was delighted to help confirm identities of those pictured for this publication.

PICTURE BY COURTESY OF HORACE HARRIS

THE KING AND QUEEN in Brighton played host to the early five-piece line up of HARRY STRUTTERS HOT RHYTHM ORCHESTRA. Pictured in mid-1968 ar PETE HILL (bass), JIM FRYER (soprano sax JIM HEATH (banjo) JOHN MUXLOW (drums) and GEOFF SIMKINS, brandishing a Grafton plastic alto sax.

PICTURE BY COURTESY OF JOHN MUXLOW

Members of the band and other musician friends strut their stuff in a seafront protest at the exclusion of local talent from the 1969 BRIGHTON FESTIVAL. JIM FRYER and GEOFF SIMKINS are the two saxophonists in the front rank, followed by PETE HILL (bass drum), JOHN MUXLOW (snare drum) and JIM HEATH (banjo). MEGS ETHERINGTON carries his cornet and behind him are trombonists IAN "SWEENEY" TODD and HARRY LEDGER (in sunglasses).

PICTURE BY COURTESY OF JOHN MUXLOW

CHAPTER 12

HARRY STRUTTERS HOT RHYTHM ORCHESTRA: A PORTRAIT

JOHN MUXLOW

IN LATE 1958, WHEN I WAS 12, there arrived at the parental home my late father's old semi-pro dance-band, The Elysians, which were formed in 1926, and had been re-convened especially for the occasion of my parents' silver wedding. All except the pianist Eric Price, then resident at Butlin's at Saltdean, had long since retired from the music scene. With the infuriating ignorance of youth, I remember thinking of them as merely quaint. True, I enjoyed jazz and swing even at that age, having been brought up with it, and can vividly remember my father going very silent one morning in 1953 as he tried to take in the *Daily Mail* headline "Django Dies". But to me The Elysians, wading gamely through their long-neglected Campbell-Connelly charts of *I Can Wiggle My Ears*, had little more than novelty value, and yet there I was with a genuine 1920s band in our living room.

I didn't know it, of course, but that evening – an echo of dad's pre-war gigs at St Augustine's Church Hall for 7/6d a man – had such a profound effect on my life that, had it not occurred, someone else might well be writing this chapter. I was fascinated by The Elysians' drum-kit, with its 28-inch bass-drum, red-and-gold temple blocks, blue velvet trap-tray, and its bizarrely-coiffed operator, the almost-eponymous Alf Ellis. He played with a smile, a quiff, a black satin cloth over the snare drum and – most weirdly – barely a sound.

Years later, I was thrilled when Dad – courtesy of Mr Ellis – presented me with the same drum-kit, just before Christmas, 1966. He said that he'd noticed me accompanying Sid Phillips' band with knitting needles on the signature tune of *Take It From Here* and keeping pretty good time, and decided that I might make a drummer. Well, thanks Dad, for the slipped disc!

I still hadn't discovered what girls were for, and in 1967 I used to go and listen to the Martinique Jazz Band, who were playing at The Imperial Hotel – presided over by Vi and Whistling Ernie – with Geoff Simkins on drums and Hugh Croxford on clarinet. When I first started going to see them, the rest of the band comprised Ian Todd on trombone, Ted Ambrose on trumpet, Pete Simkins on piano, Jim Heath on banjo and Mike "Abbo" Adams on bass.

At that time there also existed Megs Etherington's Old Timey Washboard Band, with Megs (cornet), Croxford, Jim Susans (banjo), Pete "97" Hill (bass), and Geoff Simkins (traps & washboard).

I had started sitting in with the Martinique and occasionally with Pete Simkins during the intervals at the Fox & Hounds, Haywards Heath, and at that time was not drinking enough to fall over quite so regularly. Having got to know Geoff, and having mentioned that I had "inherited" that old drum-kit, the Old Timeys asked whether I would sell it to them for Geoff to use. I did so, and as I remember agreed £5 as the price; only the balance of £2 now remains outstanding.

Then Croxford biffed off to South Africa at more or less the same time as Geoff

"Alderman" JOHN E. MUXLOW with an improvised ear trumpet, circa 1976.

PICTURE BY COURTESY OF JOHN MUXLOW

"borrowed" his first alto from brother Peter (the Grafton acrylic thing, which later melted). The Old Timeys asked me to join them on traps/washboard (thimbles supplied), while Geoff took his first not- very-faltering steps on the alto in public. This would, I reckon, have been in middle-to-late 1967. For a few weeks we did the Lamb at Lewes and the Norfolk pub (right opposite the King & Queen) in Grand Parade, Brighton. My first pay packet – Wendy Etherington having taken round the beer-mug – was 14/6d. I spent it wisely, and then drove home pissed. This is what we did in those days.

Well, we seemed to spend the next few months doing little but interval spots at places like the Sackville pub in Hove, run by the estimable Brad Bradshaw & His Moustache, for little prestige and even less money. So one night Geoff press-ganged me into marching round to Megs' house in Kemp Town with the band-fund (£1. 4s. 7d.) in a brown paper bag, and leaving the band. "OK", said Megs, and that was that. Having spoken to Jim Heath and 97, we found that we had a common yearning to play in a small band that combined some nice tight hot jazz with a leavening of humour (upon which the Martinique in particular had not seemed too keen). Local publicans' profits soared as we discussed the project, and eventually Harry Strutters were born in my old Standard Companion van outside Benny Simkins' shop in North Road. I am *absolutely certain* that I thought of the name of the band; Geoff, Jim and 97 are equally and severally certain that they did. On May 24, 1968 we burst upon an unsuspecting public, and the world has never been the same since. Nor has my liver.

The first gig was at The Eagle in Gloucester Road, Brighton. Jim had secured the engagement from what was then the Post Office. We had pledged to exercise the stated philosophy of madcappery and mayhem. Thus the floor of the function room upstairs was, by 7.30pm, absurdly covered with everything we owned which could *possibly* have done service as a neo-humorous prop, even though the precise comic function of each bit of tat (here an old gramophone, there an elk's head – oh yes, I'm afraid so) had never been defined.

At 7.50, Geoff, 97 and I sat in the public bar downstairs, contemplating our imminent public excoriation without any discernible enthusiasm.

"What are we going to *do?*" was three-quarters of Geoff's often-repeated plea. "Well, we'll just – you know. It'll be great!" was 97's considered judgment. I just sat there, mute with misery and already too many glasses of Harvey's.

At 7.56, we reached a sudden, divine, consensus. "If Jim doesn't appear by 7.59," we agreed, "it's up to The Imperial for some pinball and beers, and forget the whole thing!"

On the dot of 7.59, Jim appeared, rubbing his hands. "Hallo, boys!" he said – and changed our lives forever. In those days, you couldn't get counselling.

We secured a residency at the King & Queen under the slightly austere gaze of Ken Cook, the guv'nor, who paid us 10 shillings each for doing both Friday evenings and Sunday lunchtimes. There was no carpet, and the pub was, as my mother used mysteriously to say, "dead and alive". Within weeks we were packing the place, and in March 1969 John Marley of the *Evening Argus* wrote: "...the saloon-bar is taken over by a fascinatingly bizarre group of 'Twenties-style clown-musicians called the Harry Strutters. This Sussex quintet are one of the most colourful groups ever to have graced the inside of a local tavern, and their fans pour into the King & Queen in their hundreds.

"They spend much of their time," went on Mr Marley, getting a bit over-heated, "scouring second-hand shops for old sheet music." As I recall, we spent much of our time up at The Imperial playing the pinball machine, which, with a weekly prize of ten bob, supplied half of Geoff's income.

By this time we had recruited soprano-player Jim Fryer, whom we called "Fenton" (something to do with his raincoat) but within a year he left. Megs Etherington swam back from the wreckage of the Old Timey and clambered aboard, just after we had made our first trip overseas – to Hamburg and Neumunster, financed substantially by

Hokum and hot music. The setting is the GAY HIGHLANDER, Peacehaven, and the late 1960s Strutters line-up is augmented by two members of BOB KERR'S WHOOPEE BAND – KERR on sousaphone and (third left) banjo player VERNON DUDLEY BOWHAY-NOWELL. The regulars are JIM HEATH (second left), MAURICE DENNIS (centre), GEOFF SIMKINS (alto), JOHN MUXLOW (laughter prompter) and MIKE "MEGS" ETHERINGTON (cornet).

PICTURE BY COURTESY OF JOHN MUXLOW

saving up half our K&Q ten bobs.

Personnel changes and additions were fairly regular; for a while we had the slightly sinister Robin Fisher on baritone. Robin, with his fierce beard and impenetrable dark glasses, had the air of a Cuban freedom-fighter, and used to carry his baritone-sax around wrapped in an old raincoat (as Cuban freedom-fighters usually do). We always rehearsed in the Simkins' cellar; one evening Robin glided into what he thought was Benny's house and disappeared downstairs with his queer parcel. He emerged like a cork from a bottle when the startled old ladies who owned the place suggested that he "might try No.32".

There was the even more mysterious Blinswell, a clarinet-player we booked for one hilarious gig at Hellingly Hospital's Fun Day, at which the main "attraction" was Eileen Fowler's Keep-Fit Class, creaking around to George Mitchell Minstrel records. Maybe it was the shock of our orange-box stage collapsing in mid-*Margie*, or the mortification of being second on the bill to a group of energetic but frankly rather off-putting middle-aged ladies in grey leotards; however, we never saw Blinswell again. His name wasn't Blinswell, of course, but what else could we call the fellow?

Around the end of 1969 Peter Hill moved up to Yorkshire, where he still lives and thrives, playing occasional gigs, riding horses – which I find almost impossible to imagine – and exchanging silly correspondence with me at schoolboy-prank level. Jim Heath exhumed his old double-B-flat sousaphone while Maurice Dennis came in on banjo and guitar, and soon assumed what we loosely call "the management" of the band. He's still doing it, over 30 years later! We did residencies at the King's Head at Albourne (the place on the old A23 with the green dome, now offices) and in the days when you could still call a pub "The Gay Highlander" – The Gay Highlander at Peacehaven. The landlord was the breathless and hyper-active Brian Barratt, who was one of the best. There we were joined by Brian Hills (reeds) who, because he had actually been on the road as a "pro", was regarded with a certain amount of awe. He was as delightfully vague then as he is now, but he didn't half give the band a lift; with two saxes we could really start sounding like a proper orchestra, or so we believed.

(Oddly, I notice that we had residencies at Albourne, the Aldrington, the Alhambra, the Arlington, the Bathing Machine, the Buccaneer… was the Telephone Directory the only book we owned?)

Well, for years, we had fun, we made people laugh, and we played some pretty decent hot jazz, still with a leaning to the small American groups of the 1920s, but along the way we also gained what I feel, looking back, was a slightly unfortunate reputation, because we were widely regarded – even vilified – as little more than a "funny band", with no pretensions to playing good music. In truth, the Strutters were a fiercely swinging little outfit, dedicated to the proper presentation of tunes – in particular the inclusion of verses whenever known – and unusual tunes at that. We just didn't want to be all devout and po-faced about it, that was all. But there were not many bands in those days getting to grips with things like *Barataria, Bouncing Around*, and *Japanese Sandman*. These three appeared on our first LP, which we recorded in 1974 at Ron Geesin's studio in Heathfield. I still think it's not bad.

Geoff Simkins was phenomenal, in the context of the band. Born of a very musical family and steeped in the whole gallimaufry of the humorous side of the entertainment business, from Ally Sloper through W.C. Fields, Stan and Ollie, and Harold Lloyd, Geoff was a perfect front for the band. His alto-playing seemed, to us, fully-rounded from the word go, in the same way that Adrian Rollini and Sidney Bechet seemed to emerge from the chrysalis in full fig, and Geoff's stage-presence – deliberately aloof – was spot-on. He also made a significant contribution by insisting that, when we played incidental pieces of music to accompany the novelty stuff, we worked it out and played it *properly*. Dimwits all, we hadn't thought of that.

As early as July 1969, when Geoff had been playing alto for not much more than a year, Sam Edwards of the *Brighton & Hove Gazette* wrote that he was much impressed with his authority and poise, and his fine grasp of jazz phrasing. "I can't help feeling," wrote Edwards, "that in 12 months' time, Geoff Simkins – allowing for his current rate of development – will be heard playing in very different surroundings." This turned out to be true to a certain extent, although it was another five years before Geoff played his last official gig with the Strutters – a Gatsby Dinner for the *Evening Argus* Women's Circle. Even in those days Maurice Dennis was getting us some impressive work!

Maurice is a *rara avis* who deserves (but isn't going to get) a chapter to himself, if not a book. At our very first meeting he greeted me, not with "Hallo" or any other conventional salute, but with "I like your hat". I knew then that this was going to be interesting. I wasn't wearing a hat.

Maurice was a bit wary of us at first, partly because Jim Heath, never the most confident fellow when it comes to names, called him "Dennis" for some weeks, under the impression that his name was "Dennis Morris". ("He's a bit formal, that Jim, isn't he?" confided Maurice to me one day.) We, on the other hand, were simply terrified of Maurice – his intellect, his drive, his towering presence. Under his *aegis*, we bought an old van for a fiver – our first (and, as it transpired, our only) Harrywagon. We piled in, and Geoff lit one of his horrid little roll-ups. "For God's sake!" bellowed Maurice. "Don't you realise – this vehicle is a BOMB!" We got out again, fairly swiftly, and MD explained how he'd had to divert the petrol-line through the inside of

By 1974, when this picture was taken at a festival in South Croydon, the STRUTTERS had become an established club and cabaret attraction. BRIAN HILLS (front left) was now a regular member, along with JIM HEATH (sousaphone), MAURICE DENNIS (banjo), GEOFF SIMKINS (alto), JOHN MUXLOW (drums) and MEGS ETHERINGTON (cornet|).

PICTURE BY COURTESY OF JOHN MUXLOW

A dazzling array of props, puppets and other paraphernalia crowd detail into this shot of the Strutters at the SUSSEX PAD HOTEL at LANCING circa 1976. By then CHRIS MACDONALD (far right) had succeeded GEOFF SIMKINS in the reed section and GAVIN RUSSELL (on piano) had swelled the ranks to a seven-piece. Confusingly, Russell is pictured feigning mastery of the cornet in a military uniform (second right) while the band's regular cornet player MEGS ETHERINGTON crouches below him. MAURICE DENNIS is seated left, whilst in the foreground perches VIOLET BALLS, "the dancing doll". In the back row, JIM HEATH (left) cuddles DAISY THE COW, whilst BRIAN HILLS (with cigar) and JOHN MUXLOW (with tom tom) strike appropriate 1920s poses.

PICTURE BY COURTESY OF JOHN MUXLOW

the van on the floor between our feet. The van, instantly named The Pig, got us to the job all right, but it didn't get us back, and that was five quid gone west.

After all these years, I've never really got used to Maurice's conversational *culs-de-sac*. I was having breakfast in my bedroom at our digs one morning, when MD lumbered in. "Any ideas, John?" he asked. "Er – wha'?" I mumbled, through my Shreddies. "You never could remember anything," said Maurice, and shuffled off. "John hasn't got a clue," I expect he said to the others, and thus I was damned once again for being a useless piece of clutter.

One evening we were waiting to go on stage. I was getting anxious. "Maurice," I said, "It's nearly half-past eight." "No, John," Maurice corrected me gently, "It's not *quite* half-past eight."

When Geoff left, there were more changes. Chris Macdonald took his place in September 1974, and thus we acquired our first proper "reading" musician, which

Divested of fancy dress and props, it's easier to recognise the 1976 STRUTTERS line-up in this shot taken at the SUSSEX PAD HOTEL, LANCING. Left to right: MIKE ETHERINGTON, JIM HEATH, MAURICE DENNIS, BRIAN HILLS, JOHN MUXLOW, CHRIS MACDONALD and GAVIN RUSSELL.

PICTURE BY COURTESY OF PETE SIMKINS

was a mite frightening. Chris had been a founder-member of the Pasadena Roof Orchestra, and thus knew a thing or two. Jim Heath took an eighteenth-month sabbatical, and Yorkshireman George Flett came in on tuba. ("I once played before 60,000 people at Odsal Stadium," George told us. "Didn't you realise it was their turn then, George?" "Don't be bloody daft!")

We recorded an LP ("*That Certain Party*") for Black Lion Records at Regent Sound Studios in London (there is a famous picture of the Rolling Stones and Andrew Loog Oldham on those very premises) and for some reason were pressed upon to include a First World War medley: *Tipperary*, *Dolly Gray*, and what-not. We had a go at this, and the producer decided that some marching footstep effects would set the thing off. "We've got just the thing," he said, and produced a door (I suppose it's what producers do) upon which he assured us the Dave Clark Five had stamped their way to glory on *Bits and Pieces*. (A critic in the *Melody Maker* once described Dave Clark as being "the best drummer since Honey Lantree". He could have been serious, but I like to think he had a degree in irony.)

Anyway, six of us stamped around on this 6'x 2'6" door for much of the afternoon, and eventually the record was released without this track. We'd walked miles for nothing.

The stormer on this LP is, for me, *Ice Cream*. Chris Barber is the villain here. We'd started visiting the Continent regularly by now; little jazz-clubs at Ghent, Aalst, Oudenaarde and Dendermonde in Belgium, and better-known places like Dr Jazz in Dusseldorf. Everywhere we went, fans demanded to hear blasted *Ice Cream* "because Chris Barber always plays it". Now the German jazz-nut has a disconcertingly direct conversational style. "So!" he announces, barging in on your precious interval at the bar, while you're trying to work through as many complimentary beer-tokens as are medically advisable in *funfzehn minuten*. – "So! You are a better *Schlagzeuger* than last week, but not as good as Ron McKay! *Bitte!*" – and off he glides. But one particularly persistent cove at Dr Jazz had an obsession with *Ice Cream*. (As I say, Barber's fault.) The bloke asked us to play it. We played it. He asked for it again. We played it again.

Soon his mates joined in the game, and by the third interval we'd slogged through the damned tune half-a-dozen times. Not long into the next set: "You have not played *Ice Cream* since twenty minutes!" and Megs Etherington had an inspiration. "We'll do it," he said, "but as a waltz." So we did, with remarkable results. Half the audience leapt on to the tables and pretended it was the Munich Beer Festival. The rest showered us with empty fag-packets, beer-mats, and anything else that was within reach except – curiously – money.

Never mind – we recorded it in 3/4 time and it's pretty good, though I say it as shouldn't (another of Mum's curious expressions).

Clarinettist Peter Allen, now well known as the leader of his own very successful band, was with us on a couple of trips abroad, and wore a police-constable's uniform on stage, which had the gratifying effect of frightening the foreigners.

We pulled in Gavin Russell, a migrant from Oxford (the town, I suspect, rather than the University) on piano. Jim Heath was available again, and we asked him to return, which meant the replacement of George the Tuba; a difficult episode. But there you are. The Strutters were beginning to get a bit hard-nosed about excellence; toes, in those circumstances, are going to be trodden upon. Within the band, mutual criticism was freely and honestly dished out where necessary and for the most part sensibly accepted.

Two more LPs were recorded for Black Lion: *Rhythm King* (1977), and *Totus Porcus* (1979), on the second of which Geoff Simkins guested, to great effect, in the absence of the unavailable Chris Macdonald. In my sleeve-notes I mentioned that, whatever you may hear to the contrary, the phrase "Totus Porcus" was coined by Jim Heath in 1969, and means exactly what it says.

On November 7, 1977 Harry Strutters represented Radio Brighton in a nationally-broadcast concert at the De Montfort Hall, Leicester, to celebrate the 10th Anniversary of local radio. Tom O'Connor was the compere; other area representatives included Bobby Nutt and Pam Ayres. Reedman Bill Greenow joined us for that show, and Bill was a welcome "dep" on a number of other occasions.

Megs Etherington left the band in January 1979 and was replaced by Dave Davis on cornet, but not before Megs had contributed fully in some sessions at Brighton's Concorde Club with guests George Chisholm, Pat Halcox, Roy

The STRUTTERS were the supporting act for SPIKE MILLIGAN's one-man show at a Hove Town Hall concert in 1976. It raised a substantial sum to help save the West Pier.

COURTESY OF JOHN MUXLOW

HOVE TOWN HALL

TUESDAY, 3rd FEBRUARY, 1976

at 8 p.m.

SPIKE MILLIGAN

———

HARRY STRUTTERS HOT RHYTHM ORCHESTRA

LICENSED BAR

TICKETS: Reserved £1·50 & £1·25 ; Unreserved 75p & 50p

Available from Hove Town Hall, 10 a.m. – 12 noon & 3 p.m. – 4 p.m. or Forum Gallery, 16 Market St., Brighton (Tel. 28578) 10 a.m.–5.30 p.m. daily

Proceeds in aid of the
"WE WANT THE WEST PIER CAMPAIGN"

Printed by H. Crowhurst, 50-52 Market Street, Brighton.

West Sussex College of Design
Wednesday 3 July 1974 8 00 pm
Bar 8 00 pm to midnight

Ragtime

with Harry Strutters Hot Rythm Orchestra
and Momma Stratton's Big Band
also Absolute Horizon Disco

Ticket 50p

This attractive ticket for a 1974 STRUTTERS appearance is clearly an in-house effort by the West Sussex College of Design.

COURTESY OF JOHN MUXLOW

Williams and Alan Elsdon. Megs' departure was a touch sticky as well, but the band had settled on a direction to follow, and Davis fitted the bill. On his recommendation we acquired Mike Blakesley (trombone), who had played in Gerry Brown's band on Louis Armstrong's British tour in 1959, and suddenly the Strutters were a much more Condonesque Dixieland sort of outfit. With Davis, Blakesley and Macdonald we had a kind of Hackett-McGarity-Pee Wee front line, and the rhythm section adapted accordingly. Good band! (As a Cliff Leeman sort of chap, I enjoyed this.)

When Macdonald was unavailable for a while, Colin Bryant, from Poole in Dorset, worked with us on reeds increasingly often; a good player, and a very professional bloke, who also ran a joke shop. "Imitation dog-muck going really well this season!" he informed us one evening. "Of course it is, Col," we murmured, backing away.

On the home front, the years had seen us at a fair number of residencies, as I've previously mentioned. They all came and went, with varying degrees of success (we set fire to The Pier Hotel!) but our local following was increasing, and eventually we shimmered into the Sussex Pad at Lancing, opposite Shoreham Airport. A quite riotous few months passed at this venue – we were still in the Mike Etherington era, and he and I performed Noel Coward duets to bewildered audiences perched on wooden benches – until the Pad management announced temporary closure for refurbishment. Quite by chance, Ken Fehrenbach, the airport restaurant and bar manager, was in the Pad on that last night, and he invited the Strutters to use the Airport bar for a few weeks until the Pad was ready again.

The fact that we stayed at the Airport for seven years – almost every Sunday evening, with hardly a break except when we went abroad – and with a full house of around a hundred virtually every week, was down to three things: (1) Ken; (2) the fact that Ken, fed up with serving six semi-alcoholics and Maurice in the intervals, told us to help ourselves, and (3) No Fishing.

No Fishing equals "Jim Heath". Goodness knows how it started! (Actually, I <u>do</u> know, but this is a jazz book, and I'm conscious of my desire to present the Strutters as a serious jazz orchestra, so I don't want to dwell on *No Fishing* unduly. However, it is unquestionably part of the band's fabric.) Jim had constructed a succession of esoteric puppet-shows, one of which – *Il Pirata*"– was an elaborate reconstruction of the

Siege of Gibraltar or something, complete with defecating seagull. From these efforts there somehow emerged the anarchic episode we call *No Fishing*. As this largely consists of Jim hurling most of the contents of his kitchen and bathroom over a screen, while roaring through a kazoo, we'll leave it at that. Don't ask me why it includes an inflatable cow. But it is funny!

From 1976 to 1983 entertainment at Shoreham Airport was synonymous with Harry Strutters. (It's something I would like to emphasize in this chapter: the rise and eventual eminence as local jazz haunts of both the King & Queen and Shoreham Airport were originally down to the initiative and efforts of Harry Strutters. Don't believe any other version, even within these covers!) I think the contributions of Ken Fehrenbach, his son Paul, and his staff – Debbie, Frances and Pat – should be gratefully acknowledged here. The Strutters had a marvellous time at the Airport, and this was hugely due to the warmth and encouragement of the then management. (At Christmas 1979 we did a "This Is Your Life" for Ken – which we enjoyed, even if he didn't.)

Southern Television made a documentary about the Airport, in which the Strutters were extensively featured, and they followed up with a Christmas programme, with us and the Bernie Allen Band. BBC TV made a programme about the Piers of England, featuring ourselves, and narrated by Gavin Henderson, then the director of the Brighton Festival. We took part in ITV's *Runaround*, with Mike Reid, and made several recordings for both local radio and BBC Radio 2.

I said earlier that Geoff Simkins had played his last "official" gig with the Orchestra in 1974, but he was a frequent Shoreham Strutter, and another guest reedman on several occasions was the late Malcolm "Mogs" Everson, a baritone-player of more modern persuasion who paid the Strutters the compliment of adapting cheerfully to our style. A good nut, was Mogs, and the enormous turn-out at his funeral at New Year 1992 showed that this was a view shared by many.

And then – in 1983, there was the most enormous upheaval. Apart from anything else, Brighton & Hove Albion reached the F.A. Cup Final and, strangely enough, the Strutters had done a gig at Wembley Stadium the previous September for a greyhound meeting. Those of us with any interest in football (i.e. me) ritually trooped up to the Royal Box, accepted the imaginary Cup, and used Her Majesty's loo. "For God's sake!" said Maurice.

But I found myself getting bored with the band – not with the chaps, but with having spent 15 years lugging around and setting up and packing away a heavy "vintage" drum-kit four

Ticket for the 1978 STRUTTERS' Christmas party, an event that remains an enjoyable calendar occasion in the Brighton area.

COURTESY OF JOHN MUXLOW

or five times a week. Musically, too, I thought it was getting a little tired and formulaic, with the same tunes being called night after night – so I decided to pack it in (for ever, so I wrongly thought at the time). On June 24, 1983, we played our 15th anniversary concert at the Gardner Arts Centre at Falmer, recorded by BBC Radio Brighton, and I left. Chris Mac presented me with a bottle of something nice, and Maurice Dennis gave me a cheque for a huge sum. (Only one of these statements is true.)

The following evening – a Saturday – I sat at home and watched the telly, knowing that the boys were out doing a gig somewhere. It felt very odd; torn between being thankful that I wasn't heaving the blasted drums up some stairs, and wondering how the fellows were getting on.

By a genuine coincidence, the following Tuesday I had a call from Vince Geddes, then of Radio Brighton but shortly to transfer to the new Southern Sound Radio (now Southern FM), asking me to become the embryo station's jazz presenter. So, far from indulging in gentle semi-retirement, I stayed at Southern Sound for two years and 90 or so programmes, trying to learn how to work a wireless studio, and playing enthusiastically inept cricket for the station team.

Getting back to the Strutters upheaval: soon after my departure the band was in a kind of turmoil. Maurice had signed a contract for 10 days in Germany, while Dave Davis, Mike Blakesley and Colin Bryant had been offered a job on the *Queen Elizabeth II*, covering a similar period. Something had to give, and the three boys decided – to their advantage, as it turned out – to go maritime. (At the time of writing, I believe they're still getting the gig.)

Meanwhile, Maurice had about a week to recruit and rehearse a new front line and persuade them to leave their families for a week and-a-half's biffing up and down the Ruhr Valley. (We had a German agent named Dieter; we called him "Detour".) Miraculously, Mo signed up Johnny Tucker (for this trip only) on cornet, plus Alistair Allan (trombone) and Bill Boston (reeds), and a contractual embarrassment was averted. Not only that, but the foundation of the "modern" Harry Strutters was well and soundly laid, especially with the subsequent inclusion of the fiery Paul Lacey on trumpet.

In 1985 I was persuaded back, having been summarily dismissed by Southern Sound for having only one listener; Martin Litton soon replaced Gavin Russell on piano, and he and Lacey started contributing a stream of arrangements to supplement the excellent charts of Chris Macdonald.

In subsequent years, Alistair gave way to Bob Hunt, Paul Lacey to Mike Cotton, and Chris Mac to Tony

FERNEHAM HALL

OSBORN ROAD, FAREHAM, HAMPSHIRE, PO16 7DB.

FAREHAM BOROUGH COUNCIL'S OWN ENTERTAINMENT CENTRE

HARRY STRUTTER'S HOT RHYTHM ORCHESTRA

ROARING 20's NIGHT

FRIDAY 4th JUNE, 1982
7.30 p.m.-11.45 p.m.

Tickets £2.25(Adults)
£1.50(Children & Senior Citizens)

Cheques made payable to:
FAREHAM BOROUGH COUNCIL

Box Office opens 10th May
Tel: Box Office (0329) 231942

By 1982 bookings for the STRUTTERS had become commonplace in the South's major concert halls. COURTESY JOHN MUXLOW

An early 1990s publicity still from the latter-day life of the STRUTTERS when a number of full-time professional musicians were recruited and the bonds with the Brighton area became looser. Left to right: MAURICE DENNIS, CHRIS MACDONALD, BOB HUNT, BILLY BOSTON, JIM HEATH, MARTIN LITTON, JOHN MUXLOW, PAUL LACEY.

PICTURE BY COURTESY OF KEITH SAMUEL

Jack – an eccentric and engaging genius from Northampton – via Mac White, of Temperance Seven fame. Bobby Hunt's towering presence and brilliant arranging skills – particularly in the Ellington oeuvre – and "Red" Cotton's enormous depth of experience can truly be said to have put the finishing touches to the "modern" Strutters. In addition, we have enjoyed great success with the American singers Earlene Bentley and Shezwae Powell, the wonderful Rusty Taylor, and former Basie, Calloway and Ellington song-and-dance man Joe Chisholm. Sadly, Rusty and Joe both left the party far too early, but are fondly remembered.

I realise that I've glossed feverishly over the Strutters' last 15 or so years; that I haven't mentioned in any detail any of the Strutters' subsequent recordings on LP, cassette, and CD, or our many trips in the UK and abroad with such shows as *A Night At the Cotton Club, The Cotton Club Revue* and *Memories of Bing* (the latter with singer Roy Chappell), and that I'm bound to have omitted mentioning goodness knows how many splendid local musicians who have "depped" with the band over the years (one particularly hilarious visit to Belgium with Brighton reeds maestro Don Pashley comes to mind!). To them our thanks, and my apologies.

But the strong local connections really ended around the middle 1980s with the demise of the Shoreham Airport residency, apart from the occasional private engagement and our traditional Christmas shows at Brighton's Pavilion Theatre. Thanks to Maurice's diligence, the Strutters have undertaken no fewer than 70 trips abroad, by my reckoning, and the stories of these – and the years 1985 to 2002 – could give rise to another chapter, if not book. They will have to wait. But notebooks are being filled, even as I write.

MIKE MOUNTER

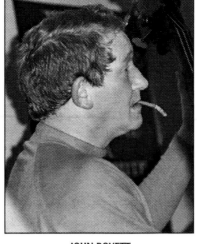

JOHN BOYETT

BILL HARVEY

PETE GODFREY

JILL STAPLES

was the unofficial court photographer to the BRIGHTON JAZZ LINE in the 1970s and 1980s. This montage from her impressive portfolio shows some of the Sussex jazz personalities of that era, plus one or two visitors.

GEORGE WALKER

DAVE GIBB

GORDON WREN

JOHN GOODRICK

DORY WHITFIELD

MIKE COLLIER (right)
and DAVE GIBB

BRIAN WHITE

SLUFF HAZELL

ROY BOWER (left) with American visitors
PEE WEE ERWIN (trumpet) and JOHNNY MINCE (clarinet).

PAUL BONNER

JACK GILBERT (soprano sax) and
GEOFF SIMKINS (alto) sit in with the
ANDERIDA JAZZ BAND.,
GERRY GEOGHEGAN is on clarinet and
GEORGE WALKER on banjo.

JOE LEE WILSON (left) and PETE SIMKINS

VIC RICHARDS

VIV BONNER

The "Guvnor" KEN COLYER guests with
GUY FENTON'S JAZZMEN.
GERRY GEOGHEGAN is on clarinet

Tailgate rambler. **SID BAILEY** in action at the **MARQUIS OF GRANBY**, Sompting, in 2001, artfully giving the impression that he is playing the trombone whilst standing on one leg!

PICTURE BY COURTESY OF SID BAILEY

Drummer-leader
BILL POLLEY
circa 1970.

PICTURE BY COURTESY OF BILL POLLEY

BRIGHTON STATION provides a platform for the music of the **ANDERIDA JAZZ BAND**, who were hired to promote the **BRIGHTON FESTIVAL** in 1988. The musicians are **JOHN GOODRICK** (clarinet) **BILL HARVEY** (trumpet), **CHRIS GIBB** (bass), **GORDON WREN** (drums) **DON WILLIAMS** (trombone) and Hampshire pianist **COLIN COLLINS**.

PICTURE BY COURTESY OF GORDON WREN

CHAPTER 13

THE
1980s AND 1990s

SID BAILEY

The unenviable task of covering the last two decades of traditional and mainstream jazz activity in the Brighton area has been tackled manfully and ably in this chapter, by Sid Bailey, with help from many others. As Sid himself has been such an important part of the scene he chronicles here, the Editors thought it appropriate that this popular Tailgate Rambler should first be encouraged to describe his own formative experiences in the jazz world.

JAZZ AND ME

I SUPPOSE IT ALL STARTED ABOUT 1954 when Al Hare, a school pal of mine, used to invite me back to his house to listen to his latest albums of Jelly or Louis. Al was a brass band trumpeter who later joined a Royal Air Force band. Under his instruction we used to mime with "air" instruments in the bicycle sheds, and I was told to do the trombone parts! Shortly after this I bought my first record player – which had to be played through a radio – and my first jazz record. This was *Bluin' the Blues/At Sundown* by Muggsy Spanier and it cost me 7/6d. I also got my first Regent narrow-bore trombone around this time. The slide was so full of holes that it had to be patched with solder every now and then. I attended music lessons with a local brass teacher.

We had all read Rex Harris's book on jazz and I used to spend my Saturday mornings with a few other friends junk-shopping for jazz and dance 78s, carrying them home in a leather satchel hanging from the crossbar of our bicycles. We regularly attended a jazz club at The Green Lounge on Stephen's Green in Dublin where we listened to The Night Owls, a popular Dixieland band. We also went to the big ballrooms when the Jimmy Compton band was down from Belfast or when the Dutch Swing College or one of the British bands was touring Ireland. I got together with some other kindred jazz spirits who had bought instruments – there were not that many of us – and we had a grand time blowing and bashing away in our parents' garages. We could, in fact, claim to be one of the first "garage bands"! Eventually we were given the odd job playing, for free admission, during the half-hour intervals at dances at suburban tennis clubs, and once we were actually paid (30 shillings, or £1.50 each) for providing "music" at a birthday party.

Things began to improve under the leadership of an English clarinet player named Denis Chapel, who was working for APV/Desco in Ireland at that time and who was older and more experienced than us. We became a bit more musically organised, had regular practice sessions and, in 1960, formed a proper band called The Eblana Jazzband (I think Eblana was an old name for Dublin). We then started our own sessions at The Green Lounge on Friday nights. This soon grew into a very popular venue and was packed to the gunnels with jiving Tradkids every week. We managed to come by other gigs at small halls around Dublin, although we were not always appreciated. "Yez are nothing but a brass band skiffle group" was the reaction of one young lady at the Carlton Hall in North Dublin. When you think about it, this is not a bad analysis of the style that we were trying to emulate.

Around 1967-68 I formed a band called the Fair City Jazzband and also the Dublin Jazz Society. Through this we arranged solo tours in Ireland – backed by the FCJB – for the English musicians Cy Laurie, Monty Sunshine and Keith Smith, for Alton Purnell, Louis Nelson and Don Ewell from the United States, and for the British bands of Ken Colyer, Barry Martyn and Monty Sunshine.

In 1970 my wife was working in a travel agency and was able to obtain discounted fares to America. We therefore managed to go on a memorable three-week holiday to New Orleans. I took my trombone (by then a respectable King 3B) and sat in at a few parties and bars there. Unfortunately, our visit coincided with the rise of the Black Panther movement and I was beaten up while I was "second-lining" on a parade with the Doc Paulin Brass Band. The police arrived in the nick of time and dumped us back in the relative safety of the tourist section, The French Quarter. Because of our experience with that mini-riot, everyone we met was extremely nice to us, compensating, I suppose, for our ordeal. We had a wonderful three weeks of listening, eating and drinking.

I moved to Shoreham-by-Sea in 1971 and shortly afterwards took a band – **Bailey's Lucky Seven** – back to Ireland for a short tour. Later on I became a member of Guy Fenton's **Luvovadur Jazz Band** for a few years, backing Ken Colyer on at least three occasions and playing regular pub jobs in Worthing and Brighton. I started sessions with my Lucky Seven at The Sussex Pad in Lancing in the early 1970s, using Pete Godfrey (piano), Ray Little (banjo), Pete Burton (drums), John Frucht (bass), Dave Greetham (trumpet) and Martin Jones (clarinet). This residency lasted for six years until the landlord moved out – the old story!

I was getting tired of trekking up to London to hear the visiting American jazzers, so in 1981 I started promoting monthly sessions at Shoreham Airport, and let them come to me! At that time Dave Bennett looked after the music for the Pizza Express in Soho and, as that venue was closed on Monday evenings, Dave helped me to book the musicians for that night at Shoreham. Using the Anderida Jazz Band as the house band, I put on Benny Waters, Hal Singer, Wild Bill Davison, Franz Jackson, Al Casey, Butch Thompson, Herbie Hall, Jimmy McPartland, Don Ewell and the Harlem Jazz and Blues Band – all from the States – as well as the gypsy jazz group WASO from Holland, the Hot Antic band from France and the Scania Jazz Band from Sweden. We had some great nights and some middlin' nights, but no bad nights.

In 1982 I played on a short tour of Germany with the New Orleans Echoes, followed by a quick trip to France with Roy Martin, a couple of visits to Belgium as a member of the Stour Valley Stompers (in 1987) and a hot weekend in Gambia organised by bass player John Roberts. Back on the Oul Sod I was happy to be able to play at three Cork Jazz Festivals before they dropped the traditional bands completely from that annual event. In the summer of 1987 I started a Sunday-night gig at my local, the Crown and Anchor in Shoreham's High Street, with Mike Mounter (trumpet), Brian Hills (clarinet), Dave Cummings (banjo), and Allan Sokell (sousaphone). One of the guests we had there was the fine French clarinettist Pierre Atlan. As the night wore on we decided to play the old favourite *I Ain't Gonna Give Nobody None of my Jelly Roll* and Pierre asked me if he could do the vocal, saying "The *double entendre* is the same in French!"

As I don't mind travelling – short distances – I used to gig with Pete Curtis's band in Tunbridge Wells, with Pete Lay in Dover and with Cuff Billett and Bob Jenkins in Portsmouth, as well as risking lip, limb and trombone playing Bonfire Night parades with Roy Martin's Expedient Brass Band. I also got, and still get, occasional work with the Excelsior Brass Band at steam rallies, etc. – and, on one memorable day, at Nat Gonella's funeral in Gosport. I began writing articles, and reviewing records and books, for various jazz magazines about this time, and I recall the hornets' nest I stirred up in *Just Jazz* when I dared to criticise Saint Colyer!

Once, I was looking for a book on the famous New Orleans trombonist Edward "Kid" Ory, but could I find any? Louis Armstrong, Sidney Bechet, George Lewis, Baby

FROM U.S.A. THE JAZZ GUITAR OF
AL CASEY

Esquire Gold Award Winner, and sideman with LOUIS ARMSTRONG, FATS WALLER etc.

WITH
LENNIE FELIX ON PIANO
AND
ANDERIDA JAZZ BAND

SHOREHAM AIRPORT LOUNGE
8·00pm Monday April 21st
Admission payable at door £1·50

A poster for the first of three appearances by American guitarist AL CASEY at Shoreham Airport lounge.
It took place in April 1980 and was one of a number of ambitious promotions staged by SID BAILEY at Shoreham in the early 1980s.
The ANDERIDA JAZZ BAND were often featured in support. Other U.S. visitors included JIMMY MCPARTLAND, DON EWELL, WILD BILL DAVISON, BENNY WATERS and the HARLEM JAZZ AND BLUES BAND.

COURTESY OF SID BAILEY

Dodds, King Oliver, Bunk Johnson and Clarence Williams have all had biographies or discographies written about them, but *not* Ory. Therefore, with the help of Lindsey Marshall (who had assisted John Collinson with his Don Ewell book), and using material I had accumulated over the years, I started to compile a discography on the man. This resulted in *Greatest Slideman Ever Born* which, to date, has sold over 300 copies and is now in its third edition. "So good it is difficult to know how it could be improved," wrote the reviewer in *Jazz Journal* – so it can't be all that bad!

In the early 1990s I joined the **Stane Street Jazzmen** in West Sussex, with Bill Harvey (trumpet), Teddy Layton (clarinet), the late Colin Collins on (piano), Butch Holden (bass guitar) and Alan Humphries (drums) – playing at The Royal Oak, Lagness, near Bognor Regis, recording for the BBC, and providing jazz music for many private jobs. We finished up at the Earl of March in Lavant with a different personnel of Roy Bower (trumpet), Chris Macdonald (clarinet), Ken Raine (bass) and Peter Godfrey (piano). Following the break-up of this band I decided to revive the **Tailgate Six** name and play a more Crescent City-style of jazz. In 1999 we played – a first, for us at least – at a service for the Church of the Good Shepherd on Shoreham beach, as part of the Adur Festival celebrations. Nowadays I play with John Maddocks Jazzmen from Bournemouth when they are gigging in the Home Counties. And I run a monthly session at the Marquis of Granby in Sompting, where I am joined in the Tailgate Six by Stu Morrison (banjo), John Boyett (bass) and Bob Jenkins (clarinet) as well as guest drummers and trumpet players such as Cuff Billett, Mike Peters and Andy Dickens. We have even been fortunate enough to have Pat Halcox joining us on three swinging occasions.

> *Sid's own story illustrates how, in some ways, Brighton has become a melting-pot for musicians, with many of the leading exponents of jazz in the area having migrated to the South Coast from all over the British Isles over the past four or five decades to augment the ranks of the highly-talented local jazzers. It is perhaps not too fanciful to compare Brighton, is this respect, with New Orleans, Chicago and New York, the jazz cities from which we have all drawn so much inspiration. Sid Bailey's summary of the traditional and mainstream scene in the 1980s and 1990s provides interesting glimpses of the musicians and bands that have formed part of the great jazz parade in Brighton and Sussex during this period. In many cases the stories of the bands and musicians stretch back to the 1970s, or even earlier. Happily many remain fully active in the 21st Century. He now takes up the narrative again:-*

The 1980s and 1990s witnessed a seesaw of activity on the local jazz scene. Many of the more popular bands played weekly pub residencies which acted as shop windows for their musical wares, and through this exposure they often procured well-paid private gigs such as parties and weddings – plus the odd corporate job in shopping malls and supermarkets, at garden fetes and the like. Nearly all of the bands in question had a regular night (or Sunday morning) at The King and Queen in Marlborough Place.

This Hollywood Tudor monstrosity actually had a sign outside claiming that it was the Home of Brighton Jazz but otherwise it rarely, if ever, advertised its jazz sessions and (under most of its landlords during this period) failed to provide a house piano, a house PA system or even a bandstand. The bands normally played in the fireplace! The money wasn't all that good either! However, to its credit, it was the only pub that continuously hired bands throughout these two decades and it *did* give BBC Radio Brighton somewhere to promote their jazz concerts during the arts festivals. I have fond memories of the night when Bob Wilber presented his tribute to Benny Goodman and also of the time when the Harlem Jazz and Blues Band played there. Somehow bandstands and PA materialised for those nights!

On a more sombre note, the **KING AND QUEEN** was judged the most appropriate venue for a memorial session to two of the most influential figures in **THE BRIGHTON JAZZ LINE**, who died in 1982. The passing of **BENNY SIMKINS** at 71 in May (recorded by Roy Bower in Chapter 8) was followed in November by a further blow – the premature death of **TED AMBROSE**. He had been suffering from a brain tumour and was just 55 years of age. He was described, very accurately, by the **EVENING ARGUS** as "a pioneer of live jazz in Brighton".

In an admirable illustration of local jazz community spirit, six bands and a number of guest soloists took the stand at the **KING AND QUEEN** on the night of Saturday April 23, 1983 to pay tribute to these two much-liked and respected trail-blazers. The bands were the re-assembled **BENNY SIMKINS SEXTET**, the **NEW EAGLE RHYTHM KINGS**, the **ANDERIDA JAZZ BAND**, the **ROYAL QUINTET** – also re-assembled for the occasion, the **NERKS Skiffle Group** and the **EXPEDIENT BRASS BAND**. The MC was Arnie King.

Describing his former colleagues in the programme for the event, Mike Collier said: "All of us had many sessions, a few drinks and a lot of good times together and, having known them for many years, I can honestly assure you that they would want everyone to enjoy themselves tonight. Please do, and our heartfelt thanks go to them for all they gave to us." Mike's enjoinders were properly taken to heart by musicians and audience members, and a memorable evening ensued.

But it was a bleak period for Sussex jazz. The deaths of pianist **HARRY WALTON** and bass-player **IAN SCRIVEN** – both very active across the county – occurred in the same period and their names were also linked to this memorial event by the organisers.   **Ed.**

Listed below are some of the area's jazz bands whose careers and histories are not covered elsewhere in the book:

THE ANDERIDA JAZZ BAND

Formed in 1971 by trombonist Geoff Hoare, this band took its name from the forests that covered Sussex in Roman times. Their first pub job was at The King's Head in

THE ANDERIDA JAZZ BAND pictured in 1977 during their long stint at the KING'S HEAD, Burgess Hill.
Left to right PETER GODFREY (piano), GEOFF HOARE (trombone), BILL HARVEY (trumpet), CHRIS GIBB (bass),
GEORGE WALKER (banjo), GORDON WREN (drums) and GERRY GEOGHEGAN (clarinet).

PICTURE BY JILL STAPLES, COURTESY OF PETER GODFREY

Cuckfield with a line-up of Doug and Doreen "Dory" Whitfield (trumpet and piano), Geoff himself (trombone), George Walker (banjo), Pete Burton (drums) and Chris Gibb (bass).

A year or so later they moved to another King's Head, this time at Burgess Hill. Here they found that much-sought-after rarity, a jazz-loving landlord in the person of Ernie Russell, who kept the band's regular Wednesday night going for five years until he gave up the pub to move to London. The personnel was revamped at this time. Chris Gibb, George Walker and Geoff remained, joined by Bill Harvey (trumpet), Gerry Geoghegan and then John Goodrick (clarinet), Pete Simkins and later Pete Godfrey (piano) and Gordon Wren (drums). Around 1975 Geoff Hoare left to live in the West Country and his place was taken by Baz Searle, with Gordon Wren taking on the mantle of bandleader.

When their stint at Burgess Hill came to an end, the Anderida moved to Shoreham Airport, playing in the restaurant there. Here, when I did some promotions in the 1980s, they backed many famous visiting American jazzmen such as Al Casey, Herb Hall, Wild Bill Davison and Benny Waters. This was a busy and a happy time for the band. They played gigs all over the county, always working as a team and without any of the niggles that so often occur.

1981 saw them start a nine-year residency at The King and Queen in Brighton, with Don Williams joining on trombone, and George Walker dropping out. They played there every other Thursday, alternating with the MC Band. When this venue abandoned its jazz policy in the early 1990s, the band decided to give up on its regular jobs and just play gigs as they came along. This decision seemed the right one because the work still keeps coming in to the present day.

THE ARUN VALLEY JAZZ BAND

Although the Arun Valley Jazz Band's name suggests a connection with the more westerly reaches of Sussex, this group's main areas of activity were in Worthing, Shoreham, Brighton and Hove. "The name tripped off the tongue nicely and that's why we chose it," says trombonist and leader John Davidson in explanation of this geographical mystery.

In 1966 the band were launched with an apt publicity picture of them playing aboard a houseboat at Shoreham owned by Tony Cooke, a local art teacher and clarinettist. With Davidson the other members were Paul Hartman (reeds), the late Dave Clifton (trumpet), Paul Gifford (bass), Neal Pilcher (drums) and Jim Susans or Howard Gabe on banjo.

After a spell at the Maltsters Arms in Worthing, Pete (Mitz) Mitton joined on trumpet and they moved to the Fountain Hotel where the weekly sessions lasted for more than two years. Bookings in Brighton included a residency at Prinny's Bar and sessions at the Chinese Jazz Club, where " Uncle" Bonny Manzi offered the band interval spots in support of the "name" attractions. Frequent substitutes in this period were Jim Heath on banjo and John Muxlow (drums). Before it too became defunct, the band gained the distinction of playing at the very last session at the Chinese Jazz Club.

THE COTTON CLUB JAZZMEN

This band was formed from the nucleus of the Sussex Jazz Kings, who in turn rose from the ashes of the Stane Street Jazzmen. The Cotton Club Jazzmen's first appearance was at the 1994 Bude Jazz Festival. It was founded by trombonist Brian Cotton, who started his jazz career at the tender age of 16 with Dick Charlesworth's City Gents and went on to play his part in the 1960s Trad Boom with the bands of Micky Ashman, Sonny Morris and Nat Gonella.

The rest of the band consists of Roy Bower (trumpet), Chris Macdonald (reeds), Jim McKay (bass), Butch Holden (guitar), Peter Burton (drums) and Pete Godfrey (piano). A seven-piece band is not a particularly economical unit in this day and age but – despite the odd criticism for not having a banjo – this group always seems to win its audiences over.

For three years running the Cotton Club Jazzmen have appeared at the jazz festival in Gran Canaria, as well as playing at the Upton on Severn, Hay on Wye and Birmingham International Jazz Festivals. They have made two well-received CDs and are resident at Shoreham Airport every

Brian Cotton's
COTTON CLUB
j a z z m e n
are

Bringing Jazz
every Sunday
evening to :

Taking Off

SHOREHAM AIRPORT
Admission £3 (£5 including supper)   Licensed Bar
For table reservations or information phone: (01273) 452300

Skilful publicity for Sunday night sessions at SHOREHAM AIRPORT featuring BRIAN COTTON'S COTTON CLUB JAZZMEN.

COURTESY OF BRIAN COTTON

The **COTTON CLUB JAZZMEN** pictured outside Doyles' Coffee Shop in Worthing in July 1999. Left to right ROY BOWER (trumpet), pianist PETE GODFREY – identifiable despite holding a clarinet, JIM MCKAY (bass), BUTCH HOLDEN (guitar), CHRIS MACDONALD (tenor sax), PETER BURTON (drums) and BRIAN COTTON (trombone).

PICTURE BY COURTESY OF PETE GODFREY

Clarinettist **KENNY DAVERN** is one of several American jazz stars to appear at the **HANBURY ARMS** in Kemp Town, Brighton in recent years. He is pictured here in January 2000 with Sussex musicians PETE GODFREY (piano), PIERS CLARK (guitar) and JIM MCKAY (bass). The hidden drummer is MALCOLM MORTIMORE.

PICTURE BY COURTESY OF PETER GODFREY

Sunday night. Brian Cotton's penchant for sailing the oceans of the world means that the band has spells in which it operates as a six-piece outfit. An especially lengthy absence took Brian out of circulation for much of 2001 and 2002.

THE FEATHERSTONE JAZZ FIVE

Among the bands to feature regularly at the Marquis of Granby at Sompting since 1997 are The Featherstone Jazz Five. They were formed in 1984 and their first date was at the splendidly named Joyful Whippet at Lancing. The personnel was: Derek

The **FEATHERSTONE JAZZ FIVE** celebrate an anniversary, circa 1990. Left to right: **JOHN DAVIDSON, DAVE CUMMINGS, RAY LITTLE, CHRIS GIBB** and **DEREK LITTLE.**

PICTURE BY COURTESY OF JOHN DAVIDSON

Little (clarinet and soprano sax), John Davidson (trombone), Ray Little – Derek's brother (drums), Dave Cummings (banjo), and Brian Finch (bass). Finch was quickly succeeded by Chris Gibb from the Anderida Jazz Band, who was a regular until his death in the mid-1990s.

The naming of the band is shrouded in near obscurity. The leader, Derek Little is a maths teacher who admired the Firehouse Five and wanted a similar alliterative name. After much contemplation (and some inspiration from a world atlas) the Featherstone Five name got the nod.

The mid-80s saw the band appearing at a number of Sussex venues, but they made their biggest impact at the Connaught Theatre, Worthing, where they played every Saturday lunchtime for six years between 1987 and 1993, often featuring guest musicians.

There were subsequent brief residencies in Worthing, Ferring, Littlehampton and at The Albion in Hove before the association with the Marquis of Granby began. Four of the original members remain in harness – the Little brothers, John Davidson and Dave Cummings. Ken Raine now plays bass with the Granby line-up, and Dave Rogers is the bass player for the band's second regular gig at the Eastney Tavern, Southsea.

THE GAVIN ALANJOHNS JAZZ BAND

The opening of a new jazz venue at the Marquis of Granby at Sompting in 1997 created opportunities for several bands. Chosen to play regularly every month from the outset were The Gavin Alanjohns Jazz Band. The band's name derives from an intriguing combination of the first names of the six regular members – Gavin Russell (piano), Alan Kennington (bass), and no fewer than four Johns – John Davidson (trombone), John Goodwin (trumpet), John Goodrick (clarinet) and John Muxlow (drums).

John Davidson, who is also a member of the NatWest Jazz Band, believes that the Gavin Alanjohns band benefits greatly from the arranging skills of John Goodwin, a comparative newcomer to the area. "This has enabled us to play many standards and also some lesser-known tunes for the benefit of our audiences."

GEORGE'S REGIS JAZZ BAND

Although most of the activities of George's Regis Jazz Band fall outside the boundaries of Brighton and mid-Sussex, it is impossible to ignore this energetic, itinerant group from West Sussex. Led by the ebullient George Bennett on drums, the band has a fluid personnel and often includes musicians from the Brighton area. "I like to share it around," is how Bennett describes his policy on hiring instrumentalists. The band was founded in 1989 and – as the name implies – regards the Bognor Regis area as home territory (George must have agonised over whether to call the band George's Jazz Kings!)

They play at regular venues such as the Royal Oak at Hooksway and the Arun Valley Leisure Centre but perhaps are best known for outdoor work on bandstands, seafront promenades, public parks and shopping malls. George's mustering instructions are legendary. "Bring a chair with you," "Wear a hat," "Be prepared to stroll and play" being among the most common enjoinders.

In their ability to deliver "feelgood" traditional jazz at social events in diverse surroundings the Regis Band echo the work schedules of those New Orleans jazz pioneers who played frequently at outdoor picnics, parties and parades.

Among the regular irregulars are Jim Chambers (reeds), Mike "Megs" Etherington (cornet), Chris Newman (piano), Geoff Steer (tuba and bass), Mary Lou Litchfield (reeds), Pete Dorday (cornet and banjo), Keith Dorday (banjo and guitar), Ron Westcott (trombone), Chris Macdonald (reeds), Derek Little (clarinet), Allan Sokell

GEORGE'S REGIS
JAZZ BAND
pictured indoors
circa 1990.
Left to right
SLUFF HAZELL,
MEGS ETHERINGTON,
JIM CHAMBERS,
GEORGE BENNETT,
DON WILLIAMS AND
ALLAN SOKELL.

PICTURE BY COURTESY OF
GEORGE BENNETT

GEORGE'S REGIS
JAZZ BAND
prepare to go walkabout at a
private engagement in West
Sussex in the mid-1990s.
Left to right
MIKE MOUNTER (trumpet),
EDDIE COOPER (tuba),
GEORGE WALKER (banjo),
GEORGE BENNETT (drums),
RON WESTCOTT (trombone),
JACK GILBERT (clarinet).

PICTURE BY COURTESY OF
GEORGE BENNETT.

(sousaphone), vocalists Julie Horton and Jo Collinson, Eddie Cooper (sousaphone), Bill Harvey (trumpet), George Walker (banjo), Don Williams (trombone), Alan Kennington (bass), Keith Samuel (trombone) and Bill Phelan (trumpet)

THE JOHNNY KING BAND

Old school chums John Frucht and Arnie King teamed up again in the early 1980s after a period of many years in which their musical paths hadn't crossed too often. Arnie had been involved in producing revues and musical shows, but they agreed it would be nice to get back to playing jazz together. Arnie had just left the New Eagle Rhythm Kings, so the time seemed ripe to form a band.

They started out with a Sunday gig at the Sea-house in Middle Street, Brighton, with Arnie (trumpet, songs and anecdotal announcements), Jack Sherriff (clarinet), John Collinson and later Ray Schooley (banjo), Brian Hussey and later Terry Shearing (drums) and John Frucht on bass. The job continued until the pub closed down about 18 months later but the band also had a midweek residency at the Fortune of War on the lower Promenade, and this kept them going. When the Sea-house gig ended, they resumed their Sunday lunchtime blow at The Adur in Hove, with Gavin Russell (piano), Pat Chapman (alto) and Bill Guy (trombone), also holding down a regular weekend job on the Palace Pier.

Following an engagement at the wedding reception of Clive Sinclair's daughter, the band decided to concentrate on providing music for this type of function – but without sacrificing their jazz credentials. The move proved successful, with the band diary filling up with well-paid private work and posh, prestigious bookings in Knightsbridge and Mayfair, along with corporate jobs. 1993 saw the Johnny King band playing Fridays at Shoreham Airport and Sundays and Tuesdays at the Albion, Hove, with Sluff Hazell (baritone) Bill Parsons (banjo) and Brian Clarke (drums) joining the

Three key members of the
JOHNNY KING BAND –
JOHN FRUCHT (bass),
ARNIE KING (cornet) and
BILL PARSONS (banjo).
This photograph was taken
in 1997 shortly before Arnie
King's untimely death.

PICTURE BY COURTESY OF JOHN FRUCHT

band. This personnel remained largely unchanged until Arnie's untimely death at the age of 57 in February 1997.

In common with Mike Collier, Arnie has a seat (and also a tree) dedicated to his memory in St Nicholas's Churchyard. The inscription reads:

> **An ash tree was planted in this garden by musicians and friends of**
> **ARNOLD KING (1939-1997)**
> **for times remembered. This bench marks that event and is to be enjoyed**
> **by all, as this jazzman could not bear to see an empty seat.**

THE JUBILEE JAZZ BAND

When Paul Bonner bought his first trumpet from Mike Mounter in 1971, little did he think that one day he would earn his living as a busy full-time musician on the London jazz scene. After running a small hotel in Wales for a few years, Paul moved back to Brighton, where I remember him sitting-in with my band at The Northern in London Road. This, he tells me, was the first time he played in public! Soon after this he was asked to join Bill Polley's New Eagle band at the Adur Social Club in Shoreham and he also enlisted as a member of Captain Roy Martin's `Bonfire Army' with the Expedient Brass Band.

The Jubilee Jazz Band was formed in 1977 and played at the Fortune of War on Brighton sea front. The band evolved from the Barry Lewis Jazzmen, who had sustained a year-long Saturday night residency at The Lamb in Lewes and then moved on to the Fortune of War. But Lewis wanted to give a full commitment as the new drummer with the busy New City Jazzmen. A capable replacement was needed and Paul Bonner relates how the Fortune of War lived up to its name when it transpired that the bar manager was an experienced, albeit slightly rusty drummer who had played in the past with the Clyde Valley Stompers. "This, of course, was Ken White. He was an old hand with much show business experience, and he turned out to be an extremely able replacement for Barry."

A new name was needed. Bass player Mike "Abbo" Adams suggested the Jubilee Jazz Band – prompted by the silver jubilee celebrations that year. The line-up then was Paul (trumpet), Roy Leith (alto sax), Mike Collier (trombone), Ray Schooley

The cover of THE JUBILEE JAZZ BAND's skilfully marketed LP record "Making Tracks", recorded in 1980.
TED AMBROSE took the pictures of the band aboard a Volks Railway train on Brighton seafront. Pictured left to
right are: PAUL BONNER (trumpet), MIKE COLLIER (trombone), KEN WHITE (drums), ROY LEITH (alto),
VIV BONNER (singer), MIKE AINSCOUGH (banjo), DAVE GIBB (bass), SLUFF HAZELL (baritone).

COURTESY OF PAUL BONNER

(banjo), Mike Adams and later Dave Gibb (bass), Ken White (drums) and Paul's wife Viv on vocals. Godfrey "Sluff" Hazell was on baritone sax. "Sluff" is a corruption of Slough, this versatile musician's hometown.

The band also started a record-breaking pub gig – by local standards, anyway – of weekly Sunday lunchtime sessions at The Adur at Hove Lagoon. This lasted for all of ten years and was extremely successful, with parents able to bring their children along to enjoy the music – hopefully opening a few young ears to jazz. Unhappily, this residency came to a sudden end when an off-duty copper dropped in one morning, was appalled to see all the families having a good time and promptly shopped the landlord!

The incident did little harm to the band, however, as they started regular nights at the King and Queen and, in 1980, recorded an LP at the Fox and Hounds, Haywards Heath. This was issued on the Flyright label under the title `Making Tracks' and featured splendid photographs taken by Ted Ambrose of the band members on a Volks Railway train on Brighton beach.

Viv Bonner was a great organiser as well as singer, and she fixed many guest jazzmen to appear with the Jubilee band, including George Chisholm, Nat Gonella, Humphrey Lyttelton and Joe Lee Wilson. A notable event organised by Viv was a gala evening at Hove Town Hall on October 17, 1979 starring Humphrey Lyttelton and his Band, American singer Joe Lee Wilson – then domiciled locally – and the Jubilee band. Before breaking-up in the late 1980s, the band made two concert tours of Holland. Paul then went on to find musical pastures new in the `Big Smoke'.

THE MC BAND

Formed in 1983 to play on Monday nights at the then Sea-house in Middle Street,

MIKE COLLIER led the MC JAZZ BAND during the 1980s. Its demise was signalled when clarinettist KEITH SLADE left Brighton for a 12-year spell in the West Country, and MIKE COLLIER emigrated to France in 1989. The band played regularly at the KING AND QUEEN, where it is pictured in 1985. JOHN MUXLOW is the drummer, ROY BOWER is on trumpet and TERRY WHITNEY on piano.

PICTURE BY COURTESY OF BEN COLLIER

Brighton, the MC Band also appeared at a concert at the Pavilion Theatre in May that year – the personnel being Mike Collier (leader and trombone), Roy Bower (trumpet, Pete Godfrey (piano), Keith Slade (clarinet and eccentric vocals), Alan Kennington (bass) and John Muxlow (drums). Later in 1983 they supplied the backing for ex-Basie tenor player Buddy Tate at a concert that I promoted in the upstairs function room of the King and Queen. The band eventually became a regular attraction there, alternating on Thursday nights with the Anderida Jazz Band. By then Terry Whitney (piano) and Roy Leith (reeds) were part of the line-up. As part of the annual Brighton Jazz Festival in the late 1980s the MC Band accompanied guests Yank Lawson (twice), Roy Williams and Humphrey Lyttelton at the King and Queen.

Another weekly gig which the band landed was at Chaplin's Bar on the sea front and they twice played at the annual French "Jam Potatoes" festival in Dieppe, alongside the Dutch Swing College and Kenny Ball bands. Mike Collier occasionally showed an abrasive side to his character and once, while playing at the King and Queen, he had an argument with a certain banjoist, whom I feel should remain anonymous. This tiff ended up with the banjo player refusing to play behind any of Mike's solos, leaving him only without any harmonic backing for the remainder of the evening.

When Mike emigrated to France in 1989 the band kept going into 1990, with Roy Leith and Neil Buckley (tenor) filling out the front line but sadly the band folded when the management at the King and Queen decided to change their music policy, leaving them without a regular session.

Tragically, in 1999, Mike had an accident and died at his home in France at the age of 69. There is now a seat dedicated to his memory in St Nicholas's Churchyard, Brighton. The story of how this came about is told in Chapter 15.

THE NEW CITY JAZZMEN

The Crawley-based New City Jazzmen have played many gigs in the Brighton area since the late 1950s. One of the longest-established traditional jazz bands in the country, the personnel has remained basically the same over the years, with Bernard

WHERE YOU FOUND SUSSEX JAZZ – IN 1980

Mike Collier, in his role as a presenter for BBC Radio Brighton (and later Radio Sussex), became a doughty champion of Sussex jazz and a valuable purveyor of publicity for events and regular sessions.

Mike compiled a fascinating "snapshot" of jazz activity in the county in May 1980 for the magazine **Jazz Journal** entitled **"Jazz Is Where You Find It".** The magazine gave it a double-page spread, with pictures of **Geoff Simkins,** the band led by his father Benny, and the **Jubilee Jazz Band**

In the Brighton and mid-Sussex area alone there was plenty going on: On Mondays, the **Jazz Four** were at **The Cat,** West Hoathly and the **New City Jazzmen** were at the Crawley Leisure Centre. On Tuesdays the **Kansas City Five** with **Mike Mounter** on trumpet were at the Lewes Arms in Lewes. The following night the **New Panama Jazz Band** (again with Mounter on trumpet) were at the **Northern Hotel** in Brighton, whilst **Geoff Simkins' Quartet** were at the **Shoreham Airport Bar.** Thursdays found the **Anderida Jazz Band** at the **King's Head,** Burgess Hill (as well as presenting occasional Sunday guest star nights at the **Fox and Hounds,** Haywards Heath), and on the same night the **Jubilee Jazz Band** were resident at the **King and Queen.** Fridays were quiet with the **Jubilee Band** planning a residency at the **Red Lion,** Ashington. Saturdays were earmarked as the day to catch the **Expedient Brass Band** playing at fetes and Bonfire Night events.

Sunday was the big day for jazz in the area, with the **Jubilee Jazz Band** holding forth at the Adur, Hove Lagoon, at lunchtimes. In the evening the **Stane Street Jazzmen** were at the **Robin Hood,** Shripney, **Harry Strutters Hot Rhythm Orchestra** was at **Shoreham Airport,** and the **Benny Simkins Band** at the **King and Queen** in Brighton.   **Ed.**

Hodgson (trumpet), Ron Westcott (trombone), Chris Jaques (clarinet), Mike Godfrey (piano), Alan Kennington (bass), Brian Nicholls and Sluff Hazell (banjo) and Barry Lewis (drums) among its long-term members. Bernie even claims to have given the young Pat Halcox his first tuition on trumpet!

The New City Jazzmen celebrated their unique longevity with a 40th birthday party at the Civic Hall, Crawley on September 20, 1997, an event attended by jazz musicians from all over Sussex. And in the spring of 2002 Bernard Hodgson published a handsomely illustrated 83-page book entitled *The New City Jazzmen:The Story* in time for the 45th birthday. The list of musicians who have deputised in the band is a veritable Who's Who of Sussex jazz.

The band has performed at venues as diverse as the Grand Hotel in Brighton on one hand and HM Prison, Lewes, on the other. With reference to the latter, Mike Godfrey, the band's diarist noted that "the atmosphere, and particularly the smell, would ensure the band's good behaviour for ever after". One night at the Devil's Dyke Hotel, the drummer had his backside bitten by the landlord's Alsatian, and was paid an extra ten shillings for the necessary trouser repairs. Was this dog a jazz lover we wonder? The band has a regular yearly booking at the St Patrick's Night celebrations in a Hove church, where, I am told, nuns and priests can be seen jiving to the New City's irresistible beat.

THE NEW EAGLE JAZZ BAND / RHYTHM KINGS : BACK O'TOWN STOMPERS

The link between the three bands named above is ex-glider pilot, racing motorcyclist and drummer-bandleader Bill Polley. When Bill decided to take up the drums at the age of 40, there were some folk who said he was too old to learn an instrument, but after a few basic lessons from Geoff Simkins – a drummer in those days – and from Sammy Bryant, he started his own band, the New Eagle Jazz Band [*once advertised, in a now legendary typographical error, as the New Evil Jazz Band – Ed.*]. Bill's reckoning was that, by starting music comparatively late in life, he hadn't much time to spare, so to form his own band seemed the quickest way to progress. He believes that this move gave him empathy for others like himself who needed a chance to play with a band. As a result he was able to give several musicians their first blow in public. Some of them have gone on to become professionals.

The New Eagle's first gig was at The Aldrington pub in Portland Road, Hove, on Thursday 12 June 1969. Alex Coughtrey was on trumpet, Jim Fryer on soprano sax (later Jack Sherriff on clarinet), Roy Osborne on trombone, Bernie Cottam on banjo, John Hearn on piano, Mike "Abbo" Adams on bass and, of course, Bill on drums. Over the next few years they played jobs all over Brighton, at venues such as the Pier Hotel, the Bird's Nest and The Gloucester, and had the odd broadcast on Radio Brighton. Around this period (1970) they were the band chosen to open the prestigious all-star jazz concert at the Dome, which also featured the Alex Welsh band, blues singer-pianist Champion Jack Dupree, and the Fourteen Foot Band with Danny Moss and Jeanie Lambe.

As well as bringing jazz back to the Fox and Hounds at Haywards Heath, Bill's band has played many eventful private engagements. A case in point was the gig one summer when they were hired to play at a riverside party in Beeding. It appears that the real ale for the band was being provided by the bucketful, and the bass player – who had got well-trousered – fell into the Adur, having to play the rest of the party with badly cut fingers, the result of hauling himself out of the river! I'm told that he carried on without a murmur of pain, proving what an anaesthetic real ale can be!

Following a few personnel changes, it was decided to change the name to the New Eagle Rhythm Kings, or NERKS as they were affectionately nicknamed. Arnie King on trumpet, Andre Eugene on piano and Mike Collier on trombone all joined the band. The NERKS played at the late Wally Vaughan's Fortune of War on Brighton sea front on Saturday nights and Sunday lunchtimes for the best part of two years – only breaking up when Wally sold the pub. After a gap of two years, during which he was involved in various business ventures, Bill decided to return to the music world, and the Back O'Town Stompers were duly born. The new line-up featured Arnie King on trumpet (later Geoff Pilgrim), Paul Hartman on clarinet and saxes, John Davidson on trombone, Dave Cummings on banjo and Abbo and Bill from the original NERKS band. They commenced playing at The Gay Highlander in Peacehaven, at the Thomas A'Becket in Worthing and at yet another new venue, The Stag in Kemp Town.

The 2002 line-up is Bill Phelan (trumpet), Paul Hartman (clarinet), Abbo Adams (bass), Dave Cummings (banjo) and Bill (drums). Bill Phelan switches to trombone when Mike Mounter guests with the band on trumpet. At the time of writing, the Stompers play monthly at the Downs Hotel, Woodingdean.

THE PANAMA JAZZ BAND

The Panama Jazz Band was originally formed by drummer/piano tuner Guy Fenton from one of his earlier aggregations, the Luvovadur Jazz Band. Following Guy's departure to the West Country in 1977, the band evolved into the "New" Panama Jazz Band.

After a spell at Shoreham Airport it was reported in the *Mid-Sussex Times* in January 1980 that the band was dropping the "New" appellation and re-forming to play at the Northern in London Road, Brighton, with Gerry Geoghegan switching from clarinet to banjo, Brian Hills joining as the new reed man, Ron Westcott from the New City Jazzmen taking over the trombone chair, and old hands Mike Mounter (trumpet), John Boyett (bass) and Brian Rickard (drums) remaining.

Clarinettist Jack Gilbert, who moved to Sussex in 1975, sat in and deputised with the band when not touring with Max Collie's Rhythm Aces, and, after leaving Collie following a three-month tour of the USA, he eventually took over the leadership in 1984-85. The line-up was then Mike Mounter (trumpet), Ron Westcott (trombone), Gerry Geoghegan (banjo), John Boyett (bass) and Ken White (drums).

The Panama band, having started out at The Northern, ended up with a very long residency at the King and Queen. George Walker re-joined on banjo and vocals, replacing Gerry Geoghegan. Following the sad death of Ken White, the drum chair

THE PANAMA JAZZ BAND pictured at THE KING AND QUEEN, Brighton, soon after Jack Gilbert joined the band in the early 1980s. He took over the leadership in 1984-5. Left to right: GERRY GEOGHEGAN (banjo), JACK GILBERT (clarinet), KEN WHITE (drums), MIKE MOUNTER (trumpet), JOHN BOYETT (bass) and RON WESTCOTT (trombone).

PICTURE BY COURTESY OF JACK GILBERT

JUMPIN' JACK GILBERT'S PANAMA JAZZ BAND pictured at one of their monthly appearances for the MID-SUSSEX JAZZ CLUB at the Clair Hall, Haywards Heath, circa 1999. Left to right: GEORGE WALKER (banjo), RON WESTCOTT (trombone), BARRY LEWIS (drums), MALCOLM WALTON (trumpet), JACK GILBERT (clarinet), JOHN BOYETT (bass).

PICTURE BY COURTESY OF JACK GILBERT

was taken over for a while by Malc Murphy, and later by Paul Norman, before Barry Lewis became the regular drummer. Barry first made his mark in the mid-1970s, leading the Stornoway Jazz Band at the Gay Highlander, Peacehaven, then later the Barry Lewis Jazz Band – which evolved into the Jubilee Jazz Band. In combining membership of the New City Jazzmen (which he joined in 1976) and the Panama band, Barry has become one of the busiest jazz drummers in the South. He also plays with the New Orleans Echoes Jazz Band

In the early 1980s, Jack Gilbert started the Mid Sussex Jazz Club and began to promote regular monthly concerts at the Clair Hall, Haywards Heath. Featuring the Panama with guest musicians such as the late Ben Cohen, Geoff Cole and Sammy Rimington, these events became very popular.

In the 1990s, with Jumpin' Jack's dynamic playing a defining feature, the Panama Band began to gain national recognition and to play at jazz clubs and festivals within an 80-mile radius. This, unfortunately, caused a few problems within the band, as some of the chaps had day jobs. In the late 1990s Mike Mounter had to leave and was replaced by Malcolm Walton on trumpet, and its members became reluctant to travel too far. Although Jack had been dogged by illness, the band remained busy on the wider jazz club circuit. But he lost his battle against cancer in October 2002.

Another of Jack's talents was as a clarinet and saxophone teacher. He worked at a local school with its own reading jazz band. One of his pupils, Adrian Cox – still a teenager at the time of writing – is now making a name for himself playing professionally with the Richard Bennett Jazz Band and helping to keep traditional jazz alive for the future.

THE SOUTH COAST STOMPERS

Another drummer-led band, the South Coast Stompers, started stomping at The Sheffield Arms, near the Bluebell Line – the well-known preserved steam railway. This was then a virgin venue, as no jazz of any kind had ever been played there up to that time. Don McMurray has a gift for boldly going where no band has gone before, having also instigated sessions at the Star of Brunswick, the Albion, the Alexander Hotel, the Berwick Arms and even at Horatio's Bar at the end of Palace Pier, as well

Clad in boaters and blazers, the SOUTH COAST STOMPERS cast off to provide
entertainment at Henley Regatta in 1990. Left to right: ANDY WOON (trumpet), BRIAN HILLS (reeds),
MIKE BELL (bass), DON MCMURRAY (drums), BILL PARSONS (banjo).

PICTURE BY COURTESY OF DON MCMURRAY

as fixing bands for two tours of Germany.

Among the local musicians Don has employed over the years are Andy Woon, Paul Bonner and Mike Mounter (trumpet); Fats Baxter and, occasionally, Sid Bailey (trombone); Brian Hills, John Goodrick and Terry Giles (clarinet); Alan Kennington, Gerry Higgins and Paul Whitten (bass); Jim Heath and Allan Sokell (sousaphone); Tony Shapiro (guitar); Bill Parsons, George Walker and Dave Cummings (banjo); and Pete Godfrey, Bob Mitchell and Paul Ward (piano).

When on holiday in New Orleans in 1992, Don met Leroy Jones, who was playing trumpet with a band in one of the bars on Bourbon Street. Don gave him his card and Leroy promised to ring if ever he came to England. A few weeks later Don got a call. Leroy was in town, playing with the Harry Connick Jnr. band at the Brighton Centre. At the time the South Coast Stompers were playing at the Yacht Club in Ship Street and Don invited Leroy down for a blow after the show. At 10.30pm he arrived with two trombone players – Craig Cline and Lucien Barbarin (Paul Barbarin's grandson) – plus the drummer Shannon Powell. I am told that the jamming went on until 2.30 in the morning – truly a session to remember.

Don seems to have established himself as the resident bandleader for the Hilton Group in Brighton and still organises trios and quartets for regular Sunday brunches at the Bedford, West Pier and Metropole Hotels.

THE SUSSEX TRUGS

The founding of the new University of Sussex in 1961 offered promising prospects for augmented jazz activity in the Brighton area. By 1966 there were about 3000 students and 300 academic and support staff. The students were more interested in rock music, although small minorities followed modern or avant-garde jazz. It fell to the academic staff to plant a flag for the classic traditional, Dixieland and swing styles of jazz.

In the vanguard was John Postgate, professor of microbiology, who played cornet and later soprano saxophone. He and Roger Taylor, pianist and chemistry lecturer, assembled a staff band named – by Taylor – the Sussex Trugs.

With them were John Rohl (clarinet), Ian Scott (tenor saxophone), Richard Veasey (bass), Jim Warren (guitar) and Ken Baker (drums). They played mostly at senior common room, departmental and private parties. In the early 1980s, weekly lunchtime sessions at the University's Gardner Centre attracted a wider audience They moved on to a more regular venue at the sports pavilion, which served drinks and snack meals, and for the next 14 years played there on Friday lunchtimes in term time, sometimes attracting substantial audiences.

Of the founder members only Postgate and Rohl stayed the course for all of the group's 33-year history. Later recruits included Bryn Bridges (piano), Graham Pratt (drums), David Dyker (guitar) and, from the University of Brighton, Paul Hartman (reeds). Dyker, a reader in economics, took over as leader when Postgate retired from the academic staff in 1987. Postgate continued to play with the band and to write knowledgeably about jazz for such publications as *Jazz Monthly* and *Jazz Journal*.

Other musicians deputised or sat-in with the Trugs, including representatives from the Brighton jazz scene such as Sid Bailey (trombone), Jack Sherriff (clarinet). Two members of the Back O'Town Stompers were regulars during the Trugs' last decade – Mike "Abbo" Adams (bass) and Bill Polley (drums).

Lunchtime audiences dwindled after the pavilion's catering facilities were pared down and the Trugs lost their venue in 1998 when the pavilion closed. Their last gig was at a party in 1999.

THE VINTAGE HOT FIVE

Formed relatively recently, in April 1993, the Vintage Hot Five's regular job is at Maxim's Winebar in Eastbourne on Sunday nights, a residency that entered its 10th year in 2002. The main mover behind this band is leader and fixer Andy Woon, Brighton-born, and an Army-trained cornet player, violinist and Clifford Brown enthusiast who has latterly come to embrace the disparate styles of both Louis Armstrong and Bix Beiderbecke. To Andy's sight-reading and transcribing expertise has been added the cornucopian knowledge, gained during nearly 50 years in music, of Brian Hills, a 78 rpm record and gramophone collector who also pays clarinet and all the saxophones, including the rarely-heard bass sax. These two musicians have harnessed their contrasting but complementary styles – along with Bill Parsons (banjo), Roger Hooper (sousaphone) and the skill of John Muxlow, honed by many years behind the drums – to produce a group that pays tribute to the classic styles of jazz with accuracy and some mild humour.

This combination started packing the people in and made a name for the band in the area, all of which led them to produce two CDs of their music, which they sell at

Immaculate in their tuxedos, **THE VINTAGE HOT FIVE**, resident at **MAXIM'S RESTAURANT** in Eastbourne since 1993, are pictured here at the **CONCORDE CLUB**, Eastleigh in 2001. Left to right: **BILL PARSONS** (banjo), **BRIAN HILLS** (reeds), **JOHN MUXLOW** (drums), **ANDY WOON** (trumpet) and **ROGER HOOPER** (sousaphone).

PICTURE BY COURTESY OF ANDY WOON

their public and private gigs. The latter have included engagements at Pinewood Film Studios, the Fishmongers' Hall in London and book launches for Gardner's every year – where they enlisted no less a person than Maureen Lipman as their number one groupie! Andy informs me that the band has a repertoire of 466 numbers, but then again he might only be blowing his own trumpet!

When the Ralph Fiennes film *The End of The Affair* was being made in Brighton, Andy got the job of providing a band for one of the scenes down by the Palace Pier. Apparently the actors' union, Equity, has an agreement with the Musicians Union that genuine musicians must be used on movies, even if they are not actually playing! Andy gathered together Carl Spencer, Gerry Smith, Jim Heath, Bill Harvey, Brian Hills, Don McMurray and a few other musicians. As the film was set in the 1940s, they all had to have their hair cut in the style of the period and were measured for, and kitted-out in, semi-military uniforms, complete with big boots! They then spent twelve hours hanging about, and miming along to a brass band tape, on a little band-stand built out on one of the jetties. Alas, it all ended up on the cutting-room floor and none of them are seen, or heard, in the finished picture as shown in the cinemas. However, they did get well paid for their efforts.

RADIO DAZE

Keith Slade, the former clarinet player with the Riverside Jump Band, had a proper job as a presenter and producer on BBC Radio Brighton – as it once was – and started giving Ted Ambrose and Mike Collier short spots on his Sunday morning shows.

Eventually Mike got his own programme. As well as playing the latest jazz discs, Mike was able to interview many American jazz visitors, chatting to Bud Freeman, Benny Morton, Al Casey, Bob Wilber, Billy Butterfield, Dick Cary, Adelaide Hall and Dick Wellstood. I'm sure they were all glad to be on air with somebody who knew what he was talking about.

Radio Brighton evolved into Radio Sussex and later this slot was taken over by Julian Rose, who had been Mike's producer. Julian introduced a popular programme called *Jazz Profiles* in which he invited local jazzers to come along and talk about their favourite musicians. Unfortunately, due to shifts in the hierarchy and policy of the BBC, the station changed its name to Southern Counties Radio and jazz was shown the proverbial door. In 1983, over on the commercial station Southern Sound (now Southern FM), which was based in Portslade, drummer John Muxlow started a two-hour (6pm to 8pm) jazz record programme on Saturday evenings. As the station had only a tiny jazz record section, he had to use discs from his own collection, coupled with what he could borrow from the local public libraries. Against all odds he still produced an eagerly anticipated, varied and interesting show. Called *Razzamajazz* – not John's idea, I can assure you – the programme was very conveniently timed, coming as it did right after Radio Three's *Jazz Record Requests*, which gave the dedicated listener three whole hours of jazz on the airwaves on Saturday evenings. After a year the show was cut down to one hour on a Sunday and was also networked with Radio Mercury, which broadcast to north Sussex. However, in this reduced format it lasted only one more year, when it too was knocked on the head!

ADRIAN COX

As the son of banjo player Graham Cox, Adrian was influenced, from an early age, by his father's love of traditional jazz and was often taken out to pubs and clubs to hear various bands. In 1991, when he was eight years old, Adrian was given a second-hand clarinet for Christmas but it wasn't until he reached the age of 12 that he became interested in having lessons. He did not wish to have clarinet tuition at school, so local clarinet maestro Jack Gilbert was contacted with a view to giving Adrian lessons. Jack's contagious enthusiasm for the music made learning fun and Adrian's own leaning towards jazz soon became very clear.

The following year he started playing with the Institute Jazz Band at Copthorne and also alongside his dad in the Clayton Jazz Band. It was while he was sitting-in with the Panama Jazz Band at a Butlin's jazz festival that Adrian was heard by Martin Bennett, the trombonist with the Phil Mason band. Martin had two sons who were forming a young band in Devon at that time, and they needed a clarinet player. When Adrian left school in 1999 at the age of 15 he played his first gig with the Richard Bennett's New Orleans Jazz Band at Farnham Maltings. Adrian soon moved to the West Country and now travels with the band around the UK jazz clubs as well as in Europe. Later, whenever they met, Jack Gilbert was always proud to sit in with his star pupil.

CHAPTER 14

THE BIG PARADE

ROY MARTIN

Roy Martin *is the parade marshal of Sussex jazz, leading the Expedient Brass Band for more than 30 years. Three generations of Sussex jazz musicians have marched to the beat of the bass drum of this former Mayor of Polegate. The Expedient band grew out of the strong base for traditional jazz established in Hastings by the success of the Dolphin Jazz Band between 1955 and 1963. The Dolphin band's natural successors, The Jazz Caverners, are now led by Roy on banjo and continue to prosper under his leadership. Trombonist Brian Towers, still active as a bandleader and resident in Toronto in 2002, was a key member of the Dolphin Jazz Band, and after its disbandment formed the Jazz Caverners with Dolphin stalwarts Chris Watford (clarinet), Ted Bishop (piano) and Geoff Coates (banjo). They recruited two Eastbourne musicians, Pete Kitcher ((trumpet) and Ian Scriven (bass). Brian recalls that "although we already had Geoff Coates on banjo, the Eastbourne guys had no transport, so we took on Roy Martin on second banjo because he had a van, didn't drink and didn't mind driving all over God's half-acre dropping off sleepy and semi-inebriated jazz musicians. As an added bonus he owned PA equipment, which he loaned to the new band. My stage appellation for Roy in those days was 'Hastings' youngest teenager' - even though he was the daddy of the band! After running the Caverners for 6 years from 1963 I left for Canada in 1969 and Roy took over the leadership and management."*

This background will help clarify the chronology and the characters as Roy Martin tells the story of the Expedient Brass Band - which has included in its ranks many members of the Brighton Jazz Line. Roy's narrative is taken from a taped memoir recorded in March 2000, transcribed by Sid Bailey and summarised by Keith Samuel.

THE STORY OF THE EXPEDIENT BRASS BAND starts in the late 1960s. There was a certain amount of animosity between the jazz bands in Brighton and Hastings in those days. So I decided that one way of restoring the balance was to form a street band, extracting members from the different bands along the

ROY MARTIN, the parade marshal of Sussex jazz, pictured in 2002. Banjo-player, drummer, singer and a former major of Polegate, Roy is the leader of the JAZZ CAVERNERS as well as the EXPEDIENT BRASS BAND.

PICTURE BY COURTESY OF ROY MARTIN

coast, so that there could be a better exchange of views and we could have a bit of fun as well!

Chris Watford (Wattie), said, "Aw you'll never do that", and of course that spurred me on a bit more. So I got this group together, some of them pretty good players. others just enthusiasts who wanted to have a go. We set out to produce a 12-piece band, which included, three trombones, three trumpets, three reeds, sousaphone, snare drum and bass drum. Very ambitious. But those were the days when people did things just for the fun of it.

The fee we charged then was just five bob! This was very affordable, and we soon infiltrated the Sussex Bonfire Society processions. On Saturday nights from the end of August, we used to work our way through all these villages, ending up on the 5th of November at Lewes.

One of the earliest members was Pete Davies (PD). He also used to play for me in a quartet that we had in Hastings, the Old Town Stompers. PD played snare drum, and the late Ian Scriven played bass drum. Pete Treger played first trumpet, and Pete Kitcher was second, a very good player in his day with the Jazz Caverners.

I think Brian Towers came in on trombone at a later date, but we had one or two other early trombone players, including a chap called Tex O'Neill.

The Expedient's first rehearsal was quiet interesting. Where the hell do you rehearse a 12 - piece street band? Some bright spark suggested we go down to the Pevensey Marshes, and try marching around in a field there. The ground there is pretty uneven. So we had all these characters marching around to *When the Saints Go*

ROY MARTIN is missing from this mid-1960s shot of the EXPEDIENT BRASS BAND as it prepares to parade at Polegate.
Back row, left to right: TONY PYKE (clarinet), JOHNNY GRIFFITHS (Eb horn), JOHN BOYETT (sousaphone), PETE KITCHER (trumpet), PETE TREGER (trumpet), ALAN WHITMORE (bass drum) TEX O'NEILL (trombone), unknown (trombone) and PETE DAVIES (snare drum).
Front row, BRIAN HILLS (alto) and TED OWEN (Eb clarinet).

PICTURE BY COURTESY OF BRIAN HILLS

Marching In and falling over hummocks now and again. It was quite a carry on. The cows down there seemed very enthusiastic about it and they all gathered around to watch us, occasionally joining in with the odd "moo".

The first gig I can recall was for the Polegate carnival. I've never seen so much rain in all my life. It absolutely teemed down; we all got soaking wet. We marched from the old railway station, up through the village, to the recreation ground, finishing the afternoon in the beer tent.

We progressed from there to carnivals at Hastings, Brighton and Haywards Heath. In that period we became very much in demand, because there didn't seem to be anything like us about, and we made quite an impact.

By that time, John Boyett became our star sousaphone player. John's sense of humour is marvellous and we had some pretty good laughs out of him. I remember once he was riding in my Hillman Minx, like the ones the RAF had with the sliding roof, and all sorts of extras. We arrived at a pedestrian crossing at Bexhill, and this very attractive young lady decided to cross in front of us. John Boyett removed the mouthpiece from his sousaphone, poked it up through the open roof and using it as a sort of loud hailer, shouted "Well done madam, well done, excellent!" She beat a hasty retreat.

Simon Medhurst (Min) was one of the characters that played in the reed section. Once in Littlehampton, Min, in one of his wilder moments, got annoyed with the fire engine that was following us. It kept blowing its very loud hooter and disrupting the

This early 1960s turn-out by the EXPEDIENT BRASS BAND includes most of the key members
of the DOLPHIN JAZZ BAND in Hastings as well as a small Brighton contingent.
Left to right: TEX O'NEILL (trombone and beer bottle), BRIAN TOWERS (trombone), PETE DAVIES (snare drum),
TED OWEN (clarinet), ALAN WHITMORE (bass drum), CHRIS WATFORD (alto sax), PETE TREGER (trumpet),
JOHNNY GRIFFITHS (Eb horn), JOHN BOYETT (sousaphone) and a be-medalled ROY MARTIN (leader).

PICTURE BY JOHN POWYS, COURTESY OF CHRIS WATFORD

music. Min thought that he would remedy the situation, so he picked up two of the bonfire procession flaming torches and put them on the bonnet of the fire engine. I've never seen a fire engine stop so quickly, the firemen leapt out and put it out. Min was then collared by a special constable, and it took me about 20 minutes to talk him out of being arrested.

The original bass drummer was the bass player Ian Scriven, who sadly died at 38 of a ghastly neurotic disease. He was a fine bass drummer, he really swung the band along, and he literally danced with the bass drum as he was going along. We all miss old Ian, he was a good lad.

Nowadays I play the bass drum whereas I used to lead as a sort of master of ceremonies in front with a little baton, which was made out of a length of tubing with two walking stick ends. It was a very useful thing on Lewes Bonfire Night because in those days it was not so tame as it is now. There used to be some aggression from bikers who tried to break up the procession. I would wade in with this thing; it was quite a handy weapon.

We now run in a format of 10, which is 2 trombones, 3 reeds (at present tenor and alto sax and clarinet) 2 trumpets but sometimes we revert to 3 trumpets and two reeds. But I do think that the format of 3 reeds and 2 trumpets (if you've got 2 good strong ones) is a better one, it balances the overall sound of the band out.

I thought deeply about the name of the band in the early days, and tried to think of something that sounded like the names that the boys in New Orleans used. There were names like the Excelsior and The Olympia, and it just occurred to me that the Expedient Brass Band was a name that sounded like them but was original.

There are so many faces that used to play with us that have sadly passed away or disappeared. We used to get a lot of people that were quite big names from the Bilk and Barber bands. They would come down just for the fun of it. I recall that Sammy Rimington sat in with us one day. Mike Pointon used to play with us a lot then, because he is a friend of PD's. PD has moved away to the West Country, so we don't see that much of him now. And Mike Collier used to play for me on trombone for a long period of time. I remember dear old Amby (Ted Ambrose) who played trumpet in the seventies with me, another one who has sadly left us. Amby and Mike Collier were great friends, and were very much into Ley lines and things like that; they used to spend weekends tracing these Ley lines. They were both pretty intelligent lads who liked a challenge.

I have always been a sort of father figure in running this band, as there has to be a compromise between being too soft and being firm about it. My proudest thing is to have sustained the Expedient band for such a long period of time. I hope the line keeps going on, as I'm in my mid 70s now and I often wonder what will happen when I go, whether anyone will take up the baton.

Leader ROY MARTIN is again missing from this mid-1960s shot of the EXPEDIENT BAND at Crowborough Bonfire Night parade. Back row, left to right: PETE CURTIS (banjo), JON FINCH (trombone), trumpeter TED AMBROSE in tropical headgear, MIKE COLLIER (trombone and cigarette), a youthful ALLAN SOKELL (sousaphone), TONY PYKE (alto), TED OWEN (clarinet), PETE TREGER (trumpet) and GERRY GEOGHEGAN (trumpet). Front: COLIN BOWDEN (bass drum), PETE DAVIES (snare drum).

PICTURE BY JOHN POWYS, COURTESY OF BEN COLLIER

The luxuriant hair-styles make it easy to date this picture from the mid-1970s. THE EXPEDIENT BRASS BAND did not win any awards for marching but their music was a hit with carnival crowds at Preston Park, Brighton, in July 1976. ROY MARTIN leads the parade and those identifiable beneath their parade caps and abundant locks and facial hair include GERRY BIRCH, ROD BROWN, MIKE COLLIER, PETE CURTIS, CHRIS HUNT, SIMON "MIN" MEDHURST, TED AMBROSE and JOHN BOYETT.

PICTURE BY COURTESY OF BEN COLLIER

Unfortunately there aren't any younger fellows in the band. I try and encourage young trumpet players , but the present education system doesn't help youngsters a lot to improvise jazz and do their own thing in that way, so consequently, there are not very many young ones coming up. Andy Woon plays in my band sometimes. He of course comes from a military background. He is one of the few people that can do a very good job of reading music and busk as well. You do find that there are buskers and there are readers, who can do one or the other, but when you find somebody that can do both you have a gem.

Coming up to date, only the big bonfire societies hire us now. To run a 10-piece band like this, it does add up when you are taking care of everybody's expenses in getting there. Some people in the Expedient come a long way. I have Mike Duckworth on trombone; he comes from Sutton in south London, so he has a long trip. Paul Bonner occasionally does it on trumpet. Paul is a busy boy in London now, but he likes to play with us.

At the moment I've got Linda Robins playing sousaphone for me. She's a good girl, and her husband Josh plays tenor. She's been playing for about ten years, an excellent sousaphone player. It amazes me how she puts up with all the nonsense, but she takes all the ribaldries, it's like water off a duck's back with her.

I've been trying to bring the band up to playing more of the modern day things. As the Expedient never gets a chance to rehearse, it stays on a staple diet of standards. In 1999 I went to New Orleans. I contacted Trevor Richards, who used to play for me when he was about 16 in the Hastings caves. He lives in New Orleans now; he's got his own quartet, and also plays drums with the Camelia Jazz Band. I stayed with him and he took me around and introduced me to all the people. I had heard a record of the Dirty Dozen Brass Band. They are a younger set carrying on the tradition, but have brought it up to date with more modern sounds. I was fortunate enough to hear them while I was there, and I was very impressed.

I was delighted to hear the Riverside Jump Band again in their millennium reunion at Lewes; it was nice to see so many people there from that way back period of good fun days, made it worth going to.

The Expedient did a week in Dieppe, France, in the 1970s. We played at a French/English exhibition. I had a bit of a problem (due to the language I suppose) they thought I was bringing two bands. What I did bring was the Expedient plus a few extra bods from the Jazz Caverners, so we could do stage work with the Caverners, and street work with the Expedient. We draped the sousaphone with the Union Jack, making it pretty plain that we were British. We were asked to parade through the aisles of a supermarket, and it was the only time I've ever seen the Expedient as a true marching band (It doesn't really march, a newspaper described it once as "the band that shuffles behind the rest of the Carnival")

Wearing elaborate uniforms, the EXPEDIENT band perform at an elevated level, circa 1979. Location unknown. ROY MARTIN is at the microphone.

PICTURE BY COURTESY OF BEN COLLIER

We are about the only jazz or street band that can handle Lewes Bonfire Night. There have been clever dicks from London who have come down, thinking they could do it. But usually they don't last very long once the old Lewes thunder flashes start flying about. It gets a bit hairy; you have to make sure there is a net over the sousaphone. Some of the crowd try to lob bangers down the spout of the sousaphone, and that can be pretty serious. Once somebody put one in Min's tenor sax at Rye, and wrote it off, it exploded inside the sax and split it from the inside. Fortunately he ended up with a new one, because it was insured.

Sid Bailey used to play for me on trombone from time to time, although he hasn't done for a little while. I think he did Lewes a few times. I saw Brian Hills recently; he was one of the original players in the Expedient. The last time I saw Arnie King was in 1997. He played at Lewes for me, played very well, but about two months after that he died. I miss him very much. One of the things about the Expedient that has been good is that there's always been a chain of friendship between the different bands and different people.

EXPEDIENT band members fortify themselves in preparation
for the LITTLEHAMPTON BONFIRE NIGHT PROCESSION, October 30, 1999.
Left to right:
PAUL HARTMAN, STEVE DAVIES, KEITH SAMUEL, LEO GOTLIFFE, BRIAN CRAIG, ANDY WOON, JOHN TANNER.
PICTURE BY COURTESY OF STEVE DAVIES

Footnote. GEOFF COATES, who played banjo with the DOLPHIN JAZZ BAND and the JAZZ CAVERNERS, now lives in Malaga and is working on a book about the story of traditional jazz in Hastings and East Sussex. He has exchanged research with the authors of this publication.

CHAPTER 15

CODA

KEITH SAMUEL

THE INSPIRATION FOR THIS BOOK has drawn impetus from a modest social get-together that takes place in Brighton roughly once a month under the banner of the Nederburg Luncheon Club.
The club has about 65 members and nearly all of them are Sussex jazz musicians of long standing. It was started in 1996 by bass player Alan Kennington and drummer John Muxlow when they retired from their daytime occupations. They were soon joined by John Boyett, George Walker, Allan Sokell and Jim Chambers. As word spread, enough musicians to form 10 bands joined the ranks – including pioneers such as Keith Slade and Terry Whitney.

Clearly, some of the communal spirit persists that enabled George Jones, and later Roy Martin, to gather together musicians from several Sussex jazz bands to form large, parade-style New Orleans marching bands.

Most of the Nederburg members are from Brighton and mid-Sussex but there is a strong contingent from West Sussex. Distinguished guests are sometimes invited. They have included Mick Mulligan, Dick Charlesworth, Campbell Burnap and Geoff Cole.

There are no quasi-Masonic rituals. The name of the club derives from the agreeable red South African wine that accompanies the meals served by attentive young catering students in the Pelham Restaurant (re-named The Gallery in late 2002) at Brighton College of Technology. This splendid establishment, near Brighton Station, is where most of the lunchtime gatherings are held.

Members who enjoy a glass of the eponymous Nederburg, and are also tempted to pause for refreshment at the Lord Nelson in Trafalgar Street, appreciate the opportunity to travel by train to these gatherings.

There are occasional forays to Chichester, usually to Roger Pocock's pub, the Bull's Head at Fishbourne – an establishment with its own niche in the history of Sussex jazz, also blessed with a nearby railway halt. Hostelries at Lewes and Cowfold are also visited from time to time.

Alan Kennington would modestly define the club's purposes as "eating, drinking and talking" but it has been the stimulus for a number of slightly more worthy activities.

Eight members of the 1960s Riverside Jump Band were reunited through the Nederburg club and were inspired to re-assemble the band for a one-off millennium performance at the Lewes Jazz Club in March 2000. This became an annual event, raising more than £2200 for charity.

More sadly, it was Alan Kennington's initiative, on behalf of the club, to raise the money to endow a wooden seat in the churchyard at St Nicholas Church in Brighton in memory of the Sussex Jazz Society's founder, Mike Collier. He died in 1999 just a few months after coming over from his retirement home in France to attend a Nederburg meeting.

An earlier precedent had been set with the dedication of a similar seat in the same churchyard in memory of Arnold King following his premature death in 1997.

The £750 cost of the Collier seat was raised by Nederburg members who contributed generously when Mike's record collection was auctioned at a well-attended meeting at the end of 1999.

The seat was dedicated at a service, attended by Mike's family, friends and many jazz colleagues, in September 2000. The inscription on the seat, located in the grounds

SUSSEX JAZZ MUSICIANS gathered en masse at the **BUSINESS CLUB** in Brighton in December 1999 for an auction to raise funds for the seat dedicated to **MIKE COLLIER** in St Nicholas's Churchyard. The initiative came from **ALAN KENNINGTON** and the members of the **NEDERBURG CLUB**. Recognisable from left to right are Barry Morgan, John Muxlow, Jim Heath, Keith Samuel, Bill Harvey, Piers Clark, Brian Hills, Robin Watt, John Boyett, Alan Kennington, Gerry Higgins, Jack Gilbert, Paul Bonner, Don Newbold, Terry Whitney, Trevor Philcox, John Collinson, George Walker, Peter Dorday, Keith Slade, John Davidson, Bernard Hodgson, George Bennett, Bill Phelan and Roger Pocock. Among those hidden are Andy Woon, Ron Westcott, Don McMurray, Roy Bower, and Bill Polley.

PICTURE BY COURTESY OF ALAN KENNINGTON

of Brighton's oldest church, close to Martha Gunn's tomb, reads:

MIKE COLLIER (1929-1999)
He loved life. He loved jazz. He loved this Church.
Presented in fond memory by his many friends in the jazz world.

The deaths of Keith Slade and Jack Gilbert occurred in the autumn of 2002 just as this book was reaching completion. Their fellow jazz musicians will wish to honour their achievements in a suitable manner.

Whatever diversities there may be in faith, all of the people who figure in this book share a common bond with Keith Slade, Jack Gilbert, Mike Collier and Arnie King in their love of life and their love of jazz.

And their collective story is far from complete. The achievements of 19-year-old clarinettist Adrian Cox described in Chapter 13 have more than a passing symbolism. The Brighton Jazz Line is not yet ready to hit the buffers.

Adrian (tutored by Jack Gilbert) and others still emerging, will be the standard bearers for jazz in the new century. And if the Brighton Jazz Line remains true to its traditions, their talent will be nurtured and championed by those that precede them.

By the time Sussex clarinettist ADRIAN COX
reached his 19th birthday in 2002,
he was already a seasoned professional musician.
He now lives in the West Country and is a member of
RICHARD BENNETT's NEW ORLEANS JAZZ BAND,
which features some of Britain's best young musicians
playing in the traditional jazz idiom.

PICTURE BY COURTESY OF GRAHAM COX

BRIGHTON JAZZ LINE
pioneer KEITH SLADE
pictured in August, 2000, two
years before his death.

PICTURE BY COURTESY OF KEITH SAMUEL

Family, friends and a big
contingent of jazz colleagues
gathered in
ST NICHOLAS CHURCHYARD
on September 12, 2000
for the unveiling of the seat
honouring the memory of
MIKE COLLIER.

PICTURE BY COURTESY OF TERRY SHEARING

MIKE COLLIER (left) pictured with
long-time friend and collaborator
TERRY WHITNEY on Mike's last
visit to Brighton in March 1998.

PICTURE BY COURTESY OF GEORGE BENNETT

NEDERBURG CLUB stalwarts sip in judgement on the latest shipment of this agreeable South African tipple at the Pelham
Restaurant, Brighton 1998. Left to right: GEORGE WALKER, BILL PHELAN, BILL HARVEY, SID BAILEY, JOHN GOODRICK and
GORDON WREN. Between them they play all the instruments required for an orthodox six-piece traditional jazz band.

PICTURE BY COURTESY OF GEORGE BENNETT

DISCOGRAPHY

BRIAN HILLS

BRIAN HILLS is a member of the VINTAGE HOT FIVE, and has played clarinet and saxophone with many of the leading Sussex bands. For this book, he has compiled this selective discography of commercially issued recordings made by Brighton and mid-Sussex jazz musicians and bands.

Les Jowett – A Tribute
12" LP -
Flyright FLY 217. Recorded Bradford - 1944/45, London - April 1951. and Brighton - August 19 or 20, 1957

Tracks:
Side A 1. Beale Street Blues
      2. House In Harlem For Sale *
      3. Jazz Me Blues
      4. Ain't Gonna Give Nobody None Of My Jelly Roll
      5. Mississippi Mud
      6. In A Mist
      7. A Monday Date
Side B 1. Louisiana **
      2. Footsteps In The Sand**
      3. Spain *
      4. Gee Ain't I Good To You
      5. It's Tight (Like That)
      6. Reefer Drag
      7. Gatemouth
      8. At The Jazz Band Ball

Personnel: Les Jowett-t; Fred Mitchell-cl; Les Newell-tb; Les Parkinson-g; Roy Edmondson-p; Frank Each-sb; Jack Scaife-d; (At The Jazz Band Ball) Bradford 1944/45.

Les Jowett-t/c; Cy Laurie-cl; Fred Hunt-p; Ron Dean-g; (Gatemouth - Reefer Drag) London April 1951.

Les Jowett-t/c; Stu Emsley-cl/as; Mike Collier-tb;

Bernie Waterman-p; Pat Benham-g; Roy Evenett-sb; Dickie Neaves-d; Brighton August 19 or 20 1957

(Lousiana - House In Harlem For Sale - Jazz Me Blues - Gee Baby Ain't I Good To You - Footsteps In The Sand - It's Tight (Like This) - Spain - I Ain't Gonna Give - Mississippi Mud - Beale St. Blues - A Monday Date)

Les Jowett-c; Stu Emsley-cl; Terry Whitney-p; Roy Evenett-sb; (In A Mist)
Notes from LP sleeve:-
All tracks are unissued apart from those marked * which were originally on '77 EP 12'. Tracks marked ** are alternative takes to those issued on that EP.

Note: Tracks B6, B7 and B8 have inferior sound quality as they were dubbed from the sole remaining acetates.

Damage to Side B Track 8 necessitated a fade.

Thanks to Doug Dobell, for use of his master tapes.
Remastered by: Ron Geesin - Product of Interstate Music Ltd.

The Dolphin Jazz Band
7" 45rpm EP
Title: 'The Dolphin Jazz Band' - VJM Records - VEP 12 Recorded in Kenton, Middlesex, December 17, 1961.

Tracks:
Side A 1. Sweet Lovin' Man
      2. Mandy Lee Blues
Side B 1. Thick Lip Stomp
      2. Parkway Stomp

Personnel: Pete Treger-c; Brian Towers-tb; Chris Watford-cl/as; John Collinson-p; Ted Bishop-bj; Johnny Griffiths-sb; Alan Whitmore-d;

The Original Downtown Syncopators
7" 45rpm EP
Title 'Original Downtown Syncopators Vol.1" - 'Soundwork' (no recording date information found)

Tracks:
Side A 1. Ostrich Walk
      2. Mournin' Blues
Side B 1. Jazz Me Blues
      2. Soudan

Personnel: Terry Parmenter-c; Bob Gordon-Walker-cl; Barry Dunning-tb; Cliff Mason-bj; Chris Gyoury-d; Recorded by: Soundwork Services, National House, 60-66 Wardour Street, London W.1.

7" 45rpm EP
Title 'It's Jass!' - Columbia SEG 8293
Recorded in London June 17, 1963

Tracks:
Side A 1. If You Knew Susie (vcl-Barry Dunning/Bob Gordon-Walker)

2. Blues My Naughty Sweetie Gives To Me (introducing: When My Baby Smiles At Me')
Side B 1. Some Of These Days (vcl-Bob Gordon-Walker)
2. Farewell Blues

Personnel: David Davis-c; Bob Gordon-Walker-cl; Barry Dunning-tb; Ron Geesin-p; Geoff Daley-d; Supervision: Denis Preston. Sleeve Design: Peter Leslie Recording first published 1964.

12" LP
Title: 'Jazz Panorama Of The Sixties' - VJM Records - VJM LC.6. containing among other tracks: (F) The Original Downtown Syncopators - Lasses Candy. Recorded in London Jan. 31, 1962. (G) The Jazz Caverners - Cole Smoak. recorded in London March 13,1966

The Indiana Jass Orchestra
7" 45 rpm EP
Title: 'The Indiana Jass Orchestra' (1965) John Hassell Recordings - HAS 609/610. Recorded at Pett Level Club, Hastings, June 1965 - limited edition of 200. (reviewed in 'Jazz Journal' September 1965)

Tracks:
Side A 1. Original Tuxedo Rag
2. Gone Daddy Blues
Side B 1. She's Forty With Me
2. Forty And Tight

Personnel: Mike Etherington-c; Brian Hills-as; Rodney Brown-cl; Pete Curtis-bj; John Edge-p; Allan Sokell-bb; Pete Davies-d; (Jack Pigott-tb added on 'Original Tuxedo Rag') (Jane Griffiths-v added on 'Gone Daddy Blues') (Brian Hills-cl/hot fountain pen; Ken Osborn-g; John Edge-p; on 'She's Forty With Me')

The Jazz Caverners
7" 45rpm EP
Title -'The Jazz Caverners' - Vintage Jazz Music Society Records - V.J.M. EC2
Recorded in London March 13, 1966.

Tracks:
Side A 1. Shout 'Em Aunt Tillie
2. Five Foot Two,Eyes Of Blue (v. Roy Martin)
Side B 1. Rickety Dan
2. Do Something (v. Geoff Coates)

Personnel: Pete Kitcher-t; Chris Watford-cl; Brian Towers-tb;Geoff Coates-bj/v; Roy Martin-bj/v; Ted Bishop-p; Ian Scriven-sb; Reg Lower-d; Engineer: J.H.J.Wadley Sleeve Design: Pete Kitcher

The Fourteen Foot Band
12" LP
Title - 'The Good Life' - 77 Records - 77LEU 12/33
Recorded at the 'Fox and Hounds' - Haywards Heath, Oct. 23, 1968

Tracks:
Side A 1. The Good Life
2. Special Delivery Stomp
3. I Want To Be Happy
4. I Want A Little Girl
5. Blue Lou
Side B 1. Squaty Roo
2. Stardust
3. You Can Depend On Me
4. Shine
5. Black Butterfly

Personnel: Ted Ambrose-t/v; Jack Jacobs-as; Danny Moss-ts; Mike Collier-tb; Terry Whitney-p; Alan Kennington-sb; Derek Middleton-d; Engineer: Don Sollash. Supervision: Doug Dobell Sleeve notes: Sam Edwards (Keith Samuel)

Ralph Sutton
12" LP
Title: 'Ralph Sutton - Live!' - Flyright FLY 204
(a CD was also issued - Flyright FLY CD 911-identical tracks). Recorded at the 'Fox and Hounds' - Haywards Heath, Sussex - Nov.16, 1975

Tracks:
Side A 1. Love Lies
2. Eye Opener
3. Echoes Of Spring
4. Morning Air
5. In The Dark

6. Viper's Drag
Side B 1. Cottage For Sale/Old Folks/T'aint So Honey, T'aint So
2. Honeysuckle Rose/Handful Of Keys//Somebody Stole My Gal
3. Ain't Misbehavin'/ Keeping Out Of Mischief Now/My Fate Is In Your Hands
4. I Found A New Baby

Recorded by: Ted Mechen Mastering By: Gem Recordings and Ron Geesin. Photo courtesy of Ralph Sutton. Sleeve Design & Artwork: W & M Etherington. Sleeve Notes: Sinclair Traill 1977 Released by exclusive arrangement with Ralph Sutton.

The New City Jazzmen
12" LP
Title: 'New Orleans To Crawley' - Fanfare Records FR 2093.
Recorded by Radio Crawley, at Civic Hall, Crawley - Nov. 15, 1974.

Tracks:
Side A 1.Travelling Blues
2. The Martinique
3. Working Man Blues
4. Chimes Blues
5. Maryland, My Maryland
Side B 1. Doctor Jazz
2. Mood Indigo
3. The Entertainer
4. Froggie Moore

Personnel: Bernard Hodgson-t; Chris Jaques-cl; Ron Westcott-tb; John Jaques-bj; Gavin Russell-p; Alan Kennington-sb; Paul Norman-d; Engineer: John Short

12" LP
Title: 'Going To Town' - Flyright FLY LP 203
Recorded March 14, 1976

Tracks:
Side A 1. Going To Town
2. Bourbon St. Parade
3. Memphis Blues
4. Dardanella
5. Jelly Bean Blues
6. Papa Dip
7. Perdido St. Blues

Side B
1. Big Bear Stomp
2. Blue Turning Grey Over You
3. Gatemouth
4. Savoy Blues
5. Saratoga Swing
6. Cushion Foot Stomp

Personnel: Bernard Hodgson-t; Chris Jaques-cl; Ron Westcott-tb; Brian Nicholls-bj; Mike Godfrey-p; Alan Kennington-sb; Paul Normand; Recording Engineer: Ron Geesin. Sleeve Notes: Bernard Hodgson.

12" LP
Title: 'To Be Collected' - Flyright FLY LP 206 Recorded at Pebble Beach Studios, Worthing, March 9, 1978.

Tracks:
Side A
1. Hiawatha Rag
2. Alexander's Ragtime Band
3. Wabash Blues
4. My Little Girl
5. Old Rugged Cross
6. Give Me Your Telephone Number
Side B
1. Muskrat Ramble
2. Blues For Jimmy
3. Yes, Yes In Your Eyes
4. Coquette
5. Candy Lips
6. At A Georgia Camp Meeting

Personnel: Bernard Hodgson-t/v; Chris Jaques-cl; Ron Westcott-tb; Brian Nicholls-bj; Mike Godfrey-p; Alan Kennington-sb; Barry Lewis-d; Sleeve Design: Ron Westcott, Gillian Hodgson. Sleeve Notes: Bernard Hodgson.

Benny Simkins Sextet
12" LP
Title: 'Linger Awhile' - Flyright FLY LP 202
Recorded at Ron Geesin Studios, Heathfield, Sussex (2 sessions) May 25 and June 22, 1975

Tracks:
Side A
1. Linger Awhile (b)
2. Haunting Blues (a)
3. 5.23 (a)
4. New Orleans (a)
5. California Here I Come (a)
Side B
1. Dear Old Southland (b)

2. What Am I Here For (a)
3. Mandy, Make Up Your Mind (a)
4. Anytime, Anyplace, Anywhere (b)
5. Swing That Music (a)

Personnel: Roy Bower-t; Benny Simkins-ts/cl; Geoff Hoare-tb;Pete Simkins-p; Alan Kennington-sb; Bernie Godfrey-d;

(a) May 25, 1975. (b) June 22, 1975 - Bob Williams replaces Alan Kennington on sb.

Billy Butterfield - with Benny Simkins Band
12" LP
Title 'Watch What Happens' - Flyright FLY LP 205
Recorded at Pebble Beach Studios, Worthing, Sussex. November 7, 1977.

(Issued in USA on George Buck's (New Orleans based) Jazzology label - 'Jazzology J-93')

Tracks:
Side A
1. Spain *
2. Someday Sweetheart
3. Don't Blame Me
4. Broadway *
5. I Can't Believe That You're In Love With Me
Side B
1. Nobody Stole Us **
2. Since My Best Girl Turned Me Down
3. Watch What Happens
4. A Hundred Years From Today
5. Oh Baby

Personnel: Billy Butterfield-t; Roy Bower-t; Randy Colville-cl/arr * Benny Simkins-ts; Geoff Simkins-as/bar; Mike Collier-tb; Pete Simkins-p/arr **; Alan Kennington-sb; Bernie Godfrey-d;

Recording and Mixing Engineer: Tony Platt Photographs: Ted Ambrose. Artwork: W.Etherington. Sleeve Notes: Alan Littlejohn

Yank Lawson - with Benny Simkins Band
12" LP
Title 'Easy To Remember' - Flyright FLY LP 208. Recorded at Ted Taylor's Studio, South London

- October 10, 1979

Tracks:
Side A
1. Meet Me Tonight In Dreamland
2. West Pier Blues
3. Three Little Words
4. Easy To Remember
Side B
1. Some Day You'll Be Sorry
2. Save It Pretty Mama
3. Sometimes I'm Happy
4. Rose Room
5. Heebie Jeebies

Personnel: Yank Lawson-t; Row Bower-t; Randy Colville-cl; Geoff Simkins-as/bar; Benny Simkins-ts; Mike Collier-tb; Pete Simkins-p; Stan Warboys-sb; Vic Richards-d; Engineer: Steve Taylor

Danny Moss Quartet featuring Geoff Simkins
12" LP -
Flyright FLY 209. Recorded at Ron Geesin's Studio, Heathfield, October 15, 1979

Tracks:
Side A
1. If Dreams Come True
2. Then I'll Be Tired Of You
3. I'm Beginning To See The Light
4. I've Got The World On A String
5. Don't Be That Way
6. The World Is Waiting For The Sunrise
Side B
1. Royal Garden Blues
2. Don't Blame Me
3. Fine And Dandy
4. You're A Weaver Of Dreams
5. Candy

Personnel: Danny Moss-ts; Geoff Simkins-as; Brian Lemon-p; Len Skeat-sb; Derek Hogg-d; Sleeve Photographs: Ted Ambrose Graphics: W. & M. Etherington

Jeanie Lambe with the Danny Moss Quartet
12" LP -
Flyright FLY 215. Recorded at Ron Geesin's Studio, Heathfield, September 5, 1980

Tracks:

Side A 1. Sittin' And A-Rockin'
2. You Don't Know What
Love Is
3. Glad To Be Unhappy
4. I Won't Dance
5. Can't We Be Friends

Side B 1. No Good Man
2. Teach Me Tonight
3. Blue Prelude
4. Sugar
5. I Wish I Was Back In
My Baby's Arms
6. Any Place I Hang My
Hat

Personnel: Danny Moss-ts; Brian
Lemon-p; Len Skeat-sb; Derek
Hogg-d; Sleeve Photography: Eric
G. Lovat Art Direction & Design:
Nigel Goodall

**Danny Moss Quartet featuring
Geoff Simkins**
12" LP -
Flyright FLY 218
Recorded at Ron Geesin's Studio,
Heathfield, April 16, 1981 (*) and
June 22, 1981

Tracks:
Side A 1. Struttin' With Some
Barbecue
2. It's Alright With Me
3. Street Of Dreams*
4. Careless Love
5. Just You, Just Me *

Side B 1. Stompin' At The Savoy
2. I Want To Be Happy
3. You've Changed*
4. Jones*
5. In A Mellotone*

Personnel: Danny Moss-ts; Geoff
Simkins-as; Brian Lemon-p; Len
Skeat-sb; Derek Hogg-d;

The Brian Rutland Band
12" LP
Title: 'Undecided' - Flyright FLY
LP 213
Recorded at Ted Taylor's Studio,
South London - July 3, 1980

Tracks:
Side A 1. Deed I Do
2. I Want A Little Girl
3. Peg Of My Heart
4. Secret Love

Side B 1. As Long As I Live
2. If I Could Be With You
3. Three Little Words

4. Don't Get Around
Much Any More
5. Undecided

Personnel: Brian Rutland-t/v; John
Barnes-cl/bar; Danny Moss-ts; Roy
Williams-tb; Terry Whitney-p;
Mike Garey-sb; Derek Hogg-d;

**Harry Strutters Hot Rhythm
Orchestra**
12" LP
Title: 'Bouncing Around' - Flyright
201
Recorded: June 16, 1974

Tracks:
Side A 1. Barataria (a)
2. Ida, Sweet As Apple
Cider (b)
3. Snake Rag (c)
4. Blue River (b)
5. Mississippi Mud (d)

Side B 1. Bouncing Around (e)
2. Clementine (f)
3. Cushion Foot Stomp (b)
4. Japanese Sandman (g)
5. New Orleans Blues (b)

Personnel: (a) Geoff Simkins-as;
Mike Etherington-c; Brian Hills-
cl/as; Jim Heath-bb; Maurice
Dennis-bj; John Muxlow-d;
(b) same as (a) but recorded May
19, 1974
(c) same as (b) but without cornet
(d) same as (b) but vocal by Geoff
Simkins
(e) same as (b) but with Brian Hills
on alto saxophone
(f) same as (b) but with vocal by
Mike Etherington and Brian Hills
on alto saxophone
(g) same as (a) but with vocal by
Mike Etherington.

Director & Distributor: Bruce
Bastin. (NB: Limited edition of
250). Recording: Ron Geesin at
Heathfield, Sx. Sleeve design: Mike
Etherington. Sleeve notes: Maurice
Dennis.

12" LP
Title: 'That Certain Party' - Bull
1003
Recorded: (?)1975 (released around
June, 1976)

Tracks:
Side A 1. That Certain Party
2. When I Take My Sugar

To Tea
3. Love Letters In The
Sand
4. I'll Never Be The Same
5. Clap Hands, Here
Comes Charlie
6. We're In The Money

Side B 1. Raining In My Heart
2. The Varsity Drag
3. Whispering
4. My Pet
5. My Blue Heaven
6. Room With A View

Recorded at: Regent Sound Studios,
London. Sleeve notes: John
Muxlow.

Personnel: Mike Etherington-c/v;
Chris Macdonald-cl/as/bar/v, Brian
Hills-cl/as; Gavin Russell-p;
Maurice Dennis-bj/g/swanee-whis-
tle; George Flett-bb; John
Muxlow-d/v;

Director & Distributor: George
Porter/Clive Stanhope for Dart
Records. (marketed by President
Records).

12" LP
Title: 'Rhythm King' - Black Lion
BLP 12130. Recorded: June 10,
1977 at Regent Sound Studios,
London.

Tracks:
Side A 1. Rhythm King
2. The Charleston
3. Am I Blue?
4. Copenhagen
5. Take Your Tomorrows
6. Ice Cream

Side B 1. How Could Red Riding
Hood?
2. Sugar Foot Strut
3. Jazz Me Blues
4. The Mooche
5. Chili Bom Bom
6. Candy Lips

Personnel: Mike Etherington-
c/bar.horn/v; Chris
Macdonald-cl/as/ts/bar; Brian
Hills-cl/ss/as/kazoo; Gavin Russell-
p/moofus; Maurice Dennis-bj/g;
Jim Heath-bb; John Muxlow-d/v

Director & Distributor: George
Porter. (marketed by Logo
Records). Sleeve notes: John
Muxlow.

12" LP
Title: 'Totus Porcus' - Black Lion
BLP 12196
Recorded: August 6, 1979 at
Plymouth Sound, Plymouth,
Devon.

Tracks:
Side A 1. It Don't Mean A Thing
2. Black And Tan Fantasy
3. If I Had A Talking
   Picture Of You
4. Hard Hearted Hannah
5. Riverboat Shuffle
6. Stevedore Stomp
Side B 1. Limehouse Blues
2. If I Could Be With You
   One Hour Tonight
3. Blue Skies
4. Squeeze Me
5. Gee Baby, Ain't I Good
   To You?
6. Buddy's Habit

Personnel: Dave Davis-c; Geoff
Simkins-as/sop; Brian Hills-
cl/sop/as/ts; Gavin Russell-p;
Maurice Dennis-bj/g; Jim Heath-
bb/v; John Muxlow-d/v.

Director & Distributor: George
Porter (marketed by Logo Records).
Recording Engineer:
Tim Mason. Sleeve Design: Harry
Moore. Sleeve Notes: John
Muxlow.

12" LP
Title: 'Borneo' - Black Lion BLM
51108
Recorded: May 25 / August 12,
1986. Recorded at: the late Ted
Taylor's Porcupine Studios,
Mottingham.

Tracks:
Side A 1. Borneo
2. Black Beauty
3. Barnacle Bill (a)
4. Rockin' In Rhythm (b)
5. Doodlin' Blue (c) -
   comp. Macdonald
6. Wherever There's Love
7. Zonky
Side B 1. Symphonic Raps
2. St.James Infirmary
   Blues (d)
3. Froggie Moore Rag (b)
4. Nagasaki (c)
5. East St. Louis Toodle-oo
6. Everybody Stomp

Personnel: Paul Lacey-tpt & voc on

a & d; Alistair Allan-tmb & voc on
e; Chris Macdonald-reeds; Bill
Boston-reeds, voc on a, bsx on c;
Martin Litton-pno, solo on b;
Maurice Dennis-bjo/gtr; Jim Heath-
brass bass, except c; John
Muxlow-dms;

Arrangements by Billy Boston, Paul
Lacey, and Chris Macdonald.
Recording Engineer: Ted Taylor.
Sleeve Notes: John Muxlow.
Director & Distributor: Alan Bates
for Phonoco

CD
Title: 'Crazy Chords' - Circle CCD-
143
Recorded London 1987

Tracks:
1. Copenhagen
2. Primrose Stomp
3. Vo-Do-Do-Deo Blues
4. Deep Henderson
5. Black And Tan Fantasy
6. Shine
7. Just An Hour Of Love
8. Mood Indigo
9. Lila
10. Cushion Foot Stomp
11. Oil Well
12. Crazy Chords
13. Rockin' In Rhythm

Personnel: Paul Lacey-c,v; Alistair
Allan-tb,v; Billy Boston-cl,as,bsx;
Chris Macdonald-cl,ss,as,ts; Martin
Litton-p; Maurice Dennis-g; Jim
Heath-bb; John Muxlow-d,v;

CD
Title: 'Memories Of Bing Crosby' -
Blueshouse BH009
Recorded: December 21, 1994 at
Nick Taylor's Porcupine Studios,
Mottingham

Tracks:
1. Deep Down South
2. Please Don't Talk About Me
   When I'm Gone
3. Angry medley -
   • Blues My Naughty Sweetie
     Gives To Me
   • What's The Reason I'm
     Not Pleasin' You
   • Angry
4. Dear Hearts And Gentle
   People
5. De Sylva, Brown and
   Henderson medley -
   • The Best Things In Life Are
     Free

• Varsity Drag
• Button Up Your Overcoat
6. One Hundred Years From
   Today
7. Baby medley -
   • When My Baby Smiles At Me
   • Baby Face
   • Everybody Loves My Baby
   • Yes Sir, That's My Baby
8. The Crosby medley -
   • Can't We Talk It Over
   • I'm Confessin'
   • Please
   • Just One More Chance
9. Jazz Me Blues
10. Blue Of The Night -
    • True Love
    • White Christmas
11. Dixie medley -
    • Is It True What They Say
      About Dixie?
    • Way Down Yonder In New
      Orleans
    • Alexander's Ragtime Band
    • The Darktown Strutter's Ball

Personnel: Mike Cotton-t; Bob
Hunt-tb/ts/t/arr; Tony Jack-
cl/as/ts; Bill Boston-cl/as/ts/bar;
Martin Litton-p; Maurice Dennis-
bj/g; Jim Heath-bb; John Muxlow-d;

Director & Distributor: Terry
Dash, Hannes Anrig / TQS Music,
Baden, Switzerland.

CD
Title: 'Hot And Bothered' -
Catalogue No. HSHROCD001

Recorded: by Nick Taylor at
Porcupine Studios, London on
November 20, 21, 2001. Editing and
Mixing by Nick Taylor, Bob Hunt
& Maurice Dennis. Produced by
Maurice Dennis & Bob Hunt.

Tracks:
1. Ellington Medley -
   • Mood Indigo
   • Hot & Bothered
   • Creole Love Call
2. My Blue Heaven
3. 100 Years From Today
4. Jungle Jamboree
5. The Clouds Will Soon Roll By
6. Bear Pit Scuffle
7. Charleston Rag
8. Stormy Weather
9. Deep Down South
10. Makin' Whoopee
11. Please Don't Talk About Me
    When I'm Gone

12. Big House Blues
13. From Monday On
14. On The Sunny Side Of The Street
15. Some Of These Days
16. Alice Blue Gown

Personnel: Mike 'Magic' Henry - t Billy Boston-clt,as,ten,bar,bsx Bob Hunt-tbn,clt,arr Tony Carter-clt,as Maurice Dennis-bjo,gtr,vcl Martin Litton-pno,arr Jim Heath-bbs,vcls,puppets John Muxlow-dms,vcl Tony Jacobs-vcls.

The Jubilee Jazz Band
12" LP
Title: 'Making Tracks' - Flyright Records - FLY 210
Recorded at the 'Fox and Hounds', Haywards Heath, courtesy of Chris Worrall. 20th Feb, 27th Feb, and 10 March 1980.

Tracks:
Side A 1. The Charleston
2. You Took Advantage Of Me
3. I Want A Big Butter And Egg Man
4. Shout 'Em Aunt Tillie
5. East St. Louis Toodle-oo
6. The Sun Has Got His Hat On
Side B 1. At The Jazz Band Ball
2. Louisiana
3. Chimes Blues
4. It Don't Mean A Thing If It Ain't Got That Swing
5. If I Could Be With You One Hour Tonight
6. Christopher Columbus

Personnel: Paul Bonner-t; Mike Collier-tb; Sluff Hazell-ts/bar; Roy Leith-as; Mike Ainscough-g/bj; Dave Gibb-sb; Ken White-d; Viv Bonner-v;

Recording: Ted Mechen Cover photos: Ted Ambrose.

Brian Cotton and the Cotton Club Jazzmen
CD
Title : 'Back in the South' : COT 001. Recorded at Chipstead Football Club, Surrey, 20th August 1997

Tracks:
1. Five Point Blues
2. Swing That Music
3. Sweeping the Blues Away
4. Jubilee (a)
5. Nobody Knows or Seems to Care (b)
6. Shimme Sha Wabble
7. Here's Freddie
8. I Never Knew (a)
9. Deed I Do
10. Stumbling
11. Spain (d)
12. Bye Bye Blues
13. I Would Do Most Anything (c)
14. There'll Come a Time, Wait and See
15. Loose Walk

Brian Cotton -tb/v ; Roy Bower - t/v ; Chris Macdonald - cl, ts, bc; Peter Godfrey - p; Jim McKay -sb; Peter Burton -d; Butch Holden -g/v.

Brian Cotton - vocal on (a)
Roy Bower - vocal on (b)
Butch Holden - vocal on (c)
Chris Macdonald - bass clarinet on (d)

Engnineer : John Softley of `Just the Job' Mobile Recordings. Sleeve notes and design by Brian Cotton. Graphics by Dave Smith.

Brian Cotton and the Cotton Club Jazzmen
CD -
Title: "100% Pure Cotton" - COT 002

Tracks:
1. Mama's Gone, Goodbye
2. Wild Man Blues
3. How Can You Face Me?
4. Heebie Jeebies
5. Linger In My Arms
6. Chimes Blues
7. You Can Depend On Me
8. Constantly
9. Once In My Life, For You
10. You're A Lucky Guy
11. Smiles
12. A Sky Blue Shirt And A Rainbow Tie

Personnel: Roy Bower - t; Brian Cotton - tb,v; Chris MacDonald - reeds; Peter Godfrey - p; Butch Holden - gtr,v; Jim McKay - bs; Peter Burton - d;

Vocal on 3 by Butch Holden
Vocals on 5,8,10, by Brian Cotton

Recorded at Chipstead Football Club, Surrey - March 3, 2000 by John Softley of 'Just The Job' Mobile Recordings

Good Vibes
CD
Title: "Raising Standards" - (no catalogue
number evident).

Titles:
1. Topsy
2. Makin' Whoopee
3. There Is No Greater Love
4. Autumn Leaves
5. Alice In Wonderland
6. Don't Blame Me
7. Yesterdays
8. Saudade
9. I Thought About You
10. Line For Lyons
11. Half Nelson
12. Love For Sale

Personnel: Dave Jones - vib; Chris Macdonald - cl,ts; Peter Godfrey - p; Frank Taylor - gtr; Jim McKay - bs; Peter Burton - d; Wendy Mills - v;

vocals on 2,4, and 9 by Wendy Mills

Recorded at Chichester College of Arts Science and Technology by Alex Zink. Mastered at Obsidian Studios by Alex Zink 2002.

Rockin' In Rhythm
CD
Title: 'Love Me Or Leave Me'. (no catalogue number).
Recorded at the Steam Rooms, Poplar, London April 8, 9, 1999.

Tracks:
1. Between The Devil And The Deep Blue Sea
2. Tickle Toe
3. 9.20 Special
4. I'm Thru With Love
5. As Long As I Live
6. Intermission Riff
7. Blue Lou
8. God Bless The Child
9. I Can't Give You Anything But Love
10. Caravan
11. Air Mail Special

12. Love Me Or Leave Me
13. In A Mellow Tone
14. Leave Us Leap
15. Jitterbug Waltz

Personnel: Jo Hunter-t; Robin Watt-ts; Tim Wade-tb; Vic Richards-vib; Piers Clark-g; Steve Ashworth-p; Dan Sheppard-sb; Dan Breslaw-d; Rachel Bundy-v; Engineered by Jon Wilkinson

---

The Vintage Hot Five
C90 Cassette Tape - Vol 1. (VHF1)
Recorded: Jan. 19/March 16, 1997 at 'Maxims Wine Bar', South Street, Eastbourne.

Tracks:
Side A 1. From Monday On
2. Weather Bird Rag
3. Miss Elizabeth Brown
4. At The Jazz Band Ball
5. Cornet Chop Suey
6. Eleven-Thirty Saturday Night
7. Muscle Shoals Blues
8. Potato Head Blues
9. Back In Your Own Backyard
Side B 1. Animal Crackers
2. Two Deuces
3. Alabamy Bound

4. Oh Baby Dear
5. She's Crying For Me
6. Futuristic Rhythm
7. My Baby Just Cares For Me
8. Wild Man Blues
9. Susie

C90 Cassette Tape - Vol 2. (VHF2)

Tracks:
Side A 1. Idolizing
2. Pretty Baby
3. Once In A While
4. A Nightingale Sang In Berkeley Square
5. After You've Gone
6. Sorry
7. Sugar
8. Sobbing Blues

Side B 1. Lila
2. Hotter Than That
3. I'm Wondering Who
4. Royal Garden Blues
5. Stardust
6. Heebie Jeebies
7. I'm Not Rough
8. Words
9. Ostrich Walk

Personnel: Andy Woon-c,v; Brian Hills-cl, as, ss, ts, bsx, v; Bill Parsons-bj,g,v; Roger Hooper-bbs; John Muxlow-d,v;

Notes: (all 'Flyright' information kindly provided by Bruce Bastin). Producer for label 'Flyright' FLY 201, 204, 205, 208, 209, 215, 217, 218 - is Bruce Bastin.
Producer for FLY 213 - is Brian Rutland.
Producer for FLY 210 - is Viv Bonner.
Producer for FLY 203 & 206 - is Bernard Hodgson.
Producer for FLY 202 - is Benny Simkins

Abbreviations – Instruments

arr	arranger
as	alto saxophone
bar	baritone saxophone
bb	brass bass (sousaphone/tuba)
bc	bass clarinet
bj	banjo
bsx	bass saxophone cornet
cl	clarinet
d	drums
g	guitar
p	piano
sb	string bass
ss	soprano saxophone
t	trumpet
tb	trombone
ts	tenor saxophone
v	vocalist
vib	vibraphone

Thanks go to Bruce Bastin, John Muxlow, Alan Kennington, Bernard Hodgson, Roy Martin, Mike Etherington, Sluff Hazel, Dave Davis, John Collinson, Piers Clark, and all for information, dates, and recording details.   Compiled by Brian Hills 2002

INDEX

DANNY MOSS

JOHN BOYETT

ALAN KENNINGTON

BRIAN HILLS

TREVOR PHILCOX

Some of the stalwarts of

THE BRIGHTON JAZZ LINE

pictured whilst this book was in preparation between August 2000 and August 2002.

STEVE DAVIES

JOHN FRUCHT

GORDON WREN

SLUFF HAZELL

JOHN GOODRICK

ROY BOWER

JIM CHAMBERS

MEGS ETHERINGTON

ROY MARTIN

ALLAN SOKELL

MAURICE DENNIS

BILL POLLEY

CHRIS MACDONALD

GEOFF SIMKINS

SID BAILEY

JACK GILBERT